100 NOVELS

THAT CHANGED
THE WORLD

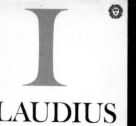

Jacqueline Susann's

Valley of the Dolls

The Quiet American

a novel

Graham Greene

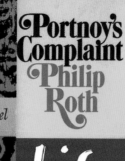

Portnoy's Complaint

Philip Roth

THE GOLDEN NOTEBOOK

BY DORIS LESSING

ERNEST HEMINGWAY

THE SUN ALSO RISES

Some of the finest and most restrained writing that this generation has produced. —New York World

le Sargasso Sea

Jean Rhys

MARGARET ATWOOD
THE HANDMAID'S TALE

Life of Pi

a novel

OVER FOURTEEN MILLION COPIES SOLD

WINNER OF THE MAN BOOKER PRIZE

Yann Martel

K2668 • 60¢ • A BANTAM SIXTY

The most powerful novel ever to come out of the Soviet Union!!!!

by Alexander Solzhenitsyn · The complete, unexpurgated translation by Ronald Hingley and Max Hayward, co-translator of *Doctor Zhivago*

one day in the life of Ivan Denisovich

A SUITABLE BOY

KAZUO ISHIGURO
The Remains of the Day

RAM SETH

KAZUO ISHIGURO
The Remains of the Day

D1619

JACK KEROUAC

ON THE ROAD

This is the bible of the "beat generation" —the explosive bestseller that tells all about today's wild youth and their frenetic search for Experience and Sensation.

A SIGNET BOOK · Complete and Unabridged

IVANHOE

~SCOTT~

DRACULA

1/6 Net.   BRAM STOKER   1/6 Net.

CATCHER
RYE

CHIMAMANDA
NGOZI ADICHIE
AUTHOR OF PURPLE HIBISCUS

Half of a Yellow Sun

The Color Purple

FRANZ KAFKA

THE METAMORPHOSIS

Pavilion
An imprint of HarperCollins*Publishers* Ltd
1 London Bridge Street
London SE1 9GF

www.harpercollins.co.uk

HarperCollins*Publishers*
Macken House, 39/40 Mayor Street Upper
Dublin 1, D01 C9W8, Ireland

10 9 8 7 6 5 4 3 2 1

First published in Great Britain by Pavilion, an imprint of HarperCollins*Publishers* Ltd 2023

Copyright © 2023

A catalogue record for this book is available from the British Library.

ISBN 978-0-008599-08-9

This book is produced from independently certified FSC™ paper
to ensure responsible forest management.

For more information visit:
www.harpercollins.co.uk/green

Printed and bound in Malaysia by Papercraft

100 NOVELS

THAT CHANGED THE WORLD

COLIN SALTER

PAVILION

Contents

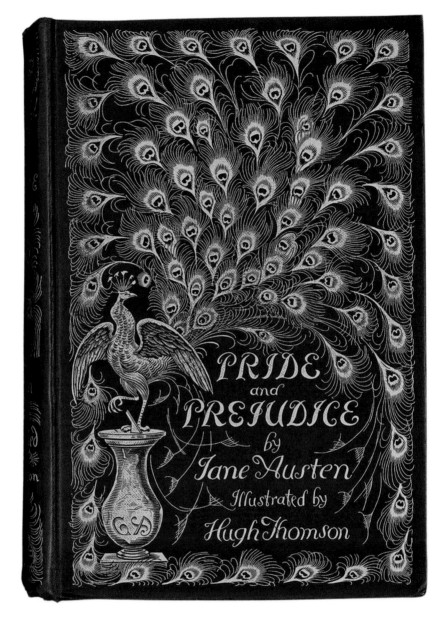

Introduction

It's a tricky list to compile. Our journey through a hundred novels begins with *The Tale of Genji*, written in around 1006, by Murasaki Shikibu, for the entertainment of her fellow Japanese ladies in waiting, who were starved of social contact in the imperial court of the time. The most recent book on the list is Bernardine Evaristo's *Girl, Woman, Other*, which looks at another group of women often marginalised by society, this time by racism experienced in modern Britain.

Between the two are many classics of world literature, and many others whose impact on literary history may be less well recognised. This is not a list of the Best Novels of All Time, but of books which made the reading world sit up and take notice. It may have been for their radical subject matter, the innovative way in which their story was told, or for their impact on that third important group in the literary transaction – the publishers. Writers write and readers read, but it's the publishers who take on the risk with innovative works of fiction, for which a potential market needs to be found.

THE ROOTS OF THE NOVEL

What is a novel? Even that is hard to answer. It's a long story, except when it's not: the beat prose of William S. Burroughs and the gonzo journalism of Hunter S. Thompson are more like impressionistic art than tales, and the colour and shade of Tracy Chevalier's *Girl with a Pearl Earring* leave the reader feeling as if they have just

emerged from a painting by Vermeer.

The original long stories were oral histories, which were embellished so much in the retelling that they became origin myths and legends, growing like pearls around grains of truth. Those fictional embellishments attach themselves partly to make the story more entertaining and partly, ironically, to make it more believable. There is, as many authors have remarked, often more truth in fiction than in fact. Myths and legends are populated by stereotypes of the human condition – heroes, villains, gods and men, wise men and fools. History, real history, is rarely so simple; but such invention offers credible explanations for events in terms which the listener or reader can understand from their own experience of other people. Some of the novels featured here do just that – Robert Graves' *I, Claudius* and Hilary Mantel's *Wolf Hall* trilogy invite the reader to re-examine real historical characters through a fictional retelling of their lives.

From the gods and men of mythical history, it is a short step to inventing new stories about well-known characters. Thus emerges the semi-legendary King Arthur, for example, and the adventures of his Knights of the Round Table; and from them the plots and subplots of many a more modern novel. *Don Quixote*, the first such work, is an inspired parody of precisely the sort of chivalric values promoted by Arthurian

One of the Great Novels of the Century

Joseph Heller

With a new preface by the author

tales. Four hundred years later the widely differing genres of science fiction, in Frank Herbert's *Dune*, and coming-of-age, in Jeanette Winterson's *Oranges Are Not the Only Fruit*, are equally happy to borrow from those ancient stories.

SOCIAL COMMENT

From its very beginnings the novel has commented on the society of the times. *Don Quixote* pokes fun at those, like his titular character, who read so many chivalric stories that their brains are weakened. A century later, *Gulliver's Travels* is a bumper book of satires aimed at various aspects of English society, so controversial at the time that the author submitted it to his publisher in someone else's handwriting; and the publisher removed and added ameliorating text to reduce the risk of offending the rich and powerful.

Gulliver's Travels is a tremendously important milestone in the history of the novel because it introduces the possibility of imaginary worlds. Thematically,

OPPOSITE: Hilary Mantel's genius in writing the Wolf Hall *trilogy was to take an episode of English history with an often-vilified figure, Thomas Cromwell, and portray him as a servant simply trying to survive the jeopardy of Henry VIII's court.*
RIGHT: Robert Louis Stevenson's Victorian novel highlighted the concept of the split personality with such force that the 'Jekyll and Hyde' trait became an easy short-cut to describe huge character swings.

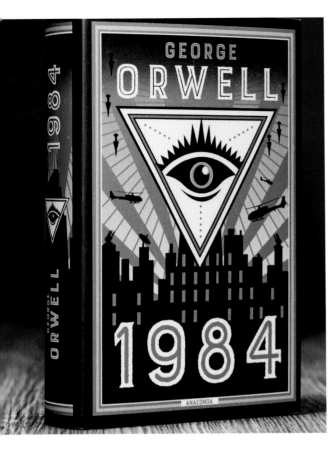

H.G. Wells, who inspired Aldous Huxley, was a pioneer of science fiction who imagined many dystopian and utopian worlds. If the best-known cruel worlds are Huxley's *Brave New World* and George Orwell's *1984*, there are many more and they seem to be appearing more frequently in recent years. *Clockwork Orange*, *V for Vendetta* and *The Handmaid's Tale* are relatively recent examples, all concerned with the violence of men towards women.

For those who prefer their fiction to be rooted in the real world (and who's to say that dystopias are not?), the works of Jane Austen, the Brontë sisters and Charles Dickens all offer critical views of society in the context of great storytelling. In this first Golden Age of the novel, French and Russian authors also make their entrance onto the literary stage. Honoré de Balzac, Gustave Flaubert and Victor Hugo paint dark pictures of social aspiration and criminal justice; and Dostoevsky's gritty St Petersburg vies with Tolstoy's imperial Moscow in a warm-up for the Russian Revolution. Crime and class are recurring themes in all these European views of society.

SHOCK HORROR

Not all fiction is preoccupied with harsh reality. The Gothic novel sits stylistically between the big stereotypes of Arthurian myth and the inner conflicts of more modern protagonists. Their characters are drawn with broad strokes and often encounter supernatural obstacles, but they also exhibit emotions, and must navigate a modern world. Horace Walpole defined the genre in

invented places allow authors to criticise real, inviolable places without being seen to pour scorn on them. Fictional lands can be better than we imagine our own to be; but in practice they are usually far worse. The land of Lilliput, Brobdingnag and the rest of Gulliver's destinations are designed to hold up a horrifying mirror to reality, and they were among the earliest dystopias in fiction. They were by no means the last.

ABOVE: Elements of Orwell's dystopian vision in 1984 have become reality in modern China where groupthink condemned the country to an extended lockdown during Covid.
RIGHT: A protestor with a V for Vendetta mask on the streets of Istanbul in 2015.

The Castle of Otranto, with its ghosts, cobwebbed corridors and creaking doors; *Frankenstein* and *Dr Jekyll and Mr Hyde* added science to the mixture; *Dracula* revelled in it; and the genre still exerts a strong influence today. By imbuing its people with thoughts and feelings, Gothic fiction is an important stage in the development of the novel. It lets the reader inside the character, and makes the character's experiences – usually shocking or horrifying – all the more entertainingly real.

Some novels take that inner thought process to its logical conclusion, either through a first-person narrative or by being entirely a stream of the protagonist's consciousness. Marcel Proust's *In Search of Lost Time* is a novel defined entirely by the narrator's sensual experience of the world. Vladimir Nabokov's sexual predator in *Lolita* was such a convincing narrator that some readers assumed that only another sexual predator could have imagined him. *Portnoy's Complaint* by Philip Roth further develops the idea by taking the form of Portnoy's confessional sessions with his psychiatrist. The psychiatrist's chair is where people unburden their innermost secrets.

TRUTH IN ANY LANGUAGE

Other fiction authors have deliberately set out to convince the reader that what they were reading was a true story. *Don Quixote*, *Robinson Crusoe* and *Gulliver's Travels* all claimed to be authentic memoirs, and the second edition of the latter even carried a letter from Gulliver complaining about the quality of the first. The novel *Tristram Shandy*, a law unto itself in so many ways, finds the supposed author Shandy not only living his life but attempting to write about it and, in yet another layer of deception, commenting on the process of writing. This must be the first example of metafiction, a trend of recent years in which characters in a novel step out of the story to comment on it. Ian McEwan's heartbreaking *Atonement* is a modern exposition of what Laurence Sterne started.

Some novels are indeed thinly veiled autobiographies – *One Day in the Life of Ivan Denisovich* is closely based on

TOP: *The majority of authors featured in this book have an acknowledged* magnum opus, *but for Charles Dickens the choice is always going to be divisive.*

Aleksandr Solzhenitsyn's time in a Soviet prison camp for political dissenters, and the family in the classic *Little Women* is almost identical in its circumstances and characteristics to that of its author Louisa May Alcott. *Milkman* by Anna Burns immerses the reader with a first-person narrative written not only in the character's thoughts but in hers and Burns' broad native Northern Irish dialect.

Language is as important to fiction as plot. In *Cloud Atlas*, for example, David Mitchell imagines what English might sound like many years from now and writes an entire chapter in an invented dialect. Authors usually, although not always, write in their native language, and that naturally shapes the rhythm of the text and the metaphors and similes within it. The Nigerian author Chinua Achebe deliberately chose to use English and not to use his native Igbo. Achebe thought that English, in all its richness, was the natural language of the novel. Authors in other languages would certainly disagree, and throughout the twentieth century and beyond, the literary canon has been greatly enriched by novels from places where English is not the first or only language. The present selection includes novels from France, Russia,

Czechoslovakia, Japan, India, Afghanistan, Africa and South America. In an increasingly global fiction market we can read these works in translation and learn not only the differences in cultures but the universal experiences of human beings.

It is almost as great a challenge to translate a novel as it is to write it in the first place, precisely because of those natural rhythms and figures of speech which make a novel successful in its original language. Russian literature has particularly suffered from poor translation: it was first brought to the attention of English readers in translations by Constance Garnett, whose grasp of Russian was not complete. She often omitted sections of text which she did not understand or approve of. It has been said that English readers could not tell the difference between Tolstoy and Dostoevsky because in Constance Garnett's hands they all sounded the same – not like either Tolstoy or Dostoevsky but like Constance Garnett. Tolstoy's *War and Peace* is interesting for another linguistic quirk. The novel was written in Russian but includes some French, which was the language of the imperial Russian court; and even in translation it has been the convention to leave the French passages in French.

CHOICES AND OBJECTIONS

The hundred titles in this list are presented chronologically – who would dare to order them by merit? The first ten were all written before Queen Victoria ruled Britain, before Andrew Jackson became president of the USA, before the discovery of electromagnetic induction. The last ten were published in the twenty-first century. It may be too soon to tell their lasting impact, but they have all made strong impressions.

Some are works of art in themselves. Others just tell a really good story – although literary scholars may turn their noses up, there's no denying the impact of popular novelists like Mark Twain, Agatha Christie and P.G. Wodehouse who were prolific and gave the reading public exactly what they wanted in terms of light entertainment.

Wodehouse once said, 'I believe there are two ways of writing novels. One is making a sort of musical comedy without music and ignoring real life altogether; the other is going deep down into life and not caring a damn.' His was the first way; but increasingly novelists are choosing

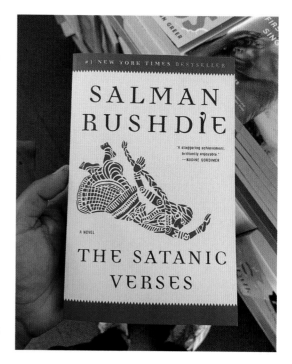

ABOVE: *Books have the power to change minds or inflame opinion. The overwhelming majority of those who objected to* The Satanic Verses *never read the book.*

BELOW: *Translator Constance Garnett didn't confine her skills to Dostoevsky and Tolstoy, she also turned her hand to short stories by Anton Chekhov.*

to go deep down into life precisely because they *do* give a damn. Many of the more recent inclusions in the list of a hundred use fiction to explore divisive social issues, including feminism, homosexuality, racism and the immigrant experience. Amy Tan's *The Joy Luck Club* centres on a Chinese American community; Alex Haley, Alice Walker and Toni Morrison all consider the African American diaspora; and Bernardine Evaristo writes the stories of Black women in Britain.

These novels and the issues they address remain controversial for some; and literature has in some parts of the world become a battleground for those with extreme views. The American Library Association keeps a record of challenges made by those who consider some books offensive. In 2015, 275 books were challenged, of which a small proportion resulted in bans. In 2022, more than 1,600 books were banned in schools and libraries across the USA.

Every reader has their own idea about what makes a good read. If you don't like plot spoilers, then please be warned, although it has been possible to avoid some of the classic plot twists, you will learn substantial amounts of detail for each novel – with notable exceptions, such as *War and Peace*. Around half of the chosen works are indisputable classics; the other half will be hotly disputed. If there are some here that you love, and some that you've never heard of, then my work is done.

ABOVE: Librarians and school boards in the USA are facing an increased climate of censorship with concerted attempts to remove books for children containing themes of race, gender and sexual identity. To Kill A Mockingbird *is frequently challenged, despite Harper Lee winning the Presidential Medal of Freedom for her book from George W. Bush in 2007.*

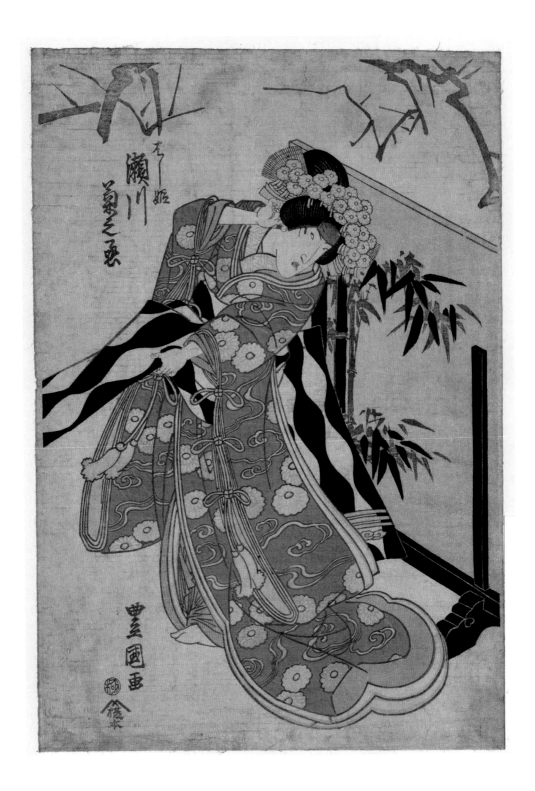

The Tale of Genji

(1008–1021)

Murasaki Shikibu (c.973–c.1025)

The Tale of Genji can claim to be the world's first novel. It was written to entertain women during Japan's Heian period and today it is required reading in every Japanese school. Its remarkable window on a different time and place is now available throughout the world, thanks to new translations.

Murasaki Shikibu was a member of the Fujiwara family, which wielded great political power in the country at the time. She was a lady in waiting in the imperial court of Japan, where she served as a companion to the emperor's daughter. It was a cosseted but isolated life for such women, removed from the rest of the population and only rarely allowed visits, even from their husbands. In that time, women, even after marriage, were obliged to live with their fathers; they should not be seen in public, and because they were considered mentally inferior to men they were not allowed to learn Chinese, the prevailing language of the court and of commerce.

Reading was permitted, in the crude kana script of the Japanese language, and typically the women of court enjoyed romances of the gods and of supernatural, magical characters. Murasaki began to write stories for the amusement of her fellow women in court who were cut off from intellectual stimulation and society. Her tales were distinguished by their modern settings and their down-to-earth characters and events, which did not rely on myth and fantasy. Their popularity spread as her friends made copies and distributed them further afield.

Although no original text by Murasaki survives, more than three hundred early copies do – and more still turn up in dusty archives from time to time.

Genji, the hero of Murasaki's story, is a handsome young noble, forced to live as a commoner despite being the son of an emperor. His life is a mixture of political intrigue and romantic episodes, and Genji experiences many successes and failures. The phrase 'the sorrow of human existence' occurs more than a thousand times in the text, like the chorus of a long ballad reiterating the novel's principal theme. The book consists of fifty-four chapters written over more than a decade and making up three distinct parts. Genji's life occupies the first two, while the third describes the changing fortunes of his son after Genji's death.

Murasaki drew her inspiration from classical historic poetry and from the contemporary prose which she and the women of the court were expected to read. Her modernity, and her intuitive grasp of human psychology, make *The Tale of Genji* a timeless work. Although its setting is eleventh-century Japan, her understanding of its characters' emotions and motives make it highly readable for a twenty-first-century audience.

LEFT: *Illustrated long after Murasaki Shikibu's time, a snow scene from* The Tale of Genji *showing courtiers from the Heian period, the last division of classical Japanese history.*
OPPOSITE: *An 1823 woodcut of Japanese actress Segawa Kikunojo in the role of Hashihime in a dramatisation of* The Tale of Genji.

Don Quixote

(1605–1615)

Miguel de Cervantes (1547–1616)

Often hailed as the first modern novel, *Don Quixote* marked a turning point in European literature and gave us one of the most memorable fictional double acts of all time in the tragicomic Don Quixote and his unfortunate sidekick Sancho Panza.

The story of a wandering knight and his squire, defeating enemies for the honour and love of his lady Dulcinea, was a conventional form. When Cervantes was writing, the dominant literary form was the chivalric romance, a mixture of prose and poetry. It told a tale of knightly chivalry of which the stories of King Arthur and the Knights of the Round Table are the best-known examples.

Cervantes set out from the start to subvert the genre. His knight, Don Quixote, is a lowly *hidalgo*, a member of the lesser Spanish nobility, whose mind has been warped by reading too many chivalric romances. It is a kind of madness which persuades Don Quixote to seek the sort of adventures which he has read about. He imagines himself a knight; and, since a knight must have a lady to serve, he invents one – Dulcinea del Toboso. His helmet is a barber's shaving bowl; his noble horse is in reality a feeble nag; the castle in which he is knighted is actually an inn; the giants whom he attacks in Dulcinea's name are mere windmills. The counterpart to Don Quixote's folly is his neighbour Sancho Panza, a down-to-earth farmer whom the faux knight enlists as his squire with the promise that he will one day make Panza a governor. Panza provides the novel's commentary on Don Quixote's deluded actions.

After one particularly bruising encounter, Don Quixote's friends burn all his romances, an act of literary symbolism which was not lost on Cervantes' readers. The book was an immediate success on its publication in 1605. When an unauthorised sequel was produced in 1614 by another writer using the pen name Avellaneda, Cervantes was persuaded to write a second book, and *Don Quixote, Part Two* appeared in 1615, only a year before his death. The two parts are now usually published together as one volume.

The book is open to widely differing interpretations. On its publication, when its readers were familiar with the romances which it satirised, it was enjoyed as a comic novel of error and misunderstanding. In the revolutionary age of the eighteenth century, Sancho Panza was celebrated for proving that lowly citizens could be wise and insightful. In the nineteenth century it was regarded as a social commentary on class structure. Since the twentieth century it has been reviewed more as a tragedy than a comedy. It portrays chivalric ideology as a delusion, and the loss of dignity in the face of harsh reality an inevitable outcome.

Don Quixote is all these things, a superficially simple adventure with a complex subtext. Its arrival signalled the demise of the chivalric romance, replacing cultural stereotypes with the personal development of its characters, and idealised situations with all the tragicomedy of real life, which – thanks to Cervantes – we can now describe as quixotic.

OPPOSITE TOP: This 1895 illustration of the wandering knight and his squire doesn't quite portray Rocinante, his 'noble steed', as a skinny and feeble old nag.
OPPOSITE BOTTOM: A time-worn First Edition of El ingenioso hidalgo Don Quixote de la Mancha (The Ingenious Gentleman Don Quixote of La Mancha).

Robinson Crusoe

(1719)

Daniel Defoe (1660–1731)

The book which invented an entire genre of castaway fiction was written so convincingly that its first readers thought it was a real-life memoir. Although it was indeed based on a true story, its colourful narrative was the invention of an author whose own troubled life reads like a novel.

Daniel Defoe was born plain and simple Dan Foe, but added the 'De' in an attempt to sound aristocratic. At various times he manufactured perfume, imported wine from Portugal, tried to overthrow King James II, spied for King William III and was imprisoned by William's successor, Queen Anne. He wrote contemporary accounts of major events, laying the foundations for modern journalism; and over 500 works of fiction and non-fiction are credited to his name.

Robinson Crusoe, which Defoe wrote at the age of fifty-nine, was the first of his eight novels. It is the story of a man shipwrecked on a deserted island, of the dangers he overcomes and the challenges to his Christian faith that they present. The only other character is an escaped native whom Crusoe names Friday after the day on which they met, and whom he educates in English and Christianity. Crusoe escapes the island after twenty-eight years and a sequel picks up the story after Crusoe settles in England.

The story was inspired by the experiences of Alexander Selkirk, a Scottish seaman who was rescued in 1709 after having been marooned on an island for over four years. Although Crusoe's adventures differ from Selkirk's, Defoe will certainly have been aware of the latter's, which were widely reported after Selkirk's return. In contrast to Crusoe, Selkirk seems to have found a measure of inner peace during his isolation. As for Crusoe's name, Defoe was at school with a boy called Caruso.

The First Edition of *The Life and Strange Surprising Adventures of Robinson Crusoe* was published in 1719 and originally purported to have been 'written by himself'.

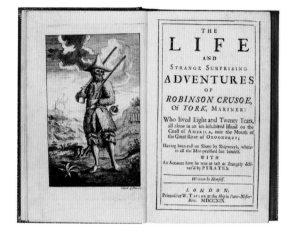

With the adventures of Alexander Selkirk still fresh in their minds, the reading public found that claim easy to believe. The book was immediately popular and was in its fourth edition by the end of the year. Its realistic voice, which made people believe in its central character, influenced the development of the novel.

It is, by some accounts, the most widely translated book apart from the Bible, and Robinson Crusoe and his man-servant Friday have become universally recognised memes, repeated in countless other books and films. *The Swiss Family Robinson* (1812) by Johann David Wyss borrows Crusoe's name and situation; the character Ben Gunn in Robert Louis Stevenson's *Treasure Island* (1883) is a parody of Crusoe.

ROBINSON CRUSOE

DANIEL DEFOE

Illustrated by N.C. WYETH

OPPOSITE: The frontispiece of the First Edition of The Life and Strange Surprizing
Adventures of Robinson Crusoe, Of York, Mariner.
*ABOVE: There have been many illustrated editions of the book, this one by respected
American illustrator N.C. Wyeth, father of realist painter Andrew Wyeth.*

GULLIVER'S TRAVELS

By
JONATHAN
SWIFT

COLOURED
ILLUSTRATIONS
BY
ARTHUR
RACKHAM

TALES
FOR
CHILDREN FROM MANY LANDS

ABOVE: What is today regarded by most as a book for children, started life as a biting repudiation of British politics.
OPPOSITE: The frontispiece of the First Edition has no mention of Jonathan Swift.

Gulliver's Travels

(1726)

Jonathan Swift (1667–1745)

Now regarded purely as a comical fantasy, *Gulliver's Travels* began life as an elaborate satire of British life and literature. It was so mocking of contemporary politicians that Jonathan Swift submitted his manuscript in another man's handwriting for fear of prosecution.

The book relates the famous adventures of Lemuel Gulliver, who is shipwrecked four times under increasingly hazardous circumstances and finds himself living among populations very different from those of his native Nottinghamshire. Swift uses these four societies to lampoon British manners and politics.

Gulliver's Travels arose from a meeting of the leading literary figures of the day: Jonathan Swift, the dramatist John Gay, physician John Arbuthnot, politician Henry St John and poets Alexander Pope and Thomas Parnell. Together they formed a group called the Scriblerus Club, whose aim was to satirise the literary forms of the day. Swift was charged with the genres of autobiography and travel, and the group's first output was a biography written in 1713–14, of Martinus Scriblerus, an invented persona under whose name they published their satires.

Swift began work on *Gulliver's Travels* in 1720. The format of the traveller's tale had only recently been popularised by Daniel Defoe's *Robinson Crusoe*, the story of a castaway on a desert island who learns to rely on his inner strength and ingenuity to survive. Where Defoe focused on the isolated person of Crusoe, Swift believed that collective society was more important than the individual.

The shores on which Gulliver is washed up are therefore far from deserted; but the societies which inhabit them are all dysfunctional in one way or another. The tiny Lilliputians are small-minded people for whom the debate about which end of an egg to crack has divided the nation. The giant Brobdingnagians,

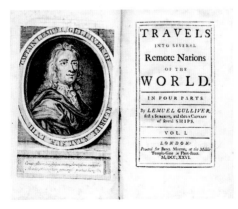

by contrast, are highly moral and rational, educated and literary; they look down on the English in every respect. The Laputans are advanced in their scientific knowledge but can find no practical use for it, Swift's way of criticising England's scientific institution the Royal Society. In his last adventure he lands among the Houyhnhnms, a sophisticated race of talking horses whose company Gulliver prefers to that of the Yahoos, the deformed, thuggish humanoids he first encountered.

Despite Jonathan Swift's efforts to disguise his authorship by having the novel redrafted, the first publisher of *Gulliver's Travels* was nervous about the reaction to it. He omitted several of the more controversial passages and added a loyal tribute to the reigning monarch in the hope of avoiding legal proceedings. Published anonymously in 1726, just seven years after *Robinson Crusoe*, *Gulliver's Travels* was an immediate success and prompted several unauthorised sequels and parodies which Swift was quick to disown.

The first authorised edition of *Gulliver's Travels*, one with the omitted sections restored and whose proofs had been read by Swift, was published in 1735. It included a letter supposedly written by Gulliver to a cousin complaining of the First Edition's liberties with the text, so great that, 'I do hardly know mine own work.' With this letter he perpetuated the idea that Gulliver was a real person and his memoirs also real, ironically one of the tricks which had made *Robinson Crusoe* so convincing.

Tom Jones

(1749)

Henry Fielding (1707–1754)

Those who think that the classic English novel is all high Victorian modesty, with authors like Jane Austen and Charles Dickens, will be surprised by this masterpiece from an earlier century. Young Tom Jones is a good man but a promiscuous one in this comedy of manners, social class and, yes, sex.

Fielding's hero is a foundling, adopted by the man in whose bed he was abandoned. His first love, Molly, is a young woman of easy virtue. There is a possibility, but no certainty, that Tom is the father of her baby. The path to the heart of his second love, Sophia, is never smooth and occupies the bulk of *Tom Jones*. In the course of it he befriends the man wrongly suspected of being his father, and accidentally sleeps with the woman falsely identified as his mother. The principal obstacles to Tom and Sophia's happiness are his illegitimate birth and his jealous, scheming half-brother, William Bilfil; but once Tom's more-respectable-if-illicit parentage is discovered, he and Sophia live happily ever after with two children and the blessings of their fathers.

The story is told by a narrator who is as much a part of the book as Tom Jones himself. The narrator provides a running commentary on the events of the novel, directly addressing the reader. By the end of the book, reader and narrator have formed an attachment and the narrator concludes by bidding a fond farewell to the reader. It's a distinctive feature of *Tom Jones*, one of the earliest stories in English to be considered a true novel.

Fielding uses the characters in the story to criticise the definitions of social class which cause Tom many of his problems. He also attacks Methodism, the brand of Christianity then gaining much ground in England; and Catholicism, which had recently been the focus of a failed

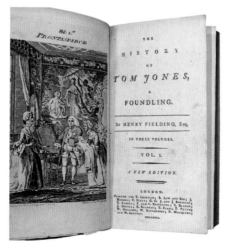

attempt to restore a Catholic, Bonnie Prince Charlie, to the British throne. Broadly speaking all the 'good' characters are Loyalists and Anglicans, and all the 'bad' ones are Methodists and Jacobites.

Tom's growth as an adult takes him through many levels of English society and he encounters people from all walks of life with every degree of moral virtue ... or the lack of it. Fielding had made his reputation not as a novelist but as a playwright, and the plot of the novel is meticulously and ingeniously crafted. Readers today enjoy it not only for its twists and turns but for its comprehensive picture of eighteenth-century life.

The frequent and complex liaisons between the many characters of *Tom Jones* led to its rediscovery at the start of the Swinging Sixties, when it chimed with the sexual freedom of the age. It was made into a very successful film in 1963, scripted by the noted anti-establishment English playwright John Osborne and starring Albert Finney as Tom. The film won four Oscars and its popularity persuaded a young Welsh singer, Thomas Woodward, to adopt the stage name Tom Jones that year.

OPPOSITE TOP: Joseph Stadler's portrait of Sophia Western, the object of Tom Jones' continuing desire.

OPPOSITE BOTTOM: A Thomas Rowlandson illustration of a typical Tom Jones pub fight.

LEFT: The frontispiece of a later edition.

Tom Jones & the Landlord, Partridge & Susan, Mrs Waters & the Landlady

Tristram Shandy

(1759–1767)

Laurence Sterne (1713–1768)

It takes the eponymous Tristram Shandy the first three volumes of his nine-volume autobiography to get to the moment of his birth. He is incapable of getting to the point of any anecdote without digressing at length in a rambling narrative. *Tristram Shandy* is at once one novel, two novels and an anti-novel.

Tristram Shandy is often called the anti-novel because Laurence Sterne's ingenious narrative technique undermines the very story which he is trying to tell. The full title of Sterne's work is *The Life and Opinions of Tristram Shandy, Gentleman*. Tristram is both the object of the tale and the woefully inadequate narrator of it. His willingness to be distracted by any topic which arises from his narration – from obstetric practices to the use of siege engines in medieval warfare – means that diversions occupy more of the novel than his life does. Thus there are two novels in *Tristram Shandy* – the biography of Tristram Shandy, gentleman; and the wit and wisdom of Tristram Shandy, storyteller.

Laurence Sterne was an exceptionally well-read author and his text is littered with literary references. *Tristram Shandy* owes a stylistic debt to Cervantes' *Don Quixote*, and rather more to several other authors. He was an admirer of Francis Bacon and François Rabelais, and of Robert Burton's remarkable seventeenth-century combination of anatomy and philosophy, *The Anatomy of Melancholy*; and on many occasions Sterne quoted his favourites verbatim, simply rearranging their clauses and sentences to support Shandy's arguments.

These borrowings were only noticed after Sterne's death and led to accusations of plagiarism. But they are just another example of the wordplay which fills *Tristram Shandy*: if narrator Tristram's frequent use of double entendres celebrates the power of words to have multiple meanings, then why should Sterne's appropriation of whole phrases not demonstrate the same power?

It has been suggested that Sterne was satirising Burton's high and solemn tone, and he was certainly influenced by the great satirists Alexander Pope and Jonathan Swift, and their fiction *Memoirs of Martinus Scriblerus*. Literary wit is Sterne's stock-in-trade.

Samuel Johnson remarked in 1776 that, 'Nothing odd will do long. *Tristram Shandy* did not last.' But a century and more later, Goethe, Schopenhauer and Karl Marx were among the book's many admirers. The narrator's polymathic and apparently irrelevant discursions anticipate the stream of consciousness of modernists like Marcel Proust and James Joyce. They help the reader to build a far more rounded sense of Tristram Shandy's character than a mere telling of his life would.

In a very modern sense, therefore, *Tristram Shandy*, despite the presence of two Tristram Shandys and a style which undermines the conventional straightforward narrative, is neither two novels nor an anti-novel but a supremely well-crafted and unified single novel.

OPPOSITE: A painting from Tate Britain by Charles Robert Leslie of a scene from Chapter 24, Volume 8. Tristram's uncle Toby is an army veteran who re-enacts historic sieges in miniature in his garden, commanding the action from a sentry box. Toby's neighbour, the widow Wadman, 'lays siege to his heart'. It is the widow who wins the battle by complaining that she has a speck of dust in her eye. Toby is entreated to look, but sees no speck – except this eye 'full of gentle salutations and soft responses'.

Horace Walpole
The Castle of Otranto

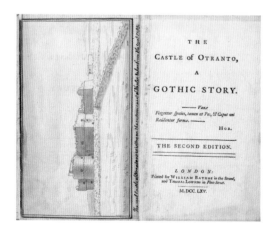

The Castle of Otranto

(1764)

Horace Walpole (1717–1797)

Widely acknowledged as the first Gothic novel, *The Castle of Otranto* single-handedly invented a new genre of fiction and its legacy can be found in everything from Bram Stoker's *Dracula* to J.K. Rowling's *Harry Potter*.

Horace Walpole, son of British Prime Minister Robert Walpole and himself a Member of Parliament for the constituency of King's Lynn, was an expert on medieval history. His affection for the period extended to building his own home, Strawberry Hill House, in the style of a medieval castle – nearly a century before the Victorian revival of Gothic architecture by Augustus Pugin and others.

Walpole's starting point for *The Castle of Otranto* was Manfred, the last king of Sicily from the Hohenstaufen dynasty, who lived in the thirteenth century and counted the real castle of Otranto among his possessions. In the novel, Manfred is haunted by an ancient prophecy that predicts the end of his line. His only son is killed just before his wedding to Isabella when a large helmet falls on him, and Manfred determines to marry the bride in order to produce an heir and to secure his claim on the castle. Isabella is rescued from her fate by a peasant, Theodore; and the rest of the book concerns Manfred's frustrated attempts to regain her.

Walpole adopted the popular literary device of claiming that his story was a translation of an old Italian text, itself based on an even earlier document from the time of the Crusades. He backed up this assertion of authenticity by writing the novel in a deliberately archaic style. Reviewers and readers were thrilled by this apparently genuine tale. When Walpole admitted his authorship in time for the second edition of the book, critics, who were embarrassed that they had fallen for his deception, attacked it as superficial romantic fiction of dubious morality.

Today *The Castle of Otranto* is recognised as having pulled off a much greater trick than merely imitating an earlier form. In his preface to the second edition, Walpole called it 'an attempt to blend the two kinds of romance, the ancient and the modern'. By 'ancient' he meant stories which relied on magical events and unlikely coincidences, for example that Theodore proves to be a prince, or that an injured knight is revealed to be Isabella's father. By 'modern' he meant a degree of realism, which he described as 'a strict adherence to common life'.

The result was a blend of the fantastic – helmets falling from the sky, portraits that walk, ghosts, haunted castle corridors and endangered maidens in need of rescue – with human motives and reactions with which the reader could identify. Reading the novel therefore became a much more immersive, satisfyingly frightening experience.

Walpole's contemporary, the poet Thomas Gray, once told him that his novel had made 'some of us cry a little, and all in general afraid to go to bed o'nights.' *The Castle of Otranto* is the template for countless Gothic horror stories which followed: it forged the association of old castles with secret passages, trapdoors, ghosts, creaking doors which open and close by themselves, and a general air of menace. Walpole made *Frankenstein* and the tales of Edgar Allan Poe possible. With some pride Walpole added a subtitle for the second edition: *The Castle of Otranto – A Gothic Story*.

OPPOSITE TOP: A contemporary edition of the book.

OPPOSITE BOTTOM: The second edition contained an illustration of the castle, Castello Aragonese in Puglia, which is little changed today.

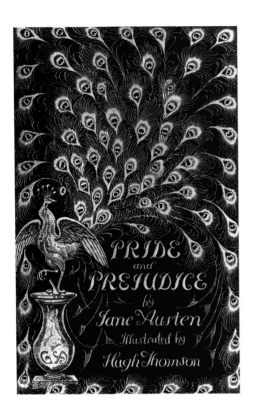

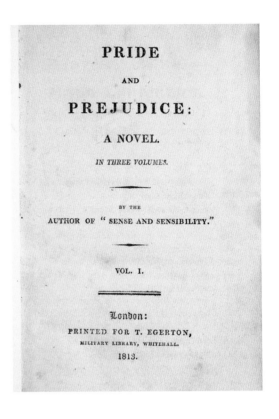

ABOVE LEFT: The first fully illustrated edition published by George Allen in 1894.
ABOVE: Jane Austen's name was omitted from all her books during her lifetime.
LEFT: The only authentic picture of Jane Austen is a pencil and watercolour sketch by her sister Cassandra, held in the National Portrait Gallery, London.

Pride and Prejudice

(1813)

Jane Austen (1775–1817)

The classic romantic comedy of manners is packed with characters who exhibit both pride and prejudice. Although the story is told through the prism of Elizabeth Bennet's thoughts, readers can identify with aspects of all the vividly drawn inhabitants of Jane Austen's Hertfordshire and Derbyshire.

The tale of Elizabeth and Mr Darcy, so obviously suited to each other but so frustratingly kept apart by their pride and prejudices, is a perfectly woven tapestry of plots. It is set in a very specific period and among a particular social class; but love is universal and so are the faults and twists of fate which often thwart it.

One of the great strengths of *Pride and Prejudice* is the affection with which Austen portrays the human failings of her characters. She is never cruel about the flaws which obstruct the path of true love and which all of her audience may have to overcome at some time. Hers is a gentle mockery of the attitudes of the emerging upper-middle class of English society, where money and a successful marriage are intertwined. Austen sets the tone with the very first line of the novel: 'It is a truth universally acknowledged, that a single man in possession of a good fortune must be in want of a wife.' She might have added that a single woman in want of a husband must be in possession of a good dowry.

Although the novel's title is apt, it was originally called *First Impressions*. Its form was different too: Austen wrote it as an epistolary novel, one told by correspondence between the characters. Elements of this version survive in the published edition, which still relies regularly on the arrival of letters. After Austen decided to make Elizabeth's perspective the reader's, the letters act as useful alternative sources of information, for example about the character of Darcy.

Between the completion of *First Impressions* and its publication, two other works with that name had appeared, forcing a change. *Pride and Prejudice* may have been chosen to capitalise on the format of Austen's previous success *Sense and Sensibility*, and *Pride and Prejudice* was credited only to 'the author of *Sense and Sensibility*'. Austen's name was not attached to any of her work during her lifetime.

The novel must be described as romantic because love triumphs in the end for Elizabeth and Darcy; but Austen also presents us with many different, well-observed pictures of marriages which achieve varying measures of success. The characters of her protagonists are not set in stone but change over the course of the story, overcoming pride and prejudice to achieve their own happy endings.

Pride and Prejudice has inspired countless retellings and sequels by other authors. *Longbourn* (2013) by Jo Baker retraces the events of the original novel through the eyes of the servants at Longbourn, the Bennet family home, which Mrs Bennet is so convinced they are going to lose. Crime novelist P.D. James' *Death Comes to Pemberley* (2011) continues Elizabeth and Darcy's story with a murder mystery. One of the most remarkable examples of Austen fan fiction was the 2009 novel *Pride and Prejudice and Zombies*, by Seth Grahame-Smith, which was as eccentric a mixture of genres as its title suggests.

Pride and Prejudice is in that sense connected to early tales of heroism and triumph against the odds, such as Homer's *Odyssey* and the epic Old-English poem *Beowulf*, in which the central character grows through adversity. Austen describes the same growth, and proves that it can take place in our living rooms just as well as in battle or the fires of hell. It has been estimated that more than twenty million copies of *Pride and Prejudice* have been bought and read since its first publication, proof that Austen's keen eye for the human condition is timeless and universally acknowledged.

Frankenstein

(1818)

Mary Shelley (1797–1851)

Few characters have so completely entered the public imagination as Frankenstein's monster. It has appeared in at least seventy-five films, few of them retaining any connection with the original story. More than a century after its creation, Mary Shelley's creature has, ironically, a life of its own.

The eruption of an Indonesian volcano blotted out the sun in the summer of 1816, and three friends retreated indoors from the cold weather to entertain themselves. The poets Byron and Shelley, and Shelley's future wife Mary, read published horror stories to each other in front of the fire. When the stories ran out they challenged each other to write some themselves. Byron's unfinished notes laid the foundation for the vampire genre, and Mary's short story became the full-length novel *Frankenstein, or the Modern Prometheus.*

Although intended as a horror story, Mary Shelley's tale also invites us to consider the nature of life and humanity. Prometheus was the Greek god who fashioned human beings for Zeus to breathe life into, and who (against Zeus's wishes) gave mankind the gift of fire. *Frankenstein* tells the tale of the young scientist Victor Frankenstein who builds a body from parts salvaged from 'the dissecting room and the slaughter-house' and reanimates it after discovering a fundamental force of life. Frankenstein regrets his decision when the new being proves not to be a perfect physical specimen. And when humans cannot accept the monster as one of them, it turns violently against humanity.

It is a sad story. The possibility that man could meet his maker, which casts Frankenstein in the role of god, raises questions about the nature and meaning of life. The book is a product of its time: its romantic and Gothic elements reflect the literary fashions of the day, while its plot owes everything to the Age of Scientific Discovery which was in full swing. Alessandro Volta invented the electric battery in 1800, opening the door for experiments with electricity, and human anatomy had become a popular interest of the educated classes after significant advances in the science during the eighteenth century.

Frankenstein uses a series of 'frame stories' to present its narrative. The reader is presented with two travellers who encounter first the monster and then an aged Frankenstein. It is in this setting that Frankenstein starts to tell the travellers (and the reader) the history of his experiments. Frankenstein at one point describes a chance meeting with the monster many years after its creation, and he relates to the travellers (and us) the tales that the monster told him. So the monster's story is framed in Frankenstein's, which is framed in the travellers', each level of framing drawing us further into the novel.

We owe many of our mental pictures of Frankenstein, his castle and his creation, to the 1931 film of a 1927 stage version of the novel, starring Boris Karloff as the monster. Karloff's make-up, designed by Hollywood artist Jack Pierce, gave us the high forehead and neck bolts. Director James Whale conceived the use of electricity from lightning to bring the creature to life; Shelley was aware of galvanism (experiments with electricity which made the limbs of dead animals move), but she does not refer to it in the novel. Colin Clive, who played Baron Frankenstein, is the role model for all subsequent depictions of the 'mad scientist'; and because Frankenstein deliberately sets out to create life, it has been argued that Shelley's novel is the first work of science fiction.

MARY SHELLEY

Frankenstein: The 1818 Text

ABOVE: Much of the iconography surrounding Frankenstein *relates to the early films and not the novel. This Penguin Classics edition has a monster very much in line with the frontispiece illustration of the 1831 edition.*

OPPOSITE: Irish painter Richard Rothwell's portrait of Mary Shelley, first shown at the Royal Academy in 1840 and accompanied by lines from Percy Shelley describing her as a 'child of love and light'.

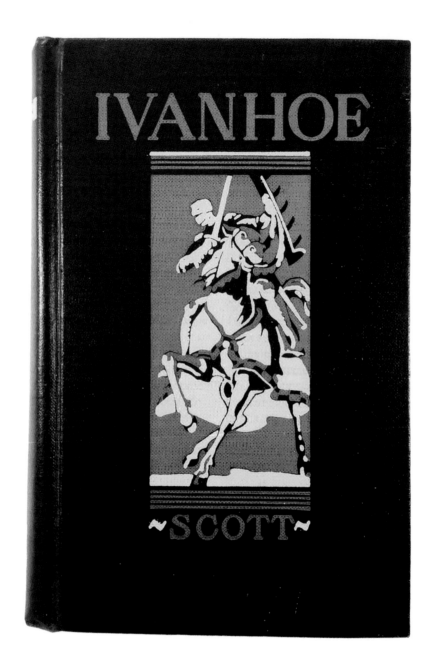

Ivanhoe

(1819)

Walter Scott (1771–1832)

Sir Walter Scott's swashbuckling tale of heroic knights and damsels in distress was one of his successful series of nineteen historical works known as the Waverley Novels. As well as creating the fictional character of Wilfrid of Ivanhoe, it also contributed to the popular image of another legendary hero, Robin Hood.

*I*vanhoe, set in 1194, has all the elements of the perfect medieval romance. The hero has been banished and disinherited by his Saxon father for supporting Richard Lionheart, a Norman king of England. Having fought for Richard on the Third Crusade, he returns to his home in disguise. There he makes life difficult for Prince John (Richard's brother, who has assumed the throne while Richard is being held for ransom in Europe) and Bois-Guilbert (a dishonourable knight trying to seduce the daughter of Ivanhoe's friend Isaac). There are jousting tournaments, castle sieges, kidnaps, the return of the king and a climactic final duel between Bois-Guilbert and Ivanhoe for the honour of Rebecca.

The original medieval romances were tales of courtly love written principally for the amusement of the ladies of European nobility. By emphasising the fighting and the heroic qualities of his principal characters, Scott caters more for his male readership. This is an adventure story for the boys.

Although it includes many of the traditional elements of a romance – chivalry, a quest, honourable and dishonourable knights, even Scott's use of archaic language – it is a subtly modernised version. Ivanhoe is certainly a noble, but he is not an important one, and acts as an everyman with whom the reader can identify. Walter Scott deploys such 'ordinary' heroes in many of his novels, making the culture and society of his chosen period more accessible to the reader.

Ivanhoe's central theme is another common device of Scott's – the tension between old ways of life and new. Here adherents to the old Saxon regime must come to terms with the new Norman overlords, and Ivanhoe acts as a go-between, finally reconciling the two when Lord Athelstane – a Saxon pretender to the throne – swears allegiance to King Richard.

The story is set in a time when the Norman dynasty had been established in England for 130 years. It was written at a time when Scotland had been in a political union with England for almost the same length of time. Scott was Scottish but an enthusiastic supporter of the new Great Britain. It has been suggested that Ivanhoe is in part an allegory for Georgian Britain, in which 'primitive' Scots and 'advanced' English all considered themselves British. Although Scott emphasises the differences between the old Saxons and the new Normans, the reality was that by 1194 the inhabitants of England considered themselves English, not Norman or Saxon.

Robin Hood and his band of outlaws play a significant supporting role in *Ivanhoe*'s drama. Scott's portrayal of them as honourable, decent, happy-go-lucky brigands defined their image in subsequent tellings of their stories. Scott gave him the title Robin of Locksley and invented his feat of splitting a willow with an arrow. In *Ivanhoe* Scott also created a new Christian name, albeit accidentally. He used many genuine Saxon names for his characters, but misspelled Ivanhoe's father Cerdic as Cedric. Many sons of Englishmen have been given the name Cedric ever since.

Le Père Goriot

(1835)

Honoré de Balzac (1799–1850)

The French language has made many contributions to world literature, and *Le Père Goriot* is one of the earliest and best. Balzac's surgically precise use of words and scenes paints a ruthless, detailed portrait of crime, marriage and family life at a turbulent time in Paris's history.

After the defeat of Napoleon, France returned to a form of monarchy with the restoration of Louis XVIII, brother of Louis XVI who had been beheaded during the French Revolution of 1789. Exiled French nobles returned to France in the hope of a return to the *Ancien Régime*; but the changes wrought by the Revolution were too deep and too well established: a restructured justice system, new levels of local government, and the emergence of a new, property-owning middle class. Tensions led to unrest between conservatives who supported the monarchy and liberals who saw not only a new, fairer society but an opportunity to advance within it.

Against this background Balzac tells the story of old man Goriot, who has impoverished himself in order to support his selfish daughters, Delphine and Anastasie, both of whom have married well. Goriot lives in a boarding house whose other guests include Eugène de Rastignac, from an aristocratic family in the provinces who is studying law in Paris, and Vautrin, a criminal. Vautrin suggests that Rastignac marry a wealthy unmarried woman. Her brother controls her fortune, so Vautrin offers to kill him.

Rastignac declines because he and Delphine have become lovers; but nevertheless he has been alerted to the possibilities of scheming to climb the social ladder. While all the other characters in the story are advancing themselves by all means possible, only honourable Père Goriot is in economic and physical decline. Only social climber Rastignac wishes to be seen at his funeral.

There are echoes of Shakespeare's *King Lear* in the relationship between father and daughters. Balzac admired Walter Scott's historical novels, and writing only a few years after the overthrow of Louis XVIII's brother Charles X, he aspired to a similar authenticity of period. He was also influenced by the American author James Fenimore Cooper, from whose depictions of American Indians he saw evidence of a brutal spirit surviving all attempts at civilisation. At one point Vautrin describes Paris as 'a forest of the New World where twenty varieties of savage tribes clash'.

Balzac's was a stark view of humanity. He was fascinated by crime and criminality. The character of Vautrin is based on a real-life criminal, Eugène François Vidocq, whom Balzac had met and whose sensational memoirs were published only six years before *Le Père Goriot*. Even those who have not yet read *Goriot* will recognise one of the most famous lines from it, later used almost verbatim in the Mario Puzo novel *The Godfather*. Vautrin hisses threateningly to Rastignac, 'I will make you an offer that no one would decline.'

Le Père Goriot marks the start of Balzac's overarching literary concept, *La Comédie humaine*, a series of novels connected by time and by shared characters. Rastignac, for example, first appeared in Balzac's earlier novel *La Peau de chagrin*. Although *Le Père Goriot* was published to mixed reviews, it was an immediate success with the public, and a profound influence on subsequent writers. The twentieth-century French novelist Félicien Marceau spoke for many when he declared, 'We are all children of *Le Père Goriot*.'

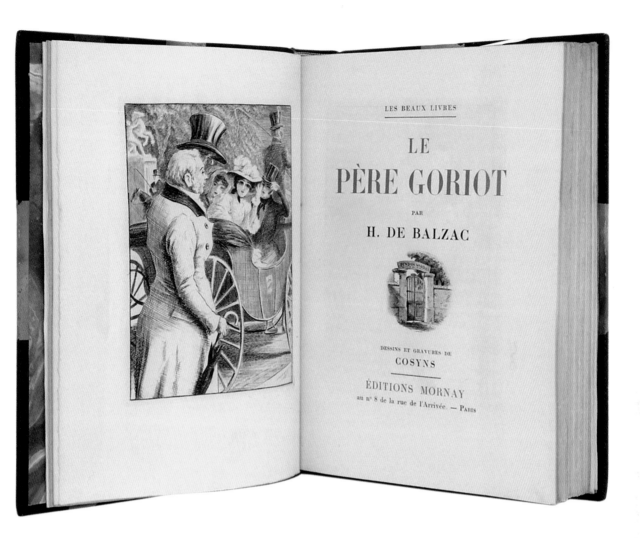

LES BEAUX LIVRES

LE
PÈRE GORIOT

PAR

H. DE BALZAC

DESSINS ET GRAVURES DE
COSYNS

ÉDITIONS MORNAY
au n° 8 de la rue de l'Arrivée. — PARIS

ABOVE: Le Père Goriot *gave rise to the French expression for an unprincipled social climber –* 'Rastignac'.

LEFT: A portrait of Balzac from the 1840s. The author spent his life dodging creditors, and guests to his house in Rue Raynouard were obliged to give a password at the door to gain entrance.

The Count of Monte Cristo

(1844)

Alexandre Dumas (1802–1870)

Dumas followed *The Three Musketeers* with another novel of non-stop action and suspense. Its setting in France's more recent turbulent past gave it a special resonance throughout Europe, where it was widely translated and became for many years the continent's best seller.

Originally published in instalments in the magazine *Journal des Débats*, *The Count of Monte Cristo* was the nineteenth-century equivalent of appointment television. New episodes were eagerly awaited and became the topic of conversation at home and on street corners for days afterwards. It was set against a background of France's fast-changing, early nineteenth-century history, when it alternated regularly between monarchy, republicanism and imperialism.

In short: after the fall of the First French Empire in 1814, the Bourbon monarchy was interrupted by the escape from Elba in 1815 of the imprisoned Napoleon and then overthrown by the July Revolution of 1830, which installed the more constitutionally limited Orléans monarchy. That lasted until the revolution of 1848, which briefly created the Second Republic before that, too, was overthrown, this time by a coup, which created the Second Empire under absolutist emperor Napoleon III.

The Count of Monte Cristo was written during the reign of Louis Philippe of Orléans. Alexandre Dumas met Napoleon III before he became emperor, sailed around the island of Monte Cristo with him, and promised him that he would write a novel with the island's name in its title.

The novel begins on the date on which Napoleon I escaped from Elba, when Edmond Dantès docks his ship at Marseille. Expecting to wed his fiancée he is instead falsely accused by jealous acquaintances of being a supporter of Napoleon and imprisoned in the notorious Château d'If. After fourteen years

he escapes with information from a fellow prisoner about a lost treasure on the island of Monte Cristo. In a succession of disguises and ruses Dantès punishes his accusers and achieves a measure of personal peace. The concluding lines of the book sum up its principal themes: 'All human wisdom is contained in these two words, "Wait and Hope".'

The story is told from many perspectives, not just by a single narrator, a device which aims to give the reader an apparently balanced view of the action. In addition to the very *live* French history in the novel, Dumas also referred to current political upheavals in Spain and Italy. The revolutionary France of *Monte Cristo* made it a favourite book of Jiang Qing, Mao Zedong's fourth wife; and the Chinese translation made after the end of the Cultural Revolution was extremely successful among China's very politically aware population.

The Count of Monte Cristo was Dumas' sixth collaboration with Auguste Maquet, who ghost-wrote rough plots and character sketches for several of Dumas' works, including *The Three Musketeers*. Dumas was already a successful writer before he met Maquet, and Maquet agreed, for a payment, that his name be omitted from their books. The relationship broke down and Maquet sued for royalties and a writing credit. He lost when a judge ruled that 'Dumas without Maquet would have been Dumas: what would Maquet have been without Dumas?'

Jane Eyre

(1847)

Charlotte Brontë (1816–1855)

The Brontës were a literary supergroup and Charlotte Brontë was their leader. *Jane Eyre* was the novel that introduced the family to the literary world. On its publication it sharply divided critics but was quickly popular with readers, for whom its ground-breaking first-person narrative struck a chord.

*J*ane Eyre was the first novel to trace its central character's personal development through that person's own thoughts. Originally titled *Jane Eyre: An Autobiography*, the book's events are unfolded for the reader in Jane's own words, in Jane's own experience of them. This now common writing technique immerses the reader in Jane Eyre's life and makes the reading of the book altogether more intense.

The story of plain-looking Jane's life, from abusive childhood, through hard work as a spinster governess, to happiness as the second wife of Edward Rochester is a superficially simple narrative, slowly transforming Jane from unloved youth to loving and finally beloved adult. But the levels of spiritual and moral development through which she passes en route not only direct but are directed by the episodes of the plot. This is a psychologically complex love story.

It's also an early contribution to feminism. Although *Jane Eyre* is not a campaigning work, Charlotte Brontë creates in it a strong-willed character who considers herself quite the equal of men, in the eyes of God if not of society, when she berates Rochester for his cruel first proposal of marriage: 'it is my spirit that addresses your spirit; just as if both had passed through the grave, and we stood at God's feet, equal, – as we are!'

Jane Eyre was published under the deliberately gender-neutral pseudonym Currer Bell, raising speculation about who the author might be. One periodical, *The Indicator*, embarrassed itself with a forthright prediction:

'No woman in all the annals of feminine celebrity ever wrote such a style, terse yet eloquent, and filled with energy bordering sometimes almost on rudeness: no woman ever conceived such masculine characters as those portrayed here ... On one assertion we are willing to risk our critical reputation – and that is, that no woman wrote it.'

Charlotte writes from a position of high Christian morality – which does not prevent her from criticising the religious and social mores of the early Victorian age. Some critics attacked the book for being anti-Christian because it attacked class inequality in Britain, which some versions of Christianity sought to perpetuate. 'Religion is stabbed in the dark,' wrote a reviewer in *The Mirror of Literature, Amusement, and Instruction*, 'our social distinctions attempted to be levelled.'

One social division which she did not attempt to subvert was that of race. Rochester's first wife, Bertha, by implication a woman of mixed race from the West Indies, is portrayed as someone of inferior mental capacity and self-control, kept out of sight, locked in a padded room in the attic. Bertha is drawn in deliberately sharp distinction to the intelligent and self-possessed Jane. Jean Rhys's 1966 novel *Wide Sargasso Sea*, which retells the story from Bertha's point of view, is an acute observation of domination, powerlessness and a mismatched marriage, which makes a fascinating companion piece to *Jane Eyre*.

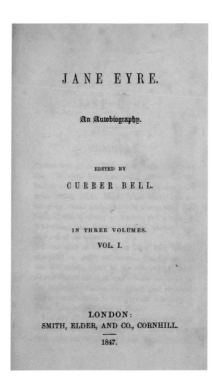

JANE EYRE.

An Autobiography.

EDITED BY

CURRER BELL.

IN THREE VOLUMES.

VOL. I.

LONDON:
SMITH, ELDER, AND CO., CORNHILL.
1847.

LEFT: The title page of Jane Eyre. The pen name Bell was adopted from the Haworth curate Arthur Bell Nicholls, who Charlotte married in 1854.
BELOW: Haworth Parsonage viewed from the cemetery of St Michael and All Angels' Church. Today it is the Brontë Museum preserving the legacy of the family, allowing visitors to experience the atmosphere in which the books were written. The family are buried in their own vault within the church.
OPPOSITE: Charlotte Brontë sketched by George Richmond in 1850.

Wuthering Heights

(1847)

Emily Brontë (1818–1848)

Emily Brontë's poll-topping masterpiece received mixed reviews on first publication. Its classic romance is underpinned with a Gothic menace as dark and bleak as the Yorkshire moors by which she lived and was inspired. The very name Heathcliff evokes danger in exposed country.

The doomed love of Heathcliff for Catherine Earnshaw is the tragic heart of *Wuthering Heights*. The affection between the characters is dashed as they grow up; and when Cathy and Linton, the children of their separate marriages, fall in love in the next generation, Cathy's happiness too is curtailed, by the death of Linton, Heathcliff's son. A recurring theme of the novel is the failure of childhood joys to be realised in later life.

The parsonage in Haworth, Yorkshire, was home to the Brontë children, whose father was the vicar at St Michael and All Angels' Church in the village. Through their father's pastoral work the children learned of some of the darker traits of humanity, and *Wuthering Heights* attracted considerable criticism for the rough language and behaviour that Emily Brontë portrayed. One review declared, 'In *Wuthering Heights* the reader is shocked, disgusted, almost sickened by details of cruelty, inhumanity, and the most diabolical hate and vengeance', but acknowledged its 'powerful testimony to the supreme power of love – even over demons in the human form'. Emily wrote under the androgynous pen name Ellis Bell, and readers were surprised when it was revealed after her death that such wild emotions had been described by a woman.

Emily's work, and that of her sisters, exists – as they did – in isolation. They were not obviously influenced by any earlier literary tradition; nor, although they had many admirers, do they seem to have directly influenced those who came after them. Their world was a closed one,

from which the wide expanses and rock outcrops of the Yorkshire moors must have seemed endlessly wild, exciting and liberating.

The Haworth parsonage was a literary hothouse. Emily and her siblings Charlotte, Anne and Branwell were all authors, encouraged in the first instance by Charlotte discovering Emily's secret poetry. Charlotte also chaperoned their legacy, outliving them all by six years before her own early death at the age of thirty-nine. Charlotte's novel *Jane Eyre* was the family's first 'hit' and was generally held to be the best of their output. But in the twentieth and twenty-first centuries *Wuthering Heights* has been re-evaluated. The true genius of Emily's poetic prose in capturing the dangerous, terrifying world of love has now been recognised. As Virginia Woolf put it, 'She looked out upon a world cleft into gigantic disorder and felt within her the power to unite it in a book.'

Emily Brontë succumbed to tuberculosis only a year after the book's publication, aged just thirty, less than three months after her brother Branwell, thirty-one, died of laudanum and alcohol poisoning. Her sister Anne also died of tuberculosis the following year, only twenty-nine years old. Only Charlotte outlasted them, but she died of complications during pregnancy. Tragically, their father lived to bury them all.

The fates of all the Brontës and the isolated lives they led have amplified their status as novelists. But Emily more than all of them had the ability to capture her world and translate it into one of the greatest romantic novels ever written.

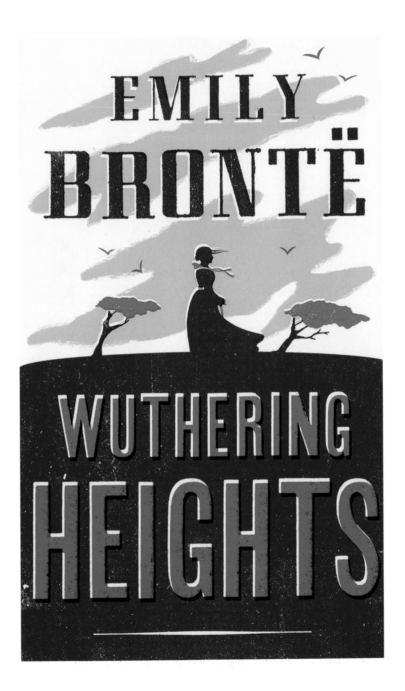

EMILY BRONTË

WUTHERING HEIGHTS

ABOVE: *A contemporary cover of Emily Brontë's classic novel.*
OPPOSITE: *The title page of the First Edition, with the author credit as Ellis Bell. It was not until 1850 that Emily Brontë appeared in print as the author, which, like Jane Austen, she never got to see.*

REBECCA'S FAREWELL.

ABOVE: *Not only was Thackeray an adroit social commentator, but also a skilful artist,
contributing his own illustrations to* Vanity Fair. *In Thackeray's hands Becky Sharp is
noticeably less fair of face than in subsequent depictions.*
OPPOSITE: *Thackeray was a fan of Charlotte Brontë's* Jane Eyre, *and she dedicated the second
edition to him.*

Vanity Fair

(1848)

William Makepeace Thackeray (1811–1863)

Love and money are the two central themes of *Vanity Fair*, the pursuit of the former taking second place to the desire for the latter. Thackeray's skewering of middle-class ideals is as sharp today as it was when Charlotte Brontë declared, 'If Truth were again a goddess, Thackeray should be her high priest.'

Vanity Fair's subtitle is *A Novel Without a Hero*. There are no noble characters here, none without flaws. Becky Sharp and Amelia, the two friends at the centre of the story, both seek love, but misguidedly. Both women are impoverished by their marriages and the novel is much concerned with their rising and falling fortunes. Becky forms relationships only if they advance her socially; and Amelia clings so desperately to the love of her dead husband, George Osborne (who betrayed her for Becky), that she misses out on the chance of true love with her lifelong admirer William Dobbin, George's best friend.

Ruthless Becky will stop at nothing, not even murder, to climb the social ladder; the widowed Amelia is too lovelorn to begin a new relationship with Dobbin, who earlier in the novel was too passive to press his own suit over Osborne's and even encouraged Amelia and George to marry. Dobbin wastes his life pining for Amelia, while Amelia's brother Jos loses his life through his infatuation with manipulative Becky. When Becky finally achieves wealth, she finds that her behaviour on the way has made her an outcast at the very level of society to which she aspired. At the end, the reader is left to ask whether any of the surviving characters will ever be really happy.

One of the features of the novel is Thackeray's authorial narrator, who not only presents the action but comments on it, gossips about it and even appears in it on occasion. He even appears to change his view of Becky's moral standing as events unfold. *Vanity Fair* is full of performances. It begins and ends with a puppet show at the Fair; and throughout the book the characters are rarely being true to themselves, whether it's Osborne and Dobbin putting on a brave face for the women before they fight at the Battle of Waterloo, or Becky supporting charitable causes to impress her society acquaintances. Amelia's devotion to her late husband is a prolonged performance; and Becky seduces a member of the nobility by her performances in a game of charades. The reader is encouraged to ask whether love is just an act.

The title of the book comes from John Bunyan's religious allegory *Pilgrim's Progress* (1678). All the people in Thackeray's orchestrated tale are in Vanity Fair, Bunyan's playground of worldly pleasures designed to distract the idle rich from a life of selfless Christian morality. As Thackeray declares at the start of the novel, 'this is VANITY FAIR; not a moral place certainly; nor a merry one, though very noisy.'

Both Becky and Amelia are on a journey of self-discovery comparable to that of Bunyan's pilgrim and face similar moral challenges along the way. Thackeray's readers would have been familiar with the reference to Bunyan's book in the title of his own, which in turn inspired the launch, in 1868, of a new magazine, *Vanity Fair*, which held a satirical mirror up to British society from then until its closure in 1914. The title was revived in the early 1980s as a glamorous society magazine, far removed from the aims of Thackeray's novel.

David Copperfield

(1850)

Charles Dickens (1812–1870)

Charles Dickens' personal favourite of his novels, *David Copperfield,* is a mixture of fiction and fact based on Dickens' own life. It marks a turning point in his writing, from the lighter works of his earlier career to the darker themes of his more mature output.

*D*avid Copperfield is, on the surface, the history of a central character in the manner of Henry Fielding's *Tom Jones* or Charlotte Brontë's *Jane Eyre.* But it is much more complicated than that, an intricately woven embroidery of autobiography, satire and social criticism. Dickens was liberated by writing *David Copperfield.* Confident in the autobiographical storyline, he was able to take on darker social issues than he had done previously. It followed the run-of-the-mill *Dombey and Son*, and was in turn followed by *Bleak House*, of which G.K. Chesterton wrote, 'Bleak House is not certainly Dickens's best book; but perhaps it is his best novel.' Dickens himself considered *David Copperfield* his 'darling', and claimed never to have read *Jane Eyre*.

There are parallels with *Jane Eyre* – Copperfield's unloved childhood, and his eventual happiness in marriage after disappointments and false starts – but Dickens, writing only two years after Brontë, digs much deeper into society's underbelly. *David Copperfield* looks critically at the prison system, at children working in factories, at prostitution, the position of women in marriage and much more. *Jane Eyre* is set in rural northern England; *David Copperfield* takes place in the industrialised south-east, in and around a rapidly expanding London. It is resolutely urban in setting and attitude.

It is striking that, in writing *David Copperfield*, Charles Dickens worked without having first drafted an outline of the plot, his more usual practice. Large parts of the story, being based on his own, were already clear in his mind. However, the story was originally published as a serial, and Dickens was flexible enough to change or add details depending on the public's response to earlier episodes. Miss Mowcher, for example (whom Copperfield encounters through his friendship with Steerforth), began life in the story as an annoyingly loud, gossipy dwarf; but when Dickens' wife's chiropodist, also a dwarf, complained to Mrs Dickens that it showed her disability in a bad light, he brought Mowcher back in later episodes with more positive characteristics.

Dickens had a genius for character, and *David Copperfield* has a full quota of them, their names as familiar as Copperfield's: David's well-meaning aunt Betsey Trotwood; the charming but ineffectual Mr and Mrs Micawber; scheming, not-so-humble Uriah Heep; dangerously charismatic James Steerforth. Many of them are potential but unsuitable father figures for Copperfield, whose own father died before he was born. Mr Micawber is at one point sent to a debtors' prison, as Dickens' father was.

There are many autobiographical details such as this in the novel. Copperfield's schools are based on those which Dickens attended. The descriptions of the lawyers' office in which Uriah Heep is the clerk are based on Dickens' own experiences as a clerk in the firm of Ellis and Blackmore, Attorneys. David's initially unrequited love for Dora Spenlow reflects Dickens' own first love, Maria Beadnell. Maria's parents put paid to that infatuation, but for the sake of the novel Dickens allows Copperfield to marry Dora. It's a happy ending to the story of a boy overcoming many setbacks on the road to adulthood and success, just as Dickens did, and it strikes a chord in all of us.

The Scarlet Letter

(1850)

Nathaniel Hawthorne (1804–1864)

Nathaniel Hawthorne's tale of shame in the darkness of Puritan society is a landmark of nineteenth-century American literature. It is set in seventeenth-century Boston, Massachusetts, but the book resonates with echoes of that century's notorious witch trials at Salem, just a few miles north of Boston.

In Boston, the Puritans gather to watch the punishment of Hester Prynne, an unmarried woman who has given birth. Her humiliation is to last not just for one day but forever, after she is ordered to wear a scarlet letter 'A' for Adultery for the rest of her life. She refuses to identify the father of the child, and her estranged husband, whom she thought dead, is the only person who thinks that the father should also be punished for conceiving the child out of wedlock.

Society shuns both Hester and her daughter, Pearl, who scrape a living at the edge of town. Meanwhile Arthur Dimmesdale, the minister of Hester's church and a pillar of the community, grows very ill. Hester's husband, a physician, tends to him, but suspects that guilt may be the root of his physical decline. At the conclusion of the novel, Dimmesdale's sin will find him out at the day of reckoning, in spite of his prayers. Hester, although she carries out charitable work, will never regain her place in the society of the town. Their parallel falls from grace echo that of Adam and Eve, punished by God and exiled from the Garden of Eden.

Puritans were often the target in Hawthorne's highly moral novels. Their dark, constricting morality offered no hope of salvation for sinners; and throughout *The Scarlet Letter* Hawthorne contrasts dark places in Boston with the light and beauty of the countryside. A rosebush, in particular, offers brightness and warmth in a cold world. Hester's daughter is another ray of light; pearls form inside seashells around specks of grit, and, like Pearl, those mere pieces of dirt become radiant jewels. Even the embroidered letter 'A' that Hester makes for herself is a beautiful thing, and in the closing paragraphs of the book, Hester, having left Boston for a new life, returns and proudly wears it again.

Hawthorne was born in Boston and lived for part of his life in Salem. The house in which he wrote *The Scarlet Letter* still stands, still a private residence. Natives of Salem, proud of their devout ancestors, complained bitterly about Hawthorne's portrayal of them in the book's introduction, but he was unrepentant. The novel contains many references to real people of the period, including Increase Mather, who was involved in the Salem witch trials, and Ann Hibbins, who was hanged for witchcraft in Boston thirty-five years before the Salem trials.

The Scarlet Letter has a place in publishing history too. It was one of the first books in America to be mass-produced instead of hand-printed and bound; and it quickly sold out its initial run of 2,500 copies. Hawthorne is believed to have based Hester on the life of Elizabeth Pain, who conceived a child before she was married. Pain's headstone stands within the King's Chapel Burying Ground in Boston, which Hawthorne names in the novel. Like Hester's fictional stone, Pain's carries a coat of arms in which can clearly be seen part of the letter 'A' for Adultery.

Moby-Dick

(1851)

Herman Melville (1819–1891)

'Call me Ishmael.' The opening imperative of *Moby-Dick; or, The Whale* grabs its readers' attention from the start and draws them into a tempestuous world as unfamiliar to twenty-first-century audiences as it was to the average American when the book was first published.

Ishmael, the novel's narrator, is a sailor serving under Captain Ahab. Ahab is a man tested to destruction by his obsessive desire for revenge on Moby Dick, the great white whale which tore off his leg. Ignoring the advice of others and the wisdom of his own experience, Ahab is trapped in his quest to seek out the great albino sperm whale.

As ever-greater disasters befall his ship, the *Pequod*, the rising sense of ill luck and doomed fate is marked by a series of encounters with other whaling ships. These 'gams' or meet-ups offer alternatives to Ahab's hell-bent determination to destroy the whale, at the risk of his crew and himself; but the ship's company cannot defy their captain. *Moby-Dick* is an immersive adventure, written with authority by a man who had himself been a sailor aboard a whaling ship.

Melville was not a nautical man by birth. His father was a Scottish émigré who became an importer of French goods in New York City. His death when Melville was only twelve left the family with debts of more than $20,000 and forced the young man to fend for himself with a variety of jobs to support his mother and siblings. He worked as a clerk, first in a bank then in the family's struggling furs business, then taught children scarcely younger than himself at a school in Massachusetts. Finally he went to sea for five years in 1839. His first published efforts as a writer were autobiographical essays on his experiences in the South Seas.

Moby-Dick; or, The Whale was his first novel. The title always includes a hyphen, although in the text the

whale is simply Moby Dick. The authenticity of Melville's descriptions of life at sea is enhanced by his extraordinary poetry of language. Owing as much to ancient sagas and to Shakespeare as to contemporary writers such as the American novelist Nathaniel Hawthorne (whom Melville admired), the text is another way of wrapping the reader up completely in the tale. While he was writing it, Melville corresponded with Richard Henry Dana Jr, author of a celebrated memoir, *Two Years Before the Mast*. In one letter he told Dana:

'The poetry runs as hard as sap from a frozen maple tree; — & to cook the thing up, one must needs throw in a little fancy, which from the nature of the thing, must be ungainly as the gambols of the whales themselves. Yet I mean to give the truth of the thing.'

Expecting to complete the novel in six months, he eventually worked on it for a year and a half.

Broadly speaking the novel was disappointingly received in America. In England the novel benefited from a long, well-established tradition of literary criticism, and reviewers were quick to recognise the power and grandeur of *Moby-Dick*. In America reviews were generally the work of staff writers who lacked a broad literary education and found the language and the setting 'difficult'. Only after Melville's death in 1891 was the book reappraised; and it now stands happily as one of the very greatest American novels ever written.

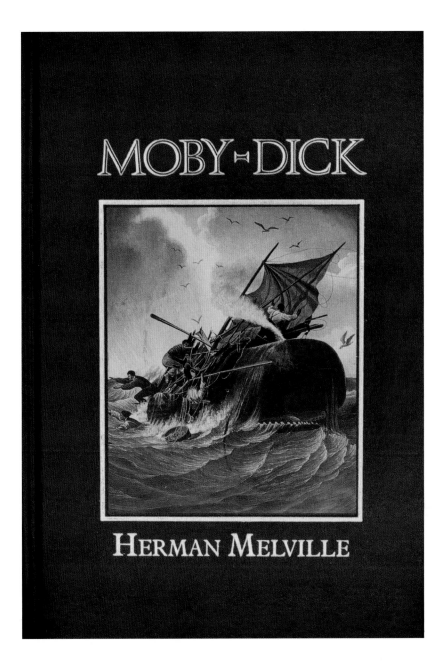

MOBY-DICK

HERMAN MELVILLE

Madame Bovary

(1856)

Gustave Flaubert (1821–1880)

Henry James thought it stood alone in its perfection. Marcel Proust admired its grammar. Vladimir Nabokov and Milan Kundera declared that it was the novel in which prose became the equal of poetry. Arbiters of taste in 1856 prosecuted it in the French courts for obscenity.

Madame Bovary's publishers were acquitted of obscenity in February 1857, and thanks to the publicity surrounding the trial, it was a bestseller by April. If its early readers were hoping for sensation, today's literati admire it for its immaculate portrayal of reality and the contrast with the unattainable romantic and economic fantasies of its central character.

Emma Bovary is a dreamer. Ironically her dreams are inspired by the popular novels of the time and she imagines the ideal marriage to the perfect man who will lavish luxury on her all her days. Like so many dreams, Emma's are elusive and disappointing in real life. Extra-marital affairs and extravagant spending do not satisfy her and destroy the lives of those around her, as well as her own.

Gustave Flaubert wrote in the emerging 'Realistic' style, a reaction to the Romantic and Gothic fiction which preceded him and which inspired Emma Bovary's fantasies. The contrast between the imperfect everyday lives of the people around her and the idealistic delusions of Madame Bovary, is at the heart of the novel; and the obscenity of which Flaubert was accused was simply the reality of humanity's attempts to carve out happiness and a little economic and emotional stability. Ordinary life in the real world thwarts Emma's unrealistic ambitions, and her selfish behaviour disrupts the efforts of others.

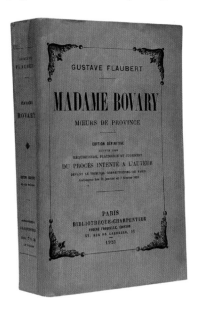

Written in the decade following the French Revolution of 1848, the novel is sometimes seen as a commentary on the foolish, acquisitive ambitions of the bourgeois. The middle classes emerged in the first half of the nineteenth century, and it was resentment of this new sector of society (rather than of the nobility) which triggered the events of 1848 and the overthrow of the last French king, Louis Philippe.

Flaubert disliked the bourgeoisie with a passion. He never married, although he had notable affairs and was extremely promiscuous. He is said to have claimed that '*Madame Bovary, c'est moi*' ('Madame Bovary is me'); but in correspondence he also declared that '*je n'y ai rien mis ni de mes sentiments ni de mon existence*' ('I have used nothing of my feelings or of my life').

He was known by other authors in his lifetime for being agonisingly perfectionist in his choice of '*le mot juste*' – the exact word for the moment – and his output was slow by the standards of the day. *Madame Bovary*, his first novel, took five years to complete: sometimes he would labour for a week over a single page of text. The result is the perfect novel, one to which almost every author since has paid tribute as the pillar around which Realism as a literary movement was built.

ABOVE: The Death of Madame Bovary *painted in 1883 by Albert Fourié.*

OPPOSITE: An early edition of the 'obscene' book. Moeurs de Province *translates as*
Provincial Manners.

COSETTE SWEEPING.

*ABOVE: An illustration of Cosette in the Thénardiers' inn at Montfermeil. Émile Bayard's work
is instantly recognisable from the* Les Misérables *musical poster.*
OPPOSITE: An etching of Victor Hugo, circa 1880.

Les Misérables

(1862)

Victor Hugo (1802–1885)

One of the longest novels ever written, *Les Misérables* runs to 655,478 words in Victor Hugo's original French. It was originally published in five volumes containing forty-eight books or sections, together made up of 365 short chapters. This is Big Literature in every sense.

Victor Hugo made notes of everything he saw, and many of the events and scenes in *Les Misérables* can be traced to his journals and diaries. Unlike his friend and fellow author Gustave Flaubert, who weighed up every word, Hugo's text poured out of him. Almost a quarter of the book consists of essays which do not move the story on at all. Instead, they either draw on Hugo's vast knowledge of history and France, or argue a socio-political perspective raised by the story. Hugo intended the book to be an encyclopaedia for the times, as he explained to his publisher:

> I don't know whether it will be read by everyone, but it is meant for everyone. ... Wherever men go in ignorance or despair, wherever women sell themselves for bread, wherever children lack a book to learn from or a warm hearth, *Les Misérables* knocks at the door and says: 'open up, I am here for you'.

Les Misérables tells the story of Jean Valjean, newly released from prison and trying to make his way honestly in a world which assumes the worst of ex-convicts. Even after he finds success under an alias, his past and the prejudices of his contemporaries threaten to destroy him. All Jean's generosity, grace and good deeds count for nothing against society's verdict; and only at the very end are his selfless acts finally attributed to him.

At its simplest, *Les Misérables* is a novel about redemption versus damnation, about society versus the individual, and crime versus punishment. Hugo himself described it as, 'a progress from evil to good, from injustice to justice, from falsehood to truth, from night to day, from appetite to conscience, from corruption to life; from bestiality to duty, from hell to heaven, from nothingness to God.'

Victor Hugo was a literary superstar in his day, famed as a poet and as the author of *The Hunchback of Notre-Dame* (*Notre-Dame de Paris*). The publication of *Les Misérables* was eagerly awaited and promoted with a large advertising budget. It marked a shift in his style, from the Gothic tragedy of *Hunchback* to an altogether grittier modern realism. Critics did not like it, complaining of Hugo's immorality in siding with the revolutionaries among whom part of the story is set, and of his sentimentality about the working classes. His fellow writers did not like it either: Flaubert thought it signalled 'the fall of a god', and the poet Charles Baudelaire managed to be supportive in public but privately found it 'repulsive and inept'.

The public, however, loved it and made it an immediate bestseller. Within a year it had been translated into several other European languages and published throughout the continent, as well as in Britain and the United States. The first film version, four and a half hours long, was made in 1932, and the long-running stage musical had its opening night in 1980. The one thing that is usually not translated is the book's title. Although it is usually understood to mean 'the miserable', 'the wretched' or 'the dispossessed', the setting and the passion of the story are so rooted in Victor Hugo's France that it would be wrong to call it anything other than *Les Misérables*.

Journey to the Centre of the Earth

(1864)

Jules Verne (1828–1905)

Verne was not the first person to explore the fictional potential of underground worlds. What marks *Journey to the Centre of the Earth* out is Verne's attention to scientific detail. Undermined by countless inaccurate screen adaptations, the original Verne version remains an outstanding work of science fantasy.

Dante Alighieri's *Divine Comedy* (1321) places Hell within the Earth's core; and a Scandinavian satire by Ludvig Holberg, *Niels Klim's Underground Travels* (1741), imagines a smaller, utopian globe contained inside our own hollow world. Verne, unlike his predecessors, was well informed about current research and the scientific context of his age.

In Verne's vision, German professor Otto Lidenbrock, his nephew Axel and their Icelandic guide Hans Bjelke enter that world through Snæfellsjökull, a real-life Icelandic volcano. In a series of adventures they encounter underground rivers and seas, prehistoric creatures, giant humans – and the remains of a modern one, suggesting that they are not the first to explore this world.

Lidenbrock and his companions encounter life-forms whose fossilised remains had only recently been discovered when Verne was writing – among them the ichthyosaurus, plesiosaurus and pterodactylus, a herd of mastodons, and forests of early forms of vegetation. The author took pains to reflect the scientific discoveries of his time.

Jules Verne is the second-most translated author in the world, ahead of Agatha Christie and beaten only by William Shakespeare. In his lifetime he published fifty-four tales of Extraordinary Journeys, beginning with *Five Weeks in a Balloon* (1863). *Journey to the Centre of the Earth* was his third novel, followed a year later by *From the Earth to the Moon* (1865). His best-known titles include *Twenty Thousand Leagues Under the Sea* (1870) and *Around the World in Eighty Days* (1872). The last, excepting posthumous publications, was a North African adventure, *The Invasion of the Sea* (1905).

In Europe he is a highly regarded literary figure; but he has been ill-served by translations into English, and in the English-speaking world he is regarded as a mere science fiction writer or, worse, a children's author. The first English translation of *Journey to the Centre of the Earth* is typical: enormous liberties were taken with the text, with details of the characters' adventures and even with their names. The unnamed translator added titles to the chapters, which Verne had only numbered, and completely rewrote whole paragraphs. Today, this version is generally regarded as the worst translation of any Jules Verne title ever published.

For those who take Verne's work seriously, *Journey to the Centre of the Earth* has been an inspiration. Arthur Conan Doyle wrote *The Lost World* in its wake, and Edgar Rice Burroughs' *Pellucidar* series of novels were all set within a hollow Earth. C.S. Lewis imagined Underland, an underground kingdom planning to invade Narnia; and in the last years of the twentieth century the novel *Indiana Jones and the Hollow Earth* by Max McCoy showed that there was plenty of life left in the concept of subterranean worlds and civilisations.

Even Jules Verne tinkered with the text. Three years after its original publication he rewrote parts of the book, adding new encounters with the dinosaurs which had proved popular in the First Edition. Verne, writing only five years after Charles Darwin published his *On the Origin of Species*, kept up to date with developments in evolutionary palaeontology. Although his tale was fantastical, it was also convincingly realistic. Readers have enjoyed his authentic *Journey* ever since.

ABOVE: *Although the original French edition was published in 1864, an expanded edition emerged in 1867 while the first English edition arrived in 1871, taking many liberties with the text.*

Alice's Adventures in Wonderland

(1865)

Lewis Carroll (1832–1898)

In Victorian Britain, children's literature was supposed to be gently entertaining, and highly educational. Reading was an act of self-improvement, and books were required to instruct children in morality and etiquette. One subversive novel turned the genre on its head.

*A*lice's Adventures in Wonderland is the first book to acknowledge the sheer delight which children derive from the utterly silly and the deliberately illogical. One can almost hear the giggles from the Liddell children as Lewis Carroll invented the story for them one golden summer afternoon in 1862. One of them, Alice Liddell, asked Carroll to write the story down for her, and two years later he presented it to her, adorned with his own illustrations and titled *Alice's Adventures Under Ground*. Carroll had also shown it to the children of Scottish fantasy author George MacDonald, and MacDonald urged him to publish it.

A contemporary magazine, *Aunt Judy's Magazine for Young People*, described the book as an 'exquisitely wild, fantastic, impossible, yet most natural history,' but without much 'knowledge in disguise'. *Alice* is in fact underpinned by arithmetic, logic, rules and wordplay, an abundance of learning which is however so heavily disguised by absurdity as to be invisible to the young reader.

The story begins with Alice falling down a rabbit hole in pursuit of a white rabbit in a waistcoat, consulting his pocket watch and complaining about being late. Alice finds herself in a world of extraordinary encounters with, among others, a caterpillar smoking a hookah;

a Cheshire cat which disappears leaving only its smile; a mad hatter at a tea party with a dormouse in a teapot (an episode not included in the original manuscript); a gryphon and a mock turtle; and the fearsome Queen of Hearts and her playing card guards.

Few novels can have been populated with so many memorable figures. These and many other characters from the book have entered the English language as idioms in their own right. Lewis Carroll drew inspiration for many of them from real people. The dodo which Alice meets is a reference to Carroll himself, who sometimes stuttered when he said his real name, Charles (Do-Do-) Dodgson.

Dodgson was a mathematician who delighted in puzzles – he invented the word ladder puzzle – and the text of *Alice* is laced with wordplay and logical conundrums. Games with unexpected rules feature frequently in the story, such as when Alice tries to play croquet using a flamingo as a mallet and a hedgehog as a ball. Food and drink also occur throughout the novel. Mock turtle is a kind of soup, not an animal; and apart from 'the stupidest tea party' that she had ever been to, Alice herself shrinks or grows in size depending on what she has eaten or drunk. *Alice's Adventures in Wonderland* is literary nonsense written by a very clever man.

Alice was originally published with illustrations based on Carroll's own sketches, but redrawn by the artist John Tenniel. His forty-two drawings remain the defining images of the characters in the book. Many other revered illustrators have risen to the challenge of capturing Carroll's surreal world, among them Arthur Rackham, Mervyn Peake, Salvador Dalí, Peter Blake and Helen Oxenbury. Alice Liddell kept the original manuscript, and a facsimile of it with Carroll's drawings was published in 1886.

ABOVE AND OPPOSITE LEFT: Sir John Tenniel's classic illustrations of the Mad Hatter's tea party and the tardy White Rabbit.
OPPOSITE RIGHT: Alice Liddell dressed up as 'the Beggar Maid' – hence the outstretched hand – and photographed by Dodgson in 1858.

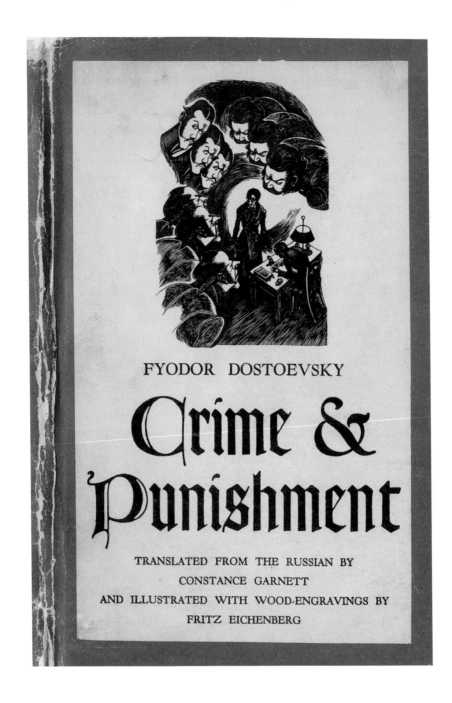

FYODOR DOSTOEVSKY

Crime & Punishment

TRANSLATED FROM THE RUSSIAN BY
CONSTANCE GARNETT
AND ILLUSTRATED WITH WOOD-ENGRAVINGS BY
FRITZ EICHENBERG

ABOVE: *A Constance Garnett translation of Dostoevsky is more of a collector's item than a text to be studied in detail, owing to her incomplete knowledge of the Russian language (see Introduction).*
OPPOSITE: *The Russian writer Fyodor Dostoevsky in 1880, aged 58.*

Crime and Punishment

(1866)

Fyodor Dostoevsky (1821–1881)

After ten years in exile in Siberia for reading banned books, Dostoevsky returned to St Petersburg and wrote with a new maturity. *Crime and Punishment* was the first truly great work to emerge from this second period of his career.

Crime and Punishment was not, as might have been expected, based on his own experiences of the Imperial Russian justice system. He wrote about that when he was first released, in the novel *The House of the Dead*. Nor was it about his narrow escape from execution in front of a firing squad, his original sentence – from which he was spared literally at the last moment by a letter from Tsar Nicholas I. *That* experience informed a later novel, *The Idiot*.

Crime and Punishment is about guilt and self-justification. In the original Russian, the word translated as 'crime' means more accurately 'transgression' and the novel is more about the moral disintegration of the central character, Rodion Raskolnikov, than about his breaking of the law. Raskolnikov first persuades himself to murder an old pawnbroker for her money, subsequently justifies his actions to himself, and is only finally convinced to set out on the road to redemption by confessing to the police.

Raskolnikov represents Dostoevsky's opposition to radical ideologies. Those who are radicalised can become dangerously intoxicated by ideas and, like drunkards, destroy the lives of those they encounter. Raskolnikov believes that the murder is justified because the money will relieve his poverty and allow him to fulfil what he sees as his extraordinary potential. Dostoevsky illustrates Raskolnikov's moral utilitarianism with other selfish characters, such as his sister's suitor. He contrasts it with the repentant fervour exhibited by Marmeladov,

a drunkard who at least admits the effect his alcoholism has had on those around him. The author draws similar parallels throughout the book. Raskolnikov sees in his sister – who will marry for money for the sake of her impoverished family – the same qualities as Marmeladov's daughter who has turned to prostitution for the same reason. Both women act as moral guides to Raskolnikov.

Deaths, and the legacies of those who die, abound in *Crime and Punishment*, whether by murder, natural causes or suicide. St Petersburg provides the background – not the glamorous tsarist city of the Winter Palace but the ubiquitous poverty that surrounded such wealth: the crowded streets, the disrepair and the grimy bars. They all reflect Raskolnikov's moral poverty. Dostoevsky was one of the first writers to use the character of a city and not merely its locations as an additional narrative tool.

Fyodor Dostoevsky was a master craftsman of language, and he uses a changing linguistic approach to reinforce the personalities of his characters. He switches from long sentences to short ones, from the present to the past, from artificial language to more natural speech, depending on the perspective of the scene in question. It was at the time an innovative style and it had a profound influence on twentieth-century modernists such as Henry James, Virginia Woolf and James Joyce. *Crime and Punishment* is a masterclass in character study and moral decline, a towering literary landmark.

Little Women

(1868)

Louisa May Alcott (1832–1888)

When Louisa Alcott's publisher suggested she write a story about girls, she protested. 'I could not write a girls' story,' she insisted, 'knowing little about any but my own sisters and always preferring boys.' She consented reluctantly, but the result was a milestone in children's literature.

Little Women is a coming-of-age tale, groundbreaking in its day for tackling the emotional and practical problems of four sisters making the transition from childhood to adulthood. It is in that sense that they are 'little' women, inhabiting the middle ground between youth and maturity.

The novel follows the lives of four Massachusetts sisters – Meg, Jo, Beth and Amy March – as they are faced with new, adult experiences in the worlds of love, work and death. Although at times sentimental and romanticised, the book's powerfully drawn female characters are an innovation. The emotional realism of *Little Women* reflected a trend in adult literature for plots driven as much by internal thought processes as by external events. It was an early attempt to adopt such an approach for children, and especially for girls.

Alcott, in proclaiming her ignorance of other girls, wisely stuck to what she did know – the four March sisters are based on herself and her three sisters: May, Lizzie and Anna. Jo March, the central character of *Little Women* is, like Louisa, a tomboy and the second child of the family. Louisa's older sister Anna was the model for glamorous Meg March; both were the first of their siblings to marry. Beth March, like Lizzie Alcott, suffers tragic ill health – Beth and Lizzie are both familiar forms of the name Elizabeth. May and Amy are anagrams of each other: in life and on the page they share an ambition to be artists. Both families live in poverty, a home called Orchard House.

The Alcotts were poor because Louisa's father was determined to establish a radical community based on the teachings of his friends, the philosophers Henry David Thoreau and Ralph Waldo Emerson. He disapproved of Louisa's tomboyish behaviour and had an old-fashioned attitude to women which, ironically, bound the girls and their mother closer together in feminist solidarity. Mr March is portrayed differently, as an army chaplain; and Louisa Alcott created an idealised father figure in the affectionate character of Professor Bhaer, who supports Jo's ambition to be a writer more than Mr Alcott ever did. Thoreau and Emerson, by contrast, were very encouraging of Louisa's early efforts.

Louisa brought in a little money by selling short stories and articles to newspapers and magazines. Although she had written long-form novels before she began *Little Women*, they had usually been Gothic potboilers published in serial form under an alias. Her most recent one had been rejected and she was planning to return to short stories when her publisher persuaded her otherwise.

'I plod away,' she wrote of the work on *Little Women*, 'although I don't enjoy this sort of thing.' In trials, however, children were enthusiastic, and when the book was published its immediate success gave Louisa and her family a security of income which they had never experienced. The public were so captivated by the March girls that they demanded sequels. *Good Wives* (1869), nowadays included as Part Two of *Little Women*, *Little Men* (1871) and *Jo's Boys* (1886) duly appeared. Unlike Jo, Louisa – a passionate feminist – never had boys or girls of her own and never married.

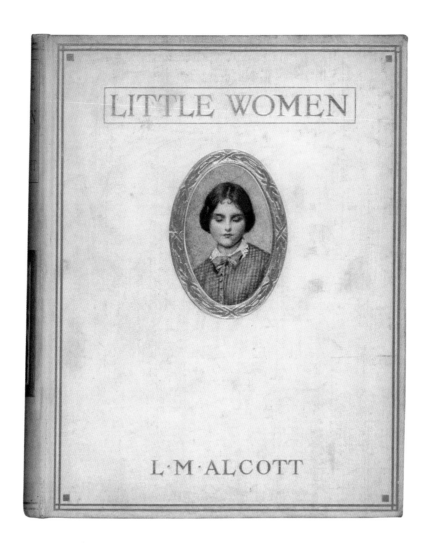

ABOVE: *Louisa May Alcott wrote accurate reflections of her siblings in Little Women, but the head of the March family was unlike her own disapproving father.*

LEFT: *The Alcotts' home, Orchard House, in Concord, Massachusetts, is open to visitors.*

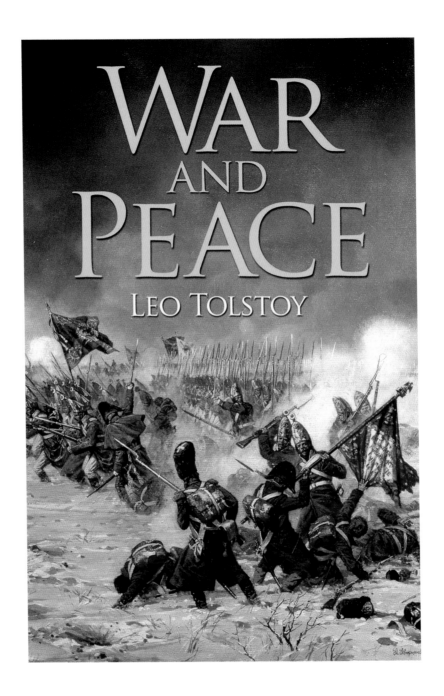

WAR AND PEACE

LEO TOLSTOY

ABOVE: With 361 chapters and 1,225 pages in the first published edition, it is an epic book on an epic subject, but spare a thought for Tolstoy's wife, Sophia Tolstaya. She copied seven separate manuscripts before Tolstoy deemed it ready for publication.

OPPOSITE: A portrait of Tolstoy from 1868.

War and Peace

(1869)

Leo Tolstoy (1828–1910)

Tolstoy's epic novel is a giant of Russian literature. Written sixty years after the events it portrays, *War and Peace* captures a Russia erased forever by twentieth-century revolutions. The implacable march of history is made personal by the fates of five aristocratic Russian families.

The wars in *War and Peace* are the Napoleonic Wars fought to restrain the imperial ambitions of Napoleon Bonaparte. They climaxed with Napoleon's ill-considered campaign to capture Moscow. His triumphant seizure of the Russian city was a pyrrhic victory. Careless French troops accidentally set fire to it, and most of Napoleon's army died during their retreat through a harsh Russian winter. The novel concludes with the surviving characters beginning to rebuild Moscow and their own lives.

Tolstoy researched the period thoroughly. Although he was born seven years after Napoleon's death, he interviewed many who had fought in the campaign, and read both French and Russian accounts of the conflict. The eventual defeat of Napoleon was a significant if expensive victory for Russia, comparable a century later to Hitler's unsuccessful siege of Leningrad. Tchaikovsky's *1812 Overture* (composed in 1880) was written to celebrate the memory of the defeat of the French that year.

The battles in *War and Peace* are battles which really took place. The central characters may be fictional, but more than 160 real people also feature in Tolstoy's telling of history. Refusing to classify the work, he said instead that it was neither a novel, nor a poem, nor a historical chronicle; and early reviewers were unsure how to approach it. Where did fiction end and fact begin? Tolstoy's contemporary, the novelist Ivan Turgenev,

attempted to sum it up when he wrote, 'It is the society epic, the history novel and the vast picture of the whole nation's life.'

The novel was praised for showing the human side of war and its impact on individuals. It was hailed for its military accuracy – Tolstoy himself had fought in Russia's Crimean campaigns – but criticised by several sections of society. The left thought it showed Russian nobility in too favourable a light; the right thought its brutal depictions of the reality of war damaged the country's patriotic pride.

The hefty novel – 361 chapters in four books with two epilogues – was written in Tolstoy's native Russian, but includes some dialogue in French. One of the ironies of Napoleon's invasion of Russia was that since the eighteenth century French had been the official language of the Russian court – Russia was at the time a Francophile nation. Modern translations usually retain the French speech of the original.

War and Peace has an undeserved reputation as a long, difficult read. It is certainly long; and Tolstoy occasionally uses unorthodox syntax. The blending of history and invention is nevertheless a powerful, engaging read, in which the greatest challenge is keeping track of the large cast of characters. There have been at least ten translations into English alone, and the best advice to those planning to read it is to find one whose style appeals to them. It is in every way a great novel.

Middlemarch

(1871)

George Eliot (1819–1880)

A tale of provincial life captured England in the throes of social, industrial and scientific change. George Eliot, who courted scandal with her unconventional private life, brought a radical eye to these changes and a compassionate one to those affected by them in the fictional town of Middlemarch.

Middlemarch is set in the years running up to the 1832 Reform Act, which greatly revised the British electoral system, redrawing parliamentary constituencies and extending the franchise. Women were still barred from voting, but it was a dramatic expansion of democracy. Written only forty years later, Eliot's novel is not generally considered to be historical fiction. But in practice the pace of change accelerated so much throughout the nineteenth century that, from 1869 when she began to write the book, 1829 (when *Middlemarch* begins) must have seemed a very different world.

In four distinct but interconnected storylines Eliot considers not only the imminent political reform but other aspects of everyday English life. Dorothea Brooke, a young woman and an orphan, is clever and wealthy but marries unwisely. Tertius Lydgate, a poor but progressive doctor, is thwarted in his scientific research by another unhappy marriage. Plain but kind Mary Garth resists the courtship of Fred Vincy until he can prove himself serious and worthy of her. Nicholas Bulstrode, a wealthy banker married to Fred's aunt, uses his religious piety to conceal a sordid past.

In retrospect this was an extraordinary period of English history in which many of the centuries-old institutions which underpinned society were being held up to the light. Low church Methodists and Baptists were challenging the role of Anglicanism. Access to education

was expanding. The traditional status of women in and out of marriage was being questioned.

Middlemarch considers the idealism and the hypocrisy surrounding this transformation of society and other welcome and unwelcome changes: a new king, William IV; new medical discoveries; the coming of the railways. For every radical new thought there is a reactionary one which defends the status quo. Although the book contains several fine comic set pieces, it is written in a realist style which presents real life and asks real questions about it. The result is a thoughtful reconstruction of time and place, an almost archaeological snapshot of Georgian Britain.

George Eliot was born Mary Ann Evans. Like the Brontë sisters she felt obliged to take a man's name to make her way in the publishing world. As a child she was considered plain in appearance and unlikely to attract a husband. Her father therefore devoted more time and money to her education than girls usually received at

that time. Education and the role of women in society are major themes of *Middlemarch*.

When the family moved to Coventry (the model for Middlemarch), Eliot mixed with a group of radical thinkers which included Ralph Waldo Emerson (then travelling through Europe) and Robert Owen. Through them she learned about liberal and

LEFT: A portrait of Mary Ann Evans by Samuel Lawrence, circa 1860.
OPPOSITE: An early twentieth-century edition.

agnostic ideologies, and eventually rejected Christianity. As if that were not shocking enough to her Victorian readers, she fell in love with a married man and lived openly with him until his death.

Contemporary reviews of *Middlemarch* were mixed. Its realistic detail was admired but some considered the emotional content to be overwritten. The psychological depth of its characters drew praise, however, and its reputation grew steadily through the twentieth century. Virginia Woolf called it 'the magnificent book that, with all its imperfections, is one of the few English novels written for grown-up people.' Today, with its insights into people and politics, it is considered one of the finest novels of its age.

The Adventures of Huckleberry Finn

(1884)

Mark Twain (1835–1910)

The sequel to *The Adventures of Tom Sawyer* is more than simply another batch of boyhood adventures. It explores much deeper moral issues such as parental cruelty, slavery and racism. 'All modern American literature,' wrote Ernest Hemingway, 'comes from one book by Mark Twain called *Huckleberry Finn*.'

The Adventures of Huckleberry Finn was extremely progressive for its time, and highly critical of the values which prevailed in the Southern States before the Civil War. Huck, on the run from his abusive father, teams up with Jim, a runaway slave. As they travel downriver on a raft, they encounter death and criminality in many forms, and even the happy ending of the book requires the deaths of Huck's father and Jim's former owner.

Twain first came to prominence as a travel writer, a journalist dispatched on journeys from which he was expected to send back entertaining reports of the sights and sounds he encountered. Although he is best known for his fiction today, the best-selling title during his lifetime was his first travel book, *The Innocents Abroad*. Throughout his career it was his observations of real-life characters and places that fed Mark Twain's imagination and fiction.

Twain, born Samuel Langhorne Clemens, grew up in Missouri. His life straddled the century that defined America, from the pioneering push westwards of the early nineteenth century, through the Civil War and the end of slavery to the industrial and urban expansion of the end of that century. Before his success as a writer he worked as a printer's apprentice, a steamboat pilot and

PUCKOGRAPHS—NEW SERIES, NO. 1.

"MARK TWAIN."
America's Best Humorist.

a silver miner. His childhood, and his working life on the Mississippi gave him the material for one of the greatest, most enduring American novels ever written. He lived the lives he wrote about.

Twain worked on *Huckleberry Finn* off and on for seven years before it reached its final form. The novel was the first publication by Twain's own publishing house, although it was a rare success for that venture. The presence of a young protagonist has sometimes meant ignoring the more adult themes and critical elements of *Huckleberry Finn* in favour of simple family entertainment. For example, the novel is notable for its use of colloquial speech from a Southern state. But it has also been criticised for its reflection of racial attitudes of the time and for its use of language considered common in the day but now regarded as racially insensitive.

The presence of *Huckleberry Finn* in the schools and public libraries of America has frequently been challenged. A 1905 ban on the moralistic grounds that Huck was described

LEFT: Twain was a gifted orator, pictured here by satirical US magazine Puck.

OPPOSITE: Twain agonised at length about the ending for Huckleberry Finn, *but the contrived final chapters were a necessary commercial addition. Louisa May Alcott still hated the book.*

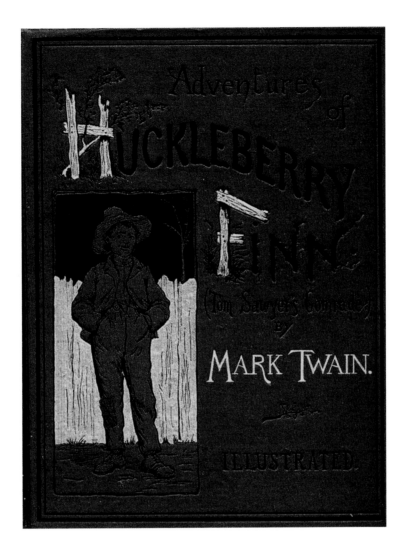

not as itching but as scratching, which was considered rude, drew a tongue-in-cheek response from Twain: he pretended to agree that children should not be exposed to such an immoral novel any more than he should have been forced to read the Bible before he was fifteen years old. 'None can do that and ever draw a clean sweet breath again on this side of the grave.'

The character of Huckleberry Finn was based on Tom Blankenship, a boyhood friend of Twain's from Hannibal, Missouri. The Blankenship family moved to Hannibal in the same year as the Twains, and Tom, whose father was a drunkard, often played truant from school. Twain wrote

in his autobiography that Tom 'was ignorant, unwashed, insufficiently fed; but he had as good a heart as ever any boy had. His liberties were totally unrestricted. He was the only really independent person – boy or man – in the community, and by consequence he was tranquilly and continuously happy and envied by the rest of us.'

As Twain once said, 'A classic is something that everybody wants to have read and nobody wants to read.' *Huckleberry Finn* is familiar even to those who have never read it. For its masterly use of the written word to capture humanity and its strengths and weaknesses, it is properly celebrated as a Great American Novel.

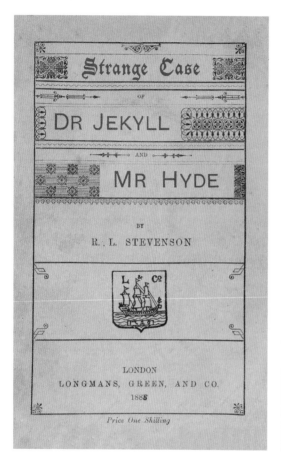

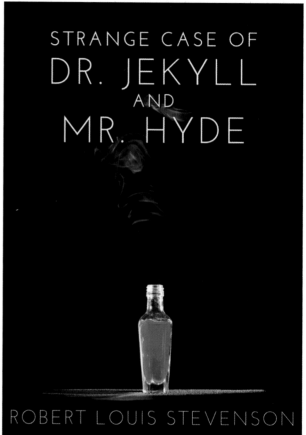

ABOVE RIGHT: A sophisticated modern cover of Jekyll, avoiding the split personalities and concentrating on the all-important serum. Alongside it is an original edition from 1886 with a hasty, hand-drawn printer's correction, after the book was delayed from 1885 to 1886.
OPPOSITE: Robert Louis Stevenson photographed in 1888.

Strange Case of Dr Jekyll and Mr Hyde

(1886)

Robert Louis Stevenson (1850–1894)

A classic of Gothic horror, Robert Louis Stevenson's novel about duality and ambiguity taps into the reader's darkest fears – that within every rational, civilised person there hides a primeval monster capable of unspeakable acts of cruelty.

The capacity to be both good and evil is often a theme of Stevenson's work. The mutineer Long John Silver in *Treasure Island*, for example, beguiles young Jim Hawkins while proving himself ruthless and treacherous to others. In *Jekyll and Hyde* he went a step further in exploring the internal tensions between these two sides of a personality.

The protagonist in the novel is Gabriel Utterson, a friend of Dr Jekyll who leads the reader through a series of shocking episodes linking the brutal Mr Hyde to the careful, diligent doctor. When part of a walking cane which Hyde used to murder a man is found in Jekyll's home, Utterson suspects that Hyde must be blackmailing Jekyll. The truth is that Jekyll has been taking a serum in an attempt to separate the evil parts of his personality from the good in him, and that Hyde is simply a different version of himself. What was once a voluntary act of transformation starts to happen more frequently, uninvited. When the antidote to the serum runs out, Jekyll is doomed to be Hyde for the rest of his life.

The story came to Stevenson in a dream and, writing it down urgently, he had completed a first draft within three days. His dream may well have been inspired by a legal trial which he attended in Edinburgh in 1878, where an apparently conventional teacher was convicted of murdering his wife (and several others over the years) with opium concealed in a snack of toasted cheese.

The idea of transformation was a challenge for movie makers, and *Jekyll and Hyde* was one of the most filmed stories of the silent movie era. The unusual surname Jekyll

belonged to a friend of Stevenson's, the Reverend Walter Jekyll, who was the younger brother of the famous garden designer Gertrude Jekyll.

There have been more than 120 dramatisations of the novel, the first only a year after its publication. The London production of it closed down in 1888 partly because of poor audiences and partly because serial killer Jack the Ripper was committing his ghastly crimes at the time. The feverish public interest in murder had led to members of the play's cast becoming suspects of real-life crimes simply because they were acting the part of a murderer. Even the director came under suspicion and wisely quit London for a tour of British provincial theatres.

Dr Jekyll and Mr Hyde was Stevenson's third novel. His breakthrough had come earlier with the pirate adventure *Treasure Island* (1883). He followed it with *Kidnapped* (1886), the first of three historical novels set against the background of Scotland's Jacobite rebellions in the early eighteenth century. He wrote in many genres, including comedy in *The Wrong Box* (1889), one of two novels which he co-wrote with his stepson Lloyd Osbourne.

Dr Jekyll and Mr Hyde was an instant success. The idea of twin characters within a single human frame was fascinating in an age of high Victorian morality, and the novel was read by people who had never before bought a book. The metaphor of Jekyll and Hyde as two contrasting aspects of the same personality very quickly established itself in the public consciousness.

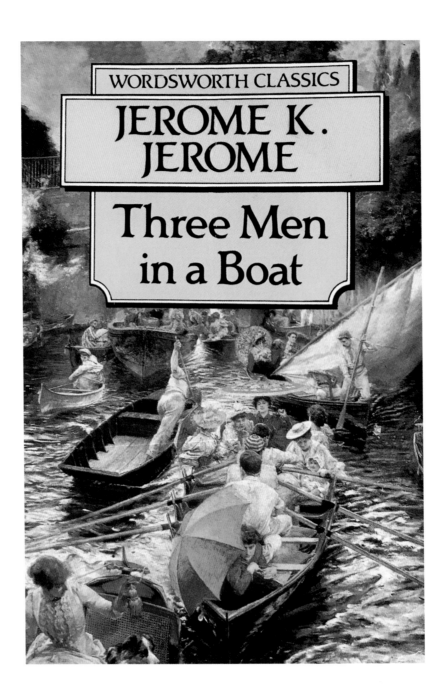

WORDSWORTH CLASSICS

JEROME K. JEROME

Three Men in a Boat

ABOVE: Many still recreate the journey of Three Men in a Boat, *and pubs such as the Barley Mow in Clifton Hampden are still open for business.*
OPPOSITE: Jerome K. Jerome has a strange link to Ernest Hemingway. Both were ambulance drivers in World War I, Jerome at age fifty-seven, Hemingway at eighteen.

Three Men in a Boat

(1889)

Jerome K. Jerome (1859–1927)

The much-loved comic novel about a chaotic boating holiday began life as a serious travel guide inspired by the author's honeymoon. But Jerome K. Jerome's ability to see the funny side of life is as fresh today as it was 130 years ago. *Three Men in a Boat* has never been out of print.

The story of the mishaps befalling three friends as they row up the Thames river from Kingston-upon-Thames to Oxford was intended as a guide to the route, and it still contains some serious passages describing historic events, buildings and other locations to be found along the way. Jerome couldn't suppress his sense of humour, however, and it is the antics of the three friends and their dog Montmorency which immediately endeared *Three Men in a Boat* to its readers.

His had been a hard life. He lost both parents and a brother before he was sixteen, and in order to support himself and his two sisters he was employed by the London and North Western Railway Company, collecting coal which had fallen beside the tracks. He aspired to some sort of creative success and joined an impoverished theatre company on tours of England. It was an unrewarding career and he next tried his hand at writing satirical or humorous articles: none were accepted for publication, until at the age of twenty-six he found success with a comical autobiography of his theatrical experiences, *On the Stage – And Off* (1885). Jerome built on that the following year with *Idle Thoughts of an Idle Fellow*, a collection of old and new articles which established his reputation as a fine humorist.

His confidence and income boosted by these hits, he married Ettie Marris, less than two weeks after she had divorced her first husband. They remained married until his death, and their honeymoon on the Thames became the source of his best-known novel. For the purposes of the book he replaced Ettie with two new characters, George and Harris, based on two real-life friends of his, and the entirely fictional hound Montmorency.

The incidents which Jerome describes are slight, the sort that might happen to anyone; and his genius lies in his success in capturing the banter and amusement of three friends on holiday together. There are encounters with fishermen and other boaters; speculation about the difficulty of learning to play the Scottish bagpipes; Montmorency's contribution of a dead rat to the friends' efforts to produce an Irish stew from leftovers. It is supremely light-hearted.

That easy wit immediately endeared the book to readers, but condemned it in the views of reviewers. There was no place for slang or repartee in literature, they felt. As Jerome himself recalled in his later autobiography, '*The Standard* spoke of me as a menace to English letters; and *The Morning Post* as an example of the sad results to be expected from the over-education of the lower orders.'

Their reviews fell on deaf ears. The first British edition sold 202,000 copies, the first American one many more, including a million in pirated versions. It was so successful in Russia that it became a school textbook, and many subsequent Russian comic novels by others claimed to have been written by Jerome K. Jerome to cash in on his success. Such was the popularity of *Three Men in a Boat* in Britain that the number of registered boats on the Thames rose by 50% in the year after its publication.

Tess of the d'Urbervilles

(1891)

Thomas Hardy (1840–1928)

The book which gave us one of the great tragic heroines of fiction was criticised for its supposedly lax moral position. Its poor reception contributed to Thomas Hardy's decision to stop writing novels; but today it is considered his masterpiece.

Tess of the d'Urbervilles takes accurate aim at social attitudes in Victorian England. A parson of the Church of England sets Tess on her fatal path at the very start of the novel, incorrectly telling her father that he is descended from a noble French family, the d'Urbervilles. Her father's drunken pleasure at belonging to a higher class leads to the family's destitution and forces her to seek work from a local family called d'Urberville. Unknown to her they have merely adopted the name in a bid for social elevation, and naive Tess loses her innocence to the family's predatory son Alec. The resulting child dies. Immorality abounds in *Tess of the d'Urbervilles*.

Later she falls in love with a gentleman farmer, Angel Clare, and hopes she can leave her unmarried past behind her; but when Angel admits to a previous liaison, she believes she can confess her own compromised maidenhood. Angel has double standards however, and, horrified, he leaves her. Alec pursues her again and, when Angel returns some years later, Tess is driven to murder Alec. Her fate is sealed.

The Church, the class system, the industrialisation of farming, and hypocritical attitudes to purity and morality all lie behind Tess's downfall. It is no wonder that the novel attracted criticism from the bulwarks of conservative England. Although there is a Gothic inevitability about Tess's fate, the story is told with realism, contrasting the brutality of the modern world with the rural idyll of Hardy's imaginary Wessex – a fictionalised version of south-western and south-central England in which many of his novels were set.

Hardy draws a contrast between wealthy industrialised towns and the impoverished Wessex countryside. Tess is pure and in touch with nature while lower middle-class Alec is abandoning his roots with an assumed name. Alec is immoral; and upper middle-class Angel, in his reaction to Tess's confession, is misguidedly moral. Some see Tess as a victim not of industrialisation but of the class struggle, and the novel was a strong influence on later writers like D.H. Lawrence and John Cowper Powys.

The novel is subtitled *A Pure Woman, Faithfully Presented*. The only point at which Hardy pulls his punches is Alec's presumed rape of Tess, where – probably on the advice of his publisher – the assault is only implied, not described. Hardy's text was further censored when it first appeared, as a serial in *The Graphic* newspaper, before it appeared in book form. The poor critical reception for *Tess of the d'Urbervilles* was followed by an even worse one for Hardy's next novel, *Jude the Obscure* (1895), which undoubtedly contains one of the bleakest moments in English literature. He never wrote another, and concentrated on poetry for the rest of his life. Tess is a finely written record of social attitudes and customs at a very particular moment in British history. In its fateful plot its underlying question is about the role of morality in shaping our lives both for better and for worse.

OPPOSITE: Two illustrations from an 1891 serialisation which appeared in The Graphic: An Illustrated Weekly Newspaper. *The upper plate shows Tess's encounter with Alec d'Urberville and below, the farm at harvest time.*

THIS NUMBER CONTAINS

The Picture of Dorian Gray.

By OSCAR WILDE.

COMPLETE.

JULY, 1890

LIPPINCOTT'S

MONTHLY MAGAZINE

CONTENTS

PRICE TWENTY-FIVE CENTS

J: B: LIPPINCOTT: Cọ: PHILADELPHIA:

LONDON: WARD, LOCK & CO.

PARIS: BRENTANO'S, 17 AVENUE DE L'OPÉRA.

ABOVE: The Picture of Dorian Gray was published in both the American and British editions of Lippincott's in July 1890.

OPPOSITE: Wilde photographed in New York by Napoleon Sarony in 1882.

The Picture of Dorian Gray

(1891)

Oscar Wilde (1854–1900)

Oscar Wilde's variation on the Faustian pact is a psychological horror story and a warning to be careful what you wish for. It has become a source of fascination, as much for its insight into Wilde's life and character as for its literary ingenuity.

The premise of *The Picture of Dorian Gray* is an intriguing one. A beautiful young man, Dorian Gray, is drawn by a libertine into a life of hedonism. As the years pass, and as the emotional damage he inflicts on others mounts up, he retains his youth and good looks. Instead, a portrait of him which he keeps in his attic shows all the lines of age and attitude, of heartlessness and selfishness, from which the man himself is spared. Realising the pain and death which he has caused his friends and lovers, he tries to make amends and to become the better man he once was; but there seems to be only one way to do so.

Oscar Wilde said of the book, his only novel, that it 'contains much of me in it – Basil Hallward [the artist who painted the portrait] is what I think I am; Lord Henry [the libertine], what the world thinks me; Dorian [the young man] is what I would like to be – in other ages, perhaps.' Wilde already had a reputation for decadence, and *Dorian Gray* only exaggerated it. Henry exhibits all the acerbic wit for which Wilde is famous; Basil is in love with Dorian, as Wilde was with Lord Alfred Douglas; and Dorian follows his path of unrestrained pleasure without suffering the wear and tear which Wilde could not avoid.

The story was originally published in *Lippincott's Monthly Magazine*, where its undertones of homoeroticism scandalised readers and critics. One review wondered 'Why must Oscar Wilde "go grubbing in muck-heaps"?' and there were calls to prosecute Wilde under laws about public morality. In response to the public outrage WH Smith, Britain's biggest bookseller at the time, withdrew all copies of the magazine from the shelves of its railway station bookstalls (although it was happy to continue selling it elsewhere).

In fact *Lippincott's* editor J.M. Stoddart had deleted many of the most shocking passages, including references to homosexuality and the use of the word 'mistress' when describing Dorian's female lovers. When it came to be published in book form, Wilde added a preface which defended his book against the criticisms. The preface has become famous in its own right as a manifesto for the artist in society and in support of art for art's sake. He added new sections which further obscured the explicitly homosexual aspects of the narrative and helped to focus on the central moral message of the novel, that unfettered hedonism destroys those with whom it comes into contact.

Nevertheless, *Dorian Gray* was described as a 'perverted novel' when it was invoked at Oscar Wilde's trial for gross indecency in 1895. Many of the critical comments about the book were actually aimed at Wilde's own character and not at the literary qualities of Wilde's writing. When a definitive version of the novel appeared a few years after Wilde's death, its publisher was a specialist in literary erotica rather than in literature. Wilde's original, uncensored novella, as first submitted to Lippincott's, was finally published in 2011.

ABOVE: *An American edition published by Berkley Books in the 1960s.*

OPPOSITE: *H.G. Wells equipped with a quill pen in 1896.*

The Time Machine

(1895)

H.G. Wells (1866–1946)

The possibility of time travel has been a boon to the creative arts. A whole sub-genre of literature, cinema and television owes its origins to one very good decision: that of Herbert George Wells to write *The Time Machine*.

The Time Machine was H.G. Wells' first novel. Its unnamed narrator travels to the year 802,701 where he finds that the human race has evolved into two distinct species. The rapacious Morlocks are descended from the working class and live underground, the result of working in dark factories for too long. The Eloi, living above ground, can trace their ancestry to the wealthy elite whose life of luxury and pleasure eventually robbed them of any intellectual capacity or curiosity.

Wells is often credited with the invention of the entire genre of science fiction, because he was among the first to approach fantasy from a scientific point of view. Where Charles Dickens transported his Scrooge back and forth in time with a ghost in *A Christmas Carol* (1843), Wells gave us a man-made machine. Such enormous strides had been made in all the sciences that by the end of the nineteenth century almost anything seemed possible.

There are at least two literary precedents, although there is no evidence that Wells read either of them. A story by Edward Page Mitchell, published in New York's *Sun* newspaper in 1881, was called *The Clock That Went Backward*. The eponymous clock enables some nineteenth-century students to avert a historical upset in the sixteenth century. The Spanish diplomat Enrique Gaspar wrote *El anacronópete* ('The man who flies against time') in 1887. In it a group of travellers, with the aid of an electro-pneumatic machine, fly further and further back in time until they reach the dawn of creation and their machine explodes.

H.G. Wells first toyed with the concept of time travel in a short story published in the student magazine of the Royal College of Science, where Wells was studying biology. This, *The Chronic Argonauts*, has several elements which recur in *The Time Machine*, although in the earlier story the inventor of the time travel machine has a companion who survives to tell the tale.

In the full-length novel, Wells is not only exploring the idea of time travel but presenting a satire of British class distinctions. The Morlocks and the Eloi are intended to hold a mirror to the late nineteenth-century divisions which had deepened since the Industrial Revolution. The rich were richer, the poor poorer and the two groups were further apart politically and economically than ever before. Wells was a convinced socialist.

The published novel ends with a distant future in which the planet itself is grinding to a halt and the last mutations of human beings (crabs and butterflies) are dying out – we can only hope that Wells (whose scientific imagination also conceived of a future with aeroplanes, military tanks, satellite television, and even a form of the internet) was wrong about this bleak final vision of humanity. Contemporary reviewers were also uncomfortable with the direction which Wells imagined humanity would take. *The Manchester Guardian* newspaper commented at the time, 'his record is anything but a "gay" picture; nor are his revelations likely to excite regret on the part of his readers at having been born 802,000 years too soon.'

Dracula

(1897)

Bram Stoker (1847–1912)

The worst contemporary reviews of *Dracula* complained that it was too frightening for its refined Victorian readership. Horror fans know 'too frightening' is the best review possible. Bram Stoker's defining novel of Gothic terror lives on long after the deaths of its author and its titular character.

Even those who have not read Stoker's original are familiar with some aspects of its plot. Jonathan Harker, a guest at Count Dracula's Transylvanian castle, encounters three female vampires. Dracula sails to England in one of several boxes filled with earth from his castle (vampires can only rest on their home soil) and begins to prey on English women including Lucy, a friend of Harker's fiancée Mina, who becomes ill. Vampire chaser Professor Abraham Van Helsing diagnoses her condition as extreme blood loss. After her death she becomes a vampire, at first preying on local children, and in a particularly gruesome scene Van Helsing drives a stake through her corpse's heart, beheads her and fills her mouth with pearls of garlic. Van Helsing and Harker place sacramental wafers inside Dracula's boxes of Transylvanian earth to make them uninhabitable to him. The Count flees with his last box back to his castle, but Harker and Van Helsing must pursue him there and destroy him in order to save Mina, on whom Dracula has also preyed.

Dracula has had an extraordinary after-life. Since it was completed and published (only six days after Stoker signed a contract with his publisher) it has become the archetypical horror movie, with classic performances as Count Dracula by Bela Lugosi, Christopher Lee, Gary Oldman and others.

In addition, academic analysis of the novel's themes and metaphors has spawned a distinct strand of literary study which has its own peer-reviewed journal and a veritable library of critical studies about the book. Those themes include gender studies. Is Dracula's draining of women's blood a metaphor for men's domination of women? They include racism. Is the arrival of the foreigner Dracula a metaphor for England's notorious fear of immigrants and invasions? In preying on English women, is he implicitly corrupting England's racial purity?

They include sexuality. Are his attacks on women sexual? Is the penetration of a stake into the heart of a vampire, the only way to kill one, a phallic metaphor? 'La petit morte', the little death, was after all a poetic metaphor for sexual climax. It is no accident that Dracula is most often shown biting the *necks* of his victims, the neck being a highly erogenous zone. When Harker is threatened by the female vampires, and Mina's friend Lucy becomes a vampire and starts to prey on men, there is an implied fear of women becoming active and men passive; and until Harker realises he is in danger he is excited at the thought of submitting to them.

Stoker wrote a hundred pages of notes in preparation for writing *Dracula*. He researched Transylvanian folklore, but opinion is divided on his source for the Count. There is no reference to the historical figure of Vlad Draculea (also known as Vlad the Impaler) in his notes; and he claimed to have believed, mistakenly, that Dracula was Romanian for 'devil'. Vampires made their first literary appearances in several eighteenth-century poems, and

Lord Byron is credited with the first piece of vampire prose, *The Vampyre* (1819), though it was actually the work of John Polidori. Stoker may have been influenced by the novel *Carmilla* (1872) by Sheridan Le Fanu, about a lesbian vampire. *Dracula* may not be the first vampire novel, but it is unequivocally the best known and most influential, defining the creature's powers and weaknesses for all the vampires that followed in its wake.

LEFT: The cover of the thirteenth edition of Dracula from 1919.
OPPOSITE: There had been vampires before Bram Stoker – photographed circa 1906 – wrote his genre-defining book.

The Hound of the Baskervilles

(1902)

Arthur Conan Doyle (1859–1930)

Sherlock Holmes' famous case merges detective fiction with Victorian horror in the most popular of Conan Doyle's four full-length novels about the sleuth. More than just another fictional detective, Holmes is a literary phenomenon who has lived many lives far beyond the pages of his original creator.

Even in Arthur Conan Doyle's incarnation, Holmes' literary life spanned forty years, from the first novel, *A Study in Scarlet* (1887), to the last short story, *The Adventure of Shoscombe Old Place* (1927). Since then the world has taken Holmes to their hearts, reinventing him in many media, relocating him in time and space, using him to investigate real-life criminals and embellishing him with characteristics and even family members of which Conan Doyle never dreamt.

The Hound of the Baskervilles tells the story of a seemingly supernatural dog, renowned in local legend, which is frightening the descendants of an ancient family – the Baskervilles – to death. Baffled by unearthly lights and howls on the moors at night, they call in Sherlock Holmes to solve the mystery.

But *The Hound of the Baskervilles* was very nearly not a Holmes story at all. Conan Doyle was a masterly author of many genres, and particularly proud of his history novels. He regarded the Holmes tales as mere money-spinning potboilers and in 1891 he killed Holmes off in the short story *The Final Problem*, because, as he put it, 'he takes my mind from better things'. There was an unprecedented public outcry at this death of a fictional character; *The Strand Magazine*, which had printed almost all the Holmes stories to date, lost 20,000 subscribers when the news came out, and although Conan Doyle put up his fees in the hope of discouraging the periodical, *The Strand* was willing to pay anything for the return of the detective to its pages. *The Hound of the Baskervilles*, set some time

before Holmes' supposed death, was the detective's return to the pages of *The Strand*, and made Conan Doyle one of the highest paid authors of his time.

Holmes himself, with his insistence on strictly logical evidence-based deductions was based in part on the methodical diagnoses of a surgeon of Conan Doyle's acquaintance. The character was so recognisable that another Scottish author, Robert Louis Stevenson, wrote to Conan Doyle to say, 'My compliments on your very ingenious and very interesting adventures of Sherlock Holmes. ... can this be my old friend Joe Bell?'

Conan Doyle acknowledged the influence of Bell on his character. Others have claimed different sources for Holmes. Holmes' creator was certainly aware of precedents, namely Auguste Dupin (the first detective in literature, created in 1841 by Edgar Allan Poe) and Monsieur Lecoq (Émile Gaboriau's detective character launched in 1866). Conan Doyle was fluent in French, and Holmes and his friend Dr Watson discuss Dupin and Lecoq in the early pages of Holmes' debut, *A Study in Scarlet*. Another French fictional detective, Henry Cauvain's *Maximilien Heller* (1871), shows many of Holmes' more antisocial character traits, including his opium addiction.

LEFT: Arthur Conan Doyle.
OPPOSITE: The cover of the First Edition. Publisher George Newnes Ltd clearly thought the 'Arthur' was superfluous.

THE HOUND
OF THE
BASKERVILLES

A.G.J.

CONAN DOYLE

ABOVE: *The Jardin du Luxembourg in Paris painted by Jean-François Raffaëlli in 1900, around the time that Lewis Strether would have been strolling through, contemplating his ambassadorial role.*

OPPOSITE: *Henry James painted by John Singer Sargent in 1913. The Metropolitan Museum of Art in New York, who loaned the picture, described them as, 'the two greatest recorders of the transatlantic social scene in their respective arts and close friends for more than forty years.'*

The Ambassadors

(1903)

Henry James (1843–1916)

Europe casts a beguiling spell over a visiting American in Henry James' dark comedy about misconceptions. Its hero must learn to make choices based on merit and experience, not on assumptions. His choices are also guided by the tension between duty and pleasure.

Lewis Lambert Strether is a fifty-something average American of limited means from fictional Woollett, Massachusetts, where they manufacture what James teasingly describes as 'a nameless little thing, a little thing they make—make better, it appears, than other people can, or than other people, at any rate, do.' His fiancée, known in the novel only as the widowed Mrs Newsome, dispatches him on a diplomatic mission to Paris, where he is to persuade her son Chad to return to Woollett and the family business. She assumes that Chad hasn't yet returned because he is having some sordid affair with a French floozie.

This is the first of many incorrect assumptions which Strether uncovers during his trip. Chad proves to be mature, polite and urbane; and so far from having an affair with elegant, virtuous Jeanne, he seems to be going out of his way to find her a wealthy husband. Strether, meanwhile, is attracted to Jeanne's mother Marie. Strether discovers a different Paris through a new friendship, with pretty Maria Gostrey, an old school friend of Marie's under whose influence he feels less inclined to return to Woollett himself, or to fulfil his task with Chad. His life in Massachusetts seems claustrophobic compared to Paris.

Strether is one of the ambassadors of the title, torn between his mission and his new experiences, between his

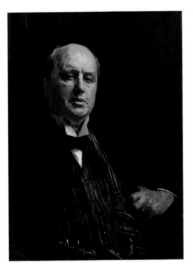

head and his heart. Frustrated at his inaction, Mrs Newsome dispatches further ambassadors in the form of a group including her daughter and son-in-law. These new arrivals reinforce each other's prejudices and do not see the situation or Paris through Chad's eyes. Their sense of duty overrides any thought for the happiness of Chad, his French lover (yes, Mrs Newsome was right) or Strether.

Throughout the book James is at pains not to over-romanticise Paris or paint it as a creative paradise compared to the limited cultural history of America. James was a fine travel writer – his *Italian Hours* is an affectionate but sometimes critical portrait of that country and he takes the same approach in *The Ambassadors*. James himself had been seduced by Europe; although a native of New York he made Britain his home and became a naturalised Englishman just before his death. It was the experience of a friend, who visited Paris and felt that his life before then had been wasted, which inspired the character of Strether.

In the end Strether must accept that his role is merely that of envoy, go-between. But James leaves open the question of whether he will find happiness back in America, and even whether Mrs Newsome, disappointed in his performance, will welcome him. There are more choices to be made, and the reader should not assume that he or she knows the answers.

In Search of Lost Time

(1913–1927)

Marcel Proust (1871–1922)

One of the first great novels of the twentieth century, Proust's book rejected the conventional realism of the nineteenth century in favour of an experimental evocation of memory. Instead of a plot driven by characters and events, he explores, through involuntary recollections, the forces which shape our life experience.

This extraordinarily passive novel is almost a meditation on reality. It observes from a distance; it recalls from the past. But it has the ring of truth about it. In the best-known passage from it, the narrator's memory of his aunt Léonie is triggered not by the sight of a madeleine cake but by the texture of it in his mouth; and he is pitched into a reverie of love from an earlier time.

By a patchwork of such moments the novel reconstructs the narrator's passage from childhood to adulthood. These isolated episodes come together almost accidentally to tell the novel's narrative. It is an indirect, lengthy process: *In Search of Lost Time* was originally published in seven volumes between 1913 and 1927. Proust continued to write and rewrite the earlier volumes even after their publication, and the final three were incomplete at the time of his death.

The identity of the narrator is concealed, and Proust toys with his readers on the question of autobiographical content: 'her first words,' he writes about the object of the narrator's affections, 'were "darling" or "my darling", followed by my Christian name, which, if we give the narrator the same name as the author of this book, would produce "darling Marcel" or "my darling Marcel".' Many of the characters are based on real-life acquaintances of Proust. He once hinted that 'one can say anything so long as one does not say "I".'

Proust, through the author-narrator, digresses at length about the nature of the arts. Many of the characters are artists – painters, novelists or composers of music – and Proust argues that everyone has the capacity of turning experiences of life into art as long as he or she has a mature understanding of them. Feelings of loss and betrayal fill *In Search of Lost Time*, whether of family members, lovers or childhood itself. Fear of abandonment makes the narrator jealous of his lovers' relationships with others, especially others of the same sex. In the final volume, *Time Regained*, the narrator at last achieves a perspective on all that has passed and all that his acquaintances have become. He finds a kind of peace and realises that his role is to write it all down.

In Search of Lost Time has been described as the first modern novel. It ushered in a new way of telling a story, through the internal monologues of its characters. Such an approach to narrative is commonplace now; but it was radical in its day. It had a large effect on those who followed, including the members of the Bloomsbury Group of writers and painters. One of them, Virginia Woolf, mused: 'Oh, if I could write like that!'

OPPOSITE TOP: The seven-volume collection was published over fourteen years.

OPPOSITE BOTTOM RIGHT: A portrait of Geneviève Straus, who created an influential salon attracting artists, politicians and nobility. She became a muse and literary confidante to Marcel Proust when he was a school friend of Straus's son.

OPPOSITE BOTTOM LEFT: Despite the elaborate bow, this is Marcel Proust photographed in 1887 as a teenager.

ABOVE: We all get out of bed on the wrong side, but for Gregor Samsa it was a Gestalt shift.

OPPOSITE: Franz Kafka died before the full literary impact of his work was felt, but the notion of absurd bureaucracy, which he touched on in Metamorphosis, has entered the dictionary as 'Kafkaesque'.

Metamorphosis

(1915)

Franz Kafka (1883–1924)

Alienation, disempowerment and rejection run like blood through Franz Kafka's most challenging work. Hotly discussed by academics, *Metamorphosis* leaves as much to the reader's imagination as it received from its author's.

It is not even certain to whom the title refers. When Gregor Samsa wakes up one morning to find that he has been transformed into 'a monstrous vermin', he can no longer work to support his family. Denied this contribution to the home, he instead becomes reliant on his parents and sister, who keep him in a locked room for fear of upsetting their lodgers and cleaner. The parents are unchanging in their view of Gregor – his father still beats him, and his mother, despite her fear, still feels maternal towards him, at least at first.

Gregor's sister Grete, however, undergoes a considerable metamorphosis, taking on more responsibility in the family and maturing through the course of the book. At first she takes on the role of carer for Gregor, but over time she finds him a burden and a constraint on her own expanding life. By the end she emerges like a butterfly having 'recently blossomed into a pretty and shapely girl', and her parents start to seek a husband for her. Gregor is in the past now and it is left to an outsider, the cleaner, to dispose of him.

There is further ambiguity about what, exactly, Gregor has become. The most frequent interpretation is that he wakes up as a cockroach; he prefers his food to be rotten, and likes to climb on the walls and ceiling of his room. But Kafka is never specific in his descriptions, and when the book was first published he insisted that there be no illustrations of Gregor. In a sense, therefore, Gregor is transformed into whatever the reader's worst fears may be.

Most critics agree that the book expresses Kafka's own alienation from his father, with whom he had only a distant, impersonal relationship, although they corresponded regularly. Others argue that Gregor's alienation from his family represents the disregard in which artists are held by a philistine society. Kafka resented the long hours which he worked for an insurance company, at the family's fancy goods store and in his brother-in-law's asbestos factory, which left him little spare time for writing.

Kafka, a Jewish German-speaking Czech, was haunted by a fear of failure, both literary and sexual. Gregor's new form deprives him of the ability to work and even speak, and may have been Kafka's attempt to describe what failure looked like to him. When he died in 1924 his work was unknown to the general public. It has been claimed that Kafka burned up to 90% of his work; and in his will he left instructions that his two unpublished novels, *The Trial* and *The Castle* be burned too. Mercifully his friend and executor Max Brod ignored his instructions.

Only after World War II was his output rediscovered and reappraised in the German-speaking world, which was itself reconsidering its identity. Since then Kafka has been a powerful influence on German literature and, when his work became known further afield in the 1960s, on the rest of the world.

The Age of Innocence

(1920)

Edith Wharton (1862–1937)

Edith Wharton's return to the period of her childhood in 1870s New York is a picture of a world lost forever in the upheaval of World War I. Amid the strict conventions of upper-class society, a man aches for liberation from their constraints, and finds real love on the eve of his wedding.

Wharton had previously revisited the era in her 1905 novel *The House of Mirth*. Both novels have ironic titles: there is little to laugh at in the former's portrayal of the loss of social status; and although the *Age of Innocence* is a kinder, gentler study, the projection of outward innocence and morality conceals darker, more passionate emotions.

The central character, Newland Archer, comes from a wealthy family. He is a successful lawyer and about to make a successful marriage, another of life's goals achieved. His bride-to-be, May Welland, has been raised according to the conventions of the day to be a perfect, passive wife. In this privileged formal environment, the arrival of May's cousin Ellen destabilises everything. Social propriety dictates that she should be frowned upon for having left her cruel husband for his secretary, for mixing with undesirable people and for treating her servant as an equal. But she is fascinating, and Newland soon falls under her spell. The book follows him as he tries to resolve his dilemma: to defy convention and elope with Ellen (with whom he shares a deep, true love), or behave as society expects by honouring his commitment to May.

The Age of Innocence is Wharton's attempt to come to terms with the paradigm shift in society which World War I wrought, by writing about the social strains of a time before that conflict. Its drama is the tension between old and new,

between the traditional subservient role of women and their new empowerment when the men went off to war. The mannered formality of the upper classes is at odds with the high passions experienced by Ellen and Newland; and in the end May too is stirred to act in a bid to save her marriage. Whether May acts out of love or in order to manipulate, she shows that even she, the most conforming of women, has feelings.

Ellen and May are polar opposites and they cannot co-exist in Newland's world. He feels a different love for each of them, one of which must remain unfulfilled. In Wharton's presentation of their psychological characters she uses many references to the elements of fire and water, which are similarly destructive of each other. Newland's solution to his dilemma leaves no one truly happy and the reader wondering what might have been.

Wharton paints a detailed picture of the world which she was recreating, especially of the sumptuous interiors of that class (she had spent time as an interior designer before becoming an author). Her unflinching examination of the clash between the old and the new made her, in 1921, the first woman to win the Pulitzer Prize for Fiction.

LEFT: *Edith Wharton was a child of America's 'Gilded Age'.*
OPPOSITE: *A centennial celebration of Wharton's greatest novel from Simon & Schuster.*

100TH
ANNIVERSARY
EDITION

THE AGE OF INNOCENCE

a novel

Edith Wharton

WINNER OF THE PULITZER PRIZE

WITH A NEW INTRODUCTION BY COLM TÓIBÍN

Ulysses

(1922)

James Joyce (1882–1941)

A giant of a book, *Ulysses* is the epitome of the modernist novel, an impressionistic stream of consciousness which conjures up the nature of one man's existence on a single Dublin day in 1904. Its complex style and structure have been debated by scholars since the day it was published.

Ulysses is the Latin form of Odysseus, the Greek hero whose twenty years of warfare and frustrated homecoming are described in Homer's *Odyssey*. Joyce offers a modern parallel, condensed into a single day in the life of Leopold Bloom. Bloom's day, 16th June 1904, divided into eighteen episodes, roughly follows the outline of Homer's twenty-four books of the *Odyssey*. Bloom fills the role of Odysseus; his wife Molly Bloom represents Odysseus's wife Penelope, left at home; and the characters whom Bloom encounters during his day out echo those met on Odysseus's journey.

Joyce adopts a bewildering variety of different styles for the episodes of *Ulysses*. One is a playscript complete with stage directions; another is a series of 309 questions and answers; another reflects the nine-month gestation of a newborn child with styles from the entire history of the English language, including Anglo-Saxon, the King James Bible, Samuel Pepys and Charles Dickens, ending with modern slang. The final episode at last gives Molly Bloom a voice in a stream of consciousness without punctuation. Elsewhere Joyce parodies scientific and legal jargon, romantic novels and boxing commentary.

It is a notoriously challenging book to read, but only because of its elaborate literary riches. Written at the same time that Marcel Proust was working on *In Search of Lost Time*, *Ulysses* goes much further in its use of internal monologue, and in its appropriation of the style and form of language, not just its meaning, to evoke the thoughts, moods and feelings of its characters. Joyce's text plays games with the reader, containing puzzles, deliberate errors and myriad allusions to classical and classic literature.

There's also quite a lot of sex, and *Ulysses* was prosecuted in the US under an old act prohibiting the distribution of obscene material. It appeared there in 1920 as a serialisation distributed by post, and the magazine in question was convicted of the crime. The US Post Office therefore burned copies of the book throughout the 1920s. Only when the publisher, Random House, allowed themselves to be caught smuggling a French copy into the country in 1932, and challenged the seizure in court, was the novel declared not pornographic. This made possible the first legal publication of the book in English; in Britain it was banned until 1936, and in Joyce's native Ireland it was not widely available until the 1960s.

The density and meaning of the novel's ideas have been the subject of passionate academic debate ever since its publication. Even the text itself is hotly disputed. The First Edition is said to have contained over 2,000 misprints, and in correcting them for the second edition many more were introduced. In addition, no one is entirely sure how many of Joyce's mistakes were mistaken or deliberate.

Ulysses is widely acknowledged by academics and authors as the finest novel of its age, and every year its admirers celebrate the date on which it is set, 16th June, as Bloomsday.

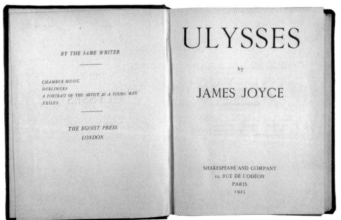

ABOVE: *Joyce with Sylvia Beach, owner of pioneering Paris bookshop Shakespeare & Co., who would often extend loans to Ernest Hemingway. A great fan of Joyce's work, she was determined to see the book published. After the German invasion of Paris an officer tried to buy her original copy of Finnegans Wake in the window. The incident prompted her to close the store for good.*
OPPOSITE: *Joyce's biographers thought he was short-sighted, like his fictional alter ego Stephen Dedalus, but researchers have noticed that his lenses were convex, suggesting far-sightedness.*

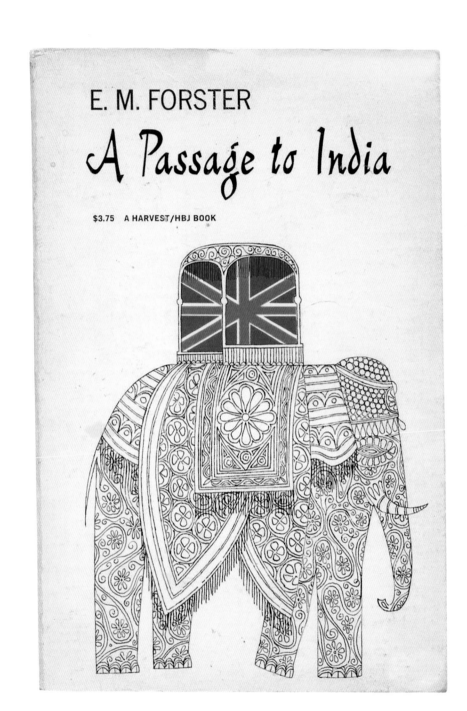

E. M. FORSTER

A Passage to India

$3.75   A HARVEST/HBJ BOOK

ABOVE: A clever graphic interpretation of the uneasy relationships portrayed in Forster's classic novel.
OPPOSITE: E.M. Forster was part of Virginia Woolf's Bloomsbury Group.

A Passage to India

(1924)

E.M. Forster (1879–1970)

Into the already socially complex world of the British upper class E.M. Forster brings the additional complications of racism, colonialism and India's growing desire to be independent of its imperial rulers. As Dr Aziz asks at the beginning of the novel, can an Indian ever be the friend of a European?

The passage to India of the title is the journey which young Adela Quested and her future mother-in-law, Mrs Moore, make to the fictional city of Chandrapore for the wedding of Adela to Mrs Moore's son Ronny. The book explores the differing attitudes to India and its people, from Ronny's unquestioning acceptance of British superiority to Mrs Moore's respectful and egalitarian treatment of Indians and their culture. Adela, who has never been to the continent, is overwhelmed by the experience and in a moment of confusion falsely accuses Dr Aziz of 'making insulting advances'. Aziz had become a friend of the European group; but as Forster examines the reactions from all sides to the accusation, wounds open up, not only between the group and Aziz but within the British contingent.

A Passage to India is as wide as the sky in scope. On the one hand it is a product of the unique place and time when it was written. Forster worked in India as a private secretary to the Maharajah of Dewas for a year from 1921 to 1922, and *A Passage to India* reflects his experience of the country. On the other hand, it holds eternal truths about humanity's treatment of those it considers inferior, whatever the colour of their skin. The British women in *A Passage to India* are subject to the same patronising attitudes from European men as the Indian population are.

Its insight on India was not, on its publication, entirely welcomed by British readers. Many thought that the interracial relationships depicted in it were inappropriate. Forster's rounded picture of Indian culture was at odds with the prevailing view of the Asian stereotype. For others who liked to think of the Far East as exotic and mysterious, Forster demystified it, presenting ordinary human beings with emotions and lives no different from anyone else's. Aziz is a doctor, not a swami; and his sometimes overwrought response to situations is Forster's way of showing that Indians have emotional depth too.

With the passage of time, much has changed. The independence movement described in the book bore fruit in 1947 when, after both peaceful and violent campaigns, India, like many outposts of empire, was granted its sovereignty. Forster's even-handed handling of the question of independence made no absolute judgement about either side in the debate. Attitudes to *A Passage to India* have changed over the years. It is now seen as a valuable witness to India's colonial history, a significant challenge to racial, imperial and sexist assumptions, and a central text for gender studies.

Forster was not a prolific author. He wrote only six novels. Four – *Where Angels Fear to Tread* (1905), *The Longest Journey* (1907), *A Room with a View* (1908) and *Howards End* (1910) – were published in the first decade of the twentieth century. In the long gap between *Howards End* and *A Passage to India* he wrote *Maurice*, a novel about homosexual love which was only published posthumously in 1971. Forster did not try to publish it in his lifetime for fear that it would contravene the prevailing laws against male homosexuality.

The Great Gatsby

(1925)

F. Scott Fitzgerald (1896–1940)

One classic American novel captures the United States at its wildest and most hedonistic, in the Jazz Age of the 1920s. Behind the raucous parties and the glamour of wealthy East Coast society, hidden from view, is a different reality. Secrets, lies and an impossible love are the flipside of the gilded coin.

Not long after F. Scott Fitzgerald's death, copies of *The Great Gatsby* were distributed to American servicemen in World War II, by the Council on Books in Wartime (motto 'weapons in the war of ideas'). This Armed Services edition prompted a large-scale reassessment of his work. Fitzgerald had died convinced he was a failure as a writer, and sales of *Gatsby* when it was first published were disappointing compared to his earlier works *This Side of Paradise* (1920) and *The Beautiful and Damned* (1922). Today, the story of the doomed love of Jay Gatsby for Daisy Buchanan may be the best-loved novel in the North American canon.

The life of Jay Gatsby closely mirror's Fitzgerald's own. The love of Fitzgerald's life was Ginevra King, daughter of a wealthy socialite; she returned his love, but her parents objected to her relationship with a lower-class Midwesterner, telling her, 'Poor boys shouldn't think of marrying rich girls'. Fitzgerald never stopped loving her, just as Gatsby clings to his love of Daisy.

Broken-hearted, Fitzgerald enlisted in the US Army in the hope of dying in combat in World War I. While he was away, Ginevra married a wealthy businessman, just as Daisy marries Tom Buchanan while Jay is posted overseas. Jay's determination to win back Daisy drives him to accumulate wealth in order to impress her. Fitzgerald pursued success partly because his future wife, Zelda, insisted on delaying the wedding until he had made his name and fortune as a writer.

Zelda and Scott settled on Long Island where they attended the sort of extravagant parties thrown in the novel by the great Gatsby. Like Gatsby, who does not join in the revelries that he hosts, Fitzgerald was an outsider at these affairs and found them morally repugnant.

Aspects of Jay's character were also inspired by the Fitzgeralds' neighbour on Long Island, Max Gerlach. Gerlach, like Gatsby, served in the war and returned to make a fortune selling bootleg liquor in the Prohibition era. Like Gatsby, Gerlach flaunted his wealth and threw wild parties. It is said that he never wore the same shirt twice and, like Gatsby, invented sensational details about his life.

Neither Gatsby nor Fitzgerald regained their lost loves. Gatsby's story ends badly when out of love he conceals Daisy's guilt in a hit-and-run accident which kills her husband's lover. Zelda Fitzgerald suffered from debilitating mental health problems, and constantly belittled her husband, much to the dismay of friend Ernest Hemingway, who wrote: 'If he could write a book as fine as *The Great Gatsby* I was sure that he could write an even better one. I did not know Zelda yet, and so I did not know the terrible odds that were against him.' Zelda died in a fire seven years after her husband, who drank himself to death. They are buried together beneath a stone on which the final line of *The Great Gatsby* is engraved:

> So we beat on, boats against the current, borne back ceaselessly into the past.

The Great Gatsby is a brilliant recreation of America's most colourful decade. If it bears the reader into the past, it also shows the contradictions that are always present: of wealth and poverty; of love and infidelity; of outward exuberance and internal sorrow; of truth and lies; of power and powerlessness; of hope and hopelessness. It is the Great American Novel.

ABOVE: The original dust jacket from the First Edition in 1925 designed by painter and graphic artist Francis Cugat. In 1925 he moved to Hollywood to design film sets for Douglas Fairbanks.

The Sun Also Rises

(1926)

Ernest Hemingway (1899–1961)

There is little difference between the characters and events of *The Sun Also Rises* and those of three visits that Ernest Hemingway made to Pamplona in northern Spain. Only the names have been changed in Hemingway's first, and finest, novel.

In 1921 Hemingway was working in Paris as European correspondent for the *Toronto Star*. He had just met and married his first wife, Hadley Richardson, and was carving out a career as a journalist. He wanted to write fiction and believed that it carried the greatest truth when based on real-life events and the author's personal experiences.

The Hemingways first visited Pamplona in 1923 and returned with guests in the following two years. Pamplona is famous for its Bull Run: bulls are driven through the city streets and young men test their manhood by running in front of them. The animals are later used in bullfighting, and Hemingway became an enthusiast of this violent sport. It forms the central sequence of *The Sun Also Rises*, when heat and testosterone mix with jealousy and lust to create an explosive denouement.

On the visit in 1925, which Hemingway drew on for much of the novel, sexual tension soon arose between those who were having affairs and those who wanted to. In the novel, Brett Ashley is the dazzling, promiscuous flame around which four moths – Jake, Mike, Robert and a local bullfighter called Romero – flap their wings. The model for Brett was Lady Twysden, a daring, adventurous British socialite who was a member of the 1925 party. When all four men come to blows in the dramatic climax of *The Sun Also Rises*, they do so because Hemingway and the writer Harold Loeb, his rival for Lady Twysden's attention, fought with fists on a public street in the city. Jake's fishing trip to Burguete is the same trip that Hemingway made with friends in 1925. Romero was based on Cayetano Ordóñez, the heroic bullfighter who won the crowds in the bullring in 1925 and who presented Hadley Hemingway with the ear of the bull which he had just killed – a great honour.

Hemingway applied the same rules of writing to his novel that he had been taught as a cub reporter on *The Kansas City Star*: 'Use short sentences. Use short first paragraphs. Use vigorous English. Be positive, not negative.' The result is an urgent, racy prose which leaves the reader breathless for more, just like Hemingway's characters. The text hauls the reader along with it, and as one reviewer wrote, it's 'as if he had never read anybody's writing, as if he had fashioned the art of writing himself'.

Critics hailed the understated approach, which left the reader feeling the emotions of the characters rather

ABOVE: *Covering old ground: Hemingway in Spain with bullfighting superstar Antonio Ordóñez, son of Cayetano, in 1960.*
OPPOSITE: *A modern cover of the novel that established Hemingway's sparse, direct style.*

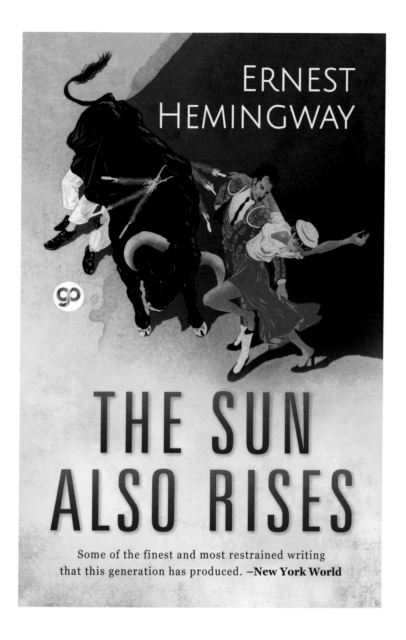

ERNEST
HEMINGWAY

THE SUN ALSO RISES

Some of the finest and most restrained writing
that this generation has produced. **—New York World**

than reading about them. Some felt that the tawdry activities of the group were not fit subjects for literature, that Hemingway's tale and fictionalised friends were simply shallow and uninteresting. His mother was horrified by it and wrote to him in a letter, 'Surely you have other words in your vocabulary than "damn" and "bitch" – Every page fills me with a sick loathing.'

Hemingway dedicated the book to his wife and son; but after its publication Hadley asked him for a divorce. He signed over all the royalties from the book to her, whether out of spite or of lingering affection, and married a further three times in the course of his hard-loving, hard-drinking life. *The Sun Also Rises* remains his best work.

*ABOVE: The Penguin re-issue that marked a sea change in legal attitudes towards works of
literature considered obscene.*

OPPOSITE: David Herbert Lawrence photographed circa 1915.

Lady Chatterley's Lover

(1928)

D.H. Lawrence (1885–1930)

Raised in a coal-mining village in Nottinghamshire D.H. Lawrence brought a rare working-class sensibility to his four novels. The controversy surrounding *Lady Chatterley's Lover* and its detailed descriptions of sex overshadowed its literary qualities, which Lawrence robustly defended.

The coarse language and the beautifully crafted but explicit sex scenes between Constance, Lady Chatterley, and her gamekeeper Oliver Mellors caused the book to be banned in Britain, the United States, Canada, Australia and Japan. In other countries the novel was only available in censored, abridged versions or on the black market. Lawrence had intended to challenge the traditional English reserve about sexual matters. He responded to the book's ban with defiance, satirical poetry and a pamphlet titled *Pornography and Obscenity.*

Thirty years after Lawrence's death, the publisher Penguin brought out a full, uncensored version of the text in a direct challenge to the new British Obscene Publications Act of 1959. The initial print run of 200,000 copies sold out within twenty-four hours, and Penguin was acquitted in court on charges of obscenity, on the grounds that the work had extenuating literary merit. The Crown's case had been undermined by the pompous prosecution barrister Mervyn Griffith-Jones who famously asked if it was a book 'you would even wish your wife or servants to read', highlighting how out of touch the British establishment had become.

Canada and the United States lifted their bans at around the same time, although Australia had to wait until 1965. The legal publication of the book is often linked to the sexual revolution of the 1960s. Penguin's edition eventually sold three million copies, mostly to readers titillated by the promise of literary pornography.

The novel is not about sex but about relationships which best succeed when there is a complete and equal connection of both mind and body. Constance's businessman husband, Lord Chatterley, represents the cold advance of industry, anathema to nature and humanity. Lord Chatterley is paralysed, symbolically, from the waist down. Constance and Mellors share

a passion for nature and each other which their membership of different social classes does not preclude.

D.H. Lawrence wrote in the Realist literary tradition in his criticism of modernity and his analysis of class. But he was also a Romantic and the contrast between natural landscape, and natural acts, and the inhuman machinery of progress, was a common theme of his work, placing him closer to Thomas Hardy than Charles Dickens.

Although Constance and Mellors have what Lawrence argues is a complete love for each other, it does not, in the end, overcome the social distinctions which it should have bridged. Mellors, dismissed from his position as gamekeeper, waits for a divorce from his wife; but although Constance leaves her husband, he refuses her a divorce. As long as she remains married, she must live not with Mellors but with her sister. The future for them remains uncertain.

Orlando

(1928)

Virginia Woolf (1882–1941)

It has been described as 'the longest and most charming love letter in literature'. Virginia Woolf's era-spanning, gender-fluid poet-hero Orlando was a literary portrait of her friend and lover Vita Sackville-West. Both women were part of the celebrated Bloomsbury Group of artists and writers.

The Bloomsbury Group was a loose collective whose members included E.M. Forster, Woolf, her husband Leonard, sister Vanessa and Vanessa's husband, Clive Bell, Vanessa's sometime lover, Duncan Grant and his sometime lovers Lytton Strachey, and John Maynard Keynes. Dorothy Parker once said of the group, 'they lived in squares, painted in circles and loved in triangles'. Besides being sexually liberal, they defined a new arts aesthetic with a left-leaning philosophy and a wilful rejection of Victorian conventions in art and in personal life. They espoused pacifism and feminism, and the group included economists and art critics as well as art practitioners.

Orlando, subtitled *A Biography*, tells the story of an Elizabethan poet who lives the first thirty years of his life as a man and, after an overnight transformation, the following three hundred years as a woman. She meets celebrated writers through the ages, including the poet Alexander Pope, and eventually finds happiness in marriage to a sea captain, in the publication of her epic work *The Oak Tree*, and in the ownership of her property after a legal challenge.

Many elements of *Orlando* are references to aspects of Vita Sackville-West's life. It was written to comfort Vita after she had, unlike Orlando, lost her family home because of the convention of inheritance through the male line. Orlando's change of gender takes place in Constantinople, which Vita had visited in 1913. Constantinople, a cultural centre under successive Greek, Roman, Christian and Muslim rule, also stands for the gender fluidity of the novel, straddling the two continents of Europe and Asia and, when Woolf was writing, having recently changed its name to Istanbul. Orlando escapes from Constantinople with the help of Romanies, a cultural group which fascinated Vita.

Vita was an aspiring writer, like Orlando. Although Woolf loved her, she held Vita's literary skills in poor regard. A recurring motif in *Orlando* is the poet's unsuccessful pursuit of a grey goose, which represented Vita's failed literary aspirations. Throughout the book Orlando struggles to find the right words, a characteristic which scholars have associated with 'the love that dare not speak its name', Vita and Virginia's lesbian love for each other. When Orlando tries to describe nature, he finds it difficult to avoid feminine metaphors – he blurts, 'the sky is like the veils which a thousand Madonnas have let fall from their hair'. Nature, Woolf implies, is inseparably bound up with femininity.

The book has become a flagship for female authorship of literature, and for gender studies. Orlando's journey through time deliberately restores a woman to the centre of history, from which so many women's lives have been excluded. Woolf uses it to satirise male-defined conventions and movements, and she is particularly critical of the very masculine British Empire. Above all it is Woolf's idealised portrait of Vita. Vita's son Nigel Nicolson wrote that in *Orlando* Woolf 'explores Vita, weaves her in and out of the centuries, tosses her from one sex to the other, plays with her, dresses her in furs, lace and emeralds, teases her, flirts with her, drops a veil of mist around her'.

ABOVE: *Apart from being a critical and financial success,* Orlando *was one of the few books that addressed gender head on.*

OPPOSITE: *Virginia Woolf photographed in 1927. Her novel* To the Lighthouse *had been published just a year before* Orlando.

100 Novels That Changed the World_____103

ABOVE: *The First Edition from 1932.*
OPPOSITE: *Aldous Huxley was nominated for a Nobel Prize for Literature many times between*
1938 and 1964, but failed to win. His half-brother, Andrew Huxley, was awarded the 1963
Nobel Prize in Physiology/Medicine for work on electrical impulses in nerve cells.

Brave New World

(1932)

Aldous Huxley (1894–1963)

What began as a parody of the utopian novels of H.G. Wells became a landmark of dystopian fiction. Very much a product of its time, *Brave New World* was written during an economic depression when the brave new world promised after the War to End All Wars had failed to materialise.

At the end of the nineteenth century it seemed that mankind had the technological knowledge and the understanding of society to fix all mankind's problems. Authors like William Morris in *News From Nowhere* (1890), H.G. Wells in *A Modern Utopia* (1905) and Alexander Bogdanov in *Red Star* (1908) offered various broadly socialist visions of this future. Others pictured a society in which gender was the key: *Sultana's Dream* (1905) by Begum Rokeya, *Beatrice the Sixteenth* (1909) by Irene Clyde and *Herland* (1915) by Charlotte Perkins Gilman all proposed feminist utopias in which education and peace were most highly prized.

The horrors of World War I dispelled the fantasy of any imminent earthly utopia. Instead of imagining an anticipated perfect world, writers turned to considering what went wrong. Aldous Huxley, who already had a reputation for satire, wrote to a friend that he had 'been having a little fun pulling the leg of H.G. Wells', but that he had 'got caught up in the excitement of my own ideas'. In fact, Wells had already produced several dystopian visions – in *The Time Machine* (1895) and *The Sleeper Awakes* (1910) – which, like *Brave New World*, addressed the question of social conditioning, and which undoubtedly influenced Huxley's novel.

Brave New World is set in the World State, a global nation founded upon the principles introduced by Henry Ford on the assembly line of his Model T vehicle: mass production, predictability, homogeneity and disposability. Babies are produced in serried ranks of incubators, not *in utero*. Through subliminal sleep-learning they are educated in approved ideas appropriate for the social caste in which they will be placed. Reading is discouraged, and although there is no religion, Ford is revered as other societies might revere a god. The Christian cross has been adapted by removing the upper limb to make the form of a T, and the years are numbered AF – After Ford. The novel takes place in the year AF 632, 632 years after the first Model T was manufactured.

The plot follows two colleagues who return from a holiday in a Savage Reservation – a place where tourists can see 'primitive' people experiencing natural birth, disease and ageing, and practicing religious rituals. They bring with them a savage mother and her adult son John. John becomes a celebrity because of his 'savagery': to the public's amusement he learned all he knows by reading Shakespeare and can only express himself in Shakespearean quotations. He, born of woman, is as indoctrinated by Shakespeare as those born in incubators are by sleep-learning. John does not fit in, and when he seeks to withdraw from this world, he is accused, incredulously, of demanding the right to be unhappy.

Brave New World is often compared to George Orwell's *1984*. Of the two dystopian visions, Orwell's is enforced by menace and violence, Huxley's by subtler social conditioning. Huxley returned to the World State in *Brave New World Revisited* (1958), a non-fiction reassessment of the ideas in his novel, which he concluded were coming to pass faster than expected. His last novel, *Island* (1962), is sometimes seen as a companion piece to *Brave New World*, presenting an island utopia.

I, Claudius

(1934)

Robert Graves (1895–1985)

A fictional autobiography of the Roman emperor who preceded Nero revolutionised the way in which both historic novels and history itself were written. Drawing on ancient historical sources Robert Graves gave Claudius a voice and challenged his long-standing reputation as a weak idiot.

Claudius suffered from a limp, a stammer, nervous tics, and slight deafness which was the legacy of a childhood illness. He was a historian, who wrote an unwisely critical account of Caesar Augustus's role in the Roman Civil Wars, while Augustus (his great-great-uncle) was still emperor. His failure to toe the family line damaged his status and nobody expected him to amount to anything. He was regarded, both during his life and by historians, as unimportant and unthreatening. Yet that very perception helped him to survive the murderous purges of the dynasty which produced the early rulers of the Roman Empire. He became the fourth emperor and is known to have written a genuine autobiography, now lost.

Robert Graves was a classical scholar who read the near-contemporary histories by Tacitus, Plutarch and Suetonius before writing the novel. His sympathetic portrayal of Claudius was at odds with the conventional view and paints a picture of a clever man who used his disabilities to his advantage. He became emperor after the assassination of his nephew Caligula (in which he was not involved, at least directly), and ruled effectively. Claudius developed the empire's network of roads and canals, presided personally over judicial proceedings and rescued Rome's finances which had been damaged by Caligula's excesses. Under Claudius's reign Rome conquered Britain.

I, Claudius was successful both as fiction and as fact. Its derivation from Latin histories was authentic and invited modern historians to reassess Claudius's life; and its first-person narrative, allied with the author's talent for storytelling, engrossed the novel-reading public. Graves later claimed that he had written the book only because he needed money after a disastrous land deal, and that the £8,000 which he made from *I, Claudius* amply cleared his debts of £4,000. Whether that is true or not,

I, Claudius and its sequel *Claudius the God* (which covers Claudius's time as emperor) broke new ground in the way that history could be told through fiction.

Graves subsequently wrote more historical fiction, including the much-admired *King Jesus* (1946), which looks at the life of Jesus from a non-religious point of view. The memoir of his early life, including his harrowing experience of World War I, *Goodbye to All That* (1929), is widely read in schools in connection with the poetry of that conflict. His two books retelling the myths and legends of ancient Greece – *The Greek Myths* (1955) and *Greek Gods and Heroes* (1960) – are standard works for anyone wishing to immerse themselves in those tales.

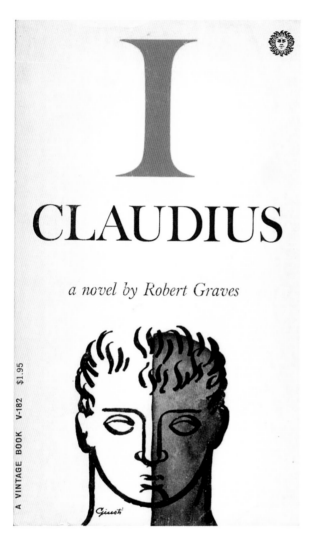

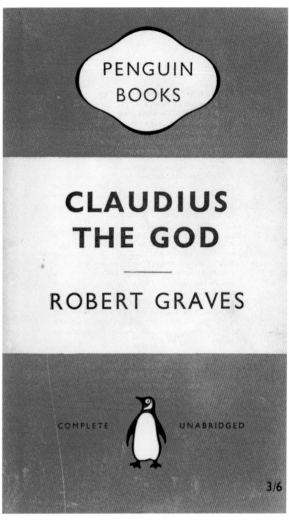

ABOVE: Graves' novels on Claudius were meticulously researched.
OPPOSITE: Graves was a war poet and friend of both T. E. Lawrence and Siegfried
Sassoon. He was so badly wounded at the Battle of the Somme that he was
reported killed in action. He published a successful biography of Lawrence in
1927 and an autobiography, including his war experiences, Goodbye to
All That in 1929.

Rebecca

(1938)

Daphne du Maurier (1907–1989)

Jealousy and resentment haunt the rooms of Manderley, the fictional country house which is the setting for *Rebecca*. Du Maurier's editor once described the place as being 'as much an atmosphere as a tangible erection of stones and mortar'. The story is Gothic to its bones and flames.

Rebecca is the late first wife of Maxim de Winter, who marries his second wife less than a year after her death. His new bride, the unnamed narrator of the novel, fears that she will not be able to fill the shoes of her predecessor, a famous beauty admired for being the perfect wife. Manderley's housekeeper, Mrs Danvers, fiercely loyal to the memory of Rebecca, resents the narrator's presence in the house and through psychological pressure encourages the narrator's belief that Maxim loves Rebecca more than her. When the truth about Rebecca's death emerges, she is found to have been manipulative, cruel and unfaithful. Although this provides some reassurance to the narrator about her marriage, Rebecca's spirit seems to be determined to make Manderley uninhabitable.

Daphne du Maurier had wanted to write a novel about jealousy ever since her marriage in 1932 to Lieutenant Colonel Tommy Browning. Her wedding, like Maxim's, followed a relatively short courtship, and du Maurier remained convinced that Browning was still in love with Jan Ricardo, a strikingly beautiful woman to whom Browning had once been engaged. These relationships form the basis for *Rebecca*.

Neither Browning nor du Maurier trusted each other, and both had affairs during World War II. A few years after the publication of *Rebecca*, Ricardo committed suicide. Du Maurier once described herself as having two sides: the public, feminine image of a faithful wife and mother; and a secret life as a lover, driven by what she called 'a decidedly male energy', which also powered her creative writing. These two personalities are the ones she ascribed to Rebecca.

Du Maurier found *Rebecca* difficult to write. She tore up the first 15,000 words in disgust, and delivered the final manuscript four months late. Her publishers were relieved to recognise its quality. The initial large print run of 20,000 was proof of their confidence in it; and only a month after publication *Rebecca* had sold more than 40,000 copies. It has never been out of print, and has been the inspiration for much fan fiction in the decades since. Du Maurier's estate has authorised three intriguing sequels: *Mrs de Winter* (1993) by Susan Hill; Maureen Freely's *The Other Rebecca* (1996); and *Rebecca's Tale* (2001) written by Sally Beauman.

Daphne du Maurier worked across many genres including biography and drama – she wrote the stage adaptation of *Rebecca* and two other original plays. Her biographies included histories of the du Maurier family and, in *The Infernal World of Branwell Brontë* (1960), of the brother of the Brontë sisters. Among her many great works of literary fiction are *Jamaica Inn* (1936), *Frenchman's Creek* (1941) and *My Cousin Rachel* (1951).

DAPHNE du MAURIER

REBECCA

A brilliant novel of an unforgettable woman,

by the author of "JAMAICA INN"

ABOVE: The American First Edition, originally priced at $2.75.
OPPOSITE: Daphne du Maurier was born into a wealthy theatrical family living in Hampstead
and, like Virginia Woolf, spending long summers in Cornwall.

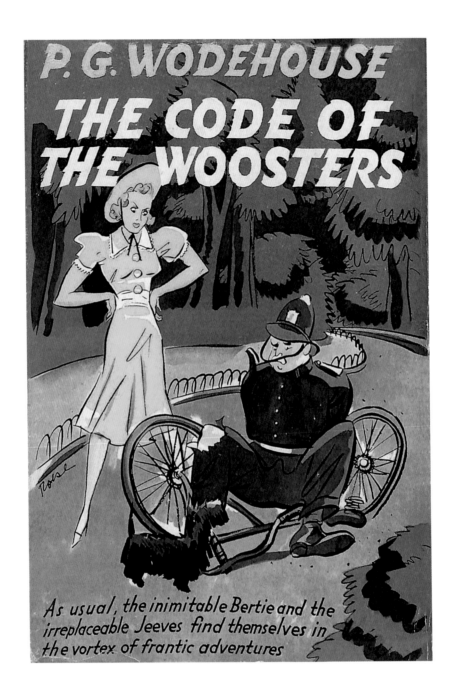

ABOVE: *A First Edition cover from 1938.*

OPPOSITE: *P.G. Wodehouse was remorseful about his World War II broadcasts for the Germans. Friend Malcolm Muggeridge defended his lack of guile: 'He is a man singularly ill-fitted to live in a time of ideological conflict, having no feelings of hatred about anyone, and no very strong views about anything.'*

The Code of the Woosters

(1938)

P.G. Wodehouse (1881–1975)

One of the greatest masters of the English language was at the top of his game when he published the third novel about his most famous creations, Bertie Wooster and his butler Jeeves. Wodehouse's dexterity of phrase, his flexibility of grammar, and his sheer inventive joy are all present and correct.

Pelham Grenville Wodehouse was a prolific humorist who published more than ninety books including novels, short story collections and three volumes of autobiography. He created many memorable characters, each appearing in their own series of stories – Lord Emsworth and his family; the golfing raconteur the Oldest Member; the many asinine members of the Drones Club; the plausible schemes of Psmith; Mr Mulliner; Ukridge; and of course the delightfully vacuous Bertie Wooster and his wise and loyal servant Jeeves.

There are eleven Jeeves novels and the pair also appear in seven volumes of short stories. By the time he approached *The Code of the Woosters*, the characters were already familiar to his readership, and this third novel introduces new recurring faces as well as continuing the adventures of supporting characters Gussie Fink-Nottle, a newt-lover and old friend of Bertie's, and Gussie's sentimental fiancée Madeline, who appeared in the earlier *Right Ho, Jeeves* (1934). The novel revolves around an antique silver cow-creamer, an object of desire for two collectors – Madeline's father, Sir Watkyn, and Bertie's uncle Tom. Wodehouse manages the story of the hapless Wooster's attempt to steal the jug back from Sir Watkyn with the theatrical flair of someone who was as comfortable writing for the stage as for the page. Jeeves, as always, saves the day.

One of the new members of Wodehouse's ensemble, cast for the first time in *The Code of the Woosters*, is the villainous Roderick Spode, 7th Earl of Sidcup. Wodehouse rarely dabbled in politics except for comic effect; and Spode is a parody of the notorious British fascist Sir Oswald Mosley, whose gangs of Blackshirt thugs attempted to sow dissent in the inter-war years. In Wodehouse's hands, Spode leads an organisation called the Saviours of Britain, whose followers must wear black schoolboy football shorts, 'because there were no shirts left'. Spode is a social outcast and a bully with messy eating habits, and unknown to his acolytes he is a designer of ladies' underwear.

Only three years after the publication of *The Code of the Woosters*, Wodehouse got into serious trouble with another political satire. Wodehouse had a house in Le Touquet in France, and when war broke out he was interned by the occupying Germans. He continued to write during his internment: he completed two novels and was persuaded by his captors to give some humorous talks for German radio, which he titled *How to be an Internee Without Previous Training*. The light-hearted reflections of his imprisonment, with gentle jibes at his German guards, were viewed in Britain as treacherous support for Germany in a time of war. After the war he chose to live in America, where his broadcasts had been seen as an act of anti-Nazi propaganda. Looking back, he wrote, 'Of course I ought to have had the sense to see that it was a loony thing to do to use the German radio for even the most harmless stuff, but I didn't. I suppose prison life saps the intellect.'

Wodehouse's first novel was published in 1902, and he completed his last in 1974. After nominations for his knighthood were blocked in 1967 and 1971 because of his wartime folly, he was finally knighted in 1975, a belated acknowledgement of one of Britain's greatest wordsmiths, who died a few weeks later, on St Valentine's Day.

And Then There Were None

(1939)

Agatha Christie (1890–1976)

Firmly established as the Queen of Detective Fiction, Agatha Christie did not confine herself to her two most celebrated detectives, Hercule Poirot and Jane Marple. In her best-selling novel, *all* the characters must become amateur detectives, and all of them are murdered before they can uncover the murderer.

And Then There Were None is a classic locked-room mystery. Eight people, strangers to each other, are unexpectedly invited to a house party on a private island, where they are met by a butler and housekeeper but not their anonymous host. The guests, the staff and the reader must search for an explanation as, one by one, each of the ten is killed. After the last death, there is no one left alive who could have committed the crimes, or could explain to the police – when they discover the grisly scene – what happened.

Agatha Christie was fascinated by the challenge which such a mystery presented to a writer. How to retain the reader's interest after so many murders? How to present so many deaths one after the other without the sequence becoming farcical? And how to write such a story without making the identity of the murderer obvious? Christie planned the story thoroughly before starting to write it, and considered it the hardest of her sixty-six novels to have written. Looking back on the experience, she wrote in her autobiography, 'I do think in some ways that it is a better piece of craftsmanship than anything else I have written.'

A largely forgotten American novel by Gwen Bristow and Bruce Manning, *The Invisible Host*, was published in 1930 and soon adapted for Broadway and Hollywood. Its plot bears an uncanny similarity to *And Then There Were None*; but there is no evidence that Christie, living and

writing in the English country village of Wallingford in Oxfordshire, read or saw it. *And Then There Were None* has itself been the source of more adaptations than any other of Christie's novels, many of them changing the setting, the characters or other details. Christie herself changed the bleak ending of the original for a more upbeat one when she adapted it for the stage in 1943.

The title itself has been altered several times. It is the last line of a children's counting rhyme which has occurred in various forms in both the United Kingdom and the United States. It has always been published in America under its present title, *And Then There Were None*, but Christie's original title, under which it was published in the UK until 1985, was the first line of the rhyme as she knew it. The book follows the structure of the verse, counting down how many are left until 'there were none'. Christie, living in rural England, did not comprehend the racial impact of what is now dubbed 'the n-word'. In the US the poem has been known as *Ten Little Indians*, and the book was sometimes published under that name, with a sensitivity edit applied to Christie's text.

And Then There Were None has sold more than 100 million copies to date, making it not only the most popular of Agatha Christie's novels but the best-selling crime book of all time, and the sixth most successful book in *any* genre. There is no mystery about how the Queen of Crime won her crown.

LEFT: *A rare copy of the US First Edition from 1940, featuring a country house not unlike the Burgh Island Hotel.*

BELOW: *Agatha Christie wrote two novels while staying on the Devon island which is cut off from the mainland at high tide. Guests are ferried to the island using an elevated tractor transport.*

OPPOSITE: *Agatha Christie photographed in the mid 1920s.*

The Big Sleep

(1939)

Raymond Chandler (1888–1959)

The book which introduced hard-boiled detective Philip Marlowe, elevated the crime novel from pulp fiction to literature. Raymond Chandler wrote both, and *The Big Sleep* shows how he converted the former into the latter.

It is Chandler's ability to conjure atmosphere that marks him out from other crime writers of the period. From the dusty grandeur of General Sternwood's residence where Marlowe begins his investigation, the action moves to the shopfront and lurid love nest of the gay pornographer Arthur Geiger.

Chandler weaves a complex storyline. Geiger is blackmailing Sternwood's wild daughter, Carmen, and the husband of Carmen's sister Vivian has disappeared. Gangster Eddie Mars seems to be involved in both cases, and Mars' wife Mona and Geiger's receptionist Agnes serve as irresistible red herrings until Marlowe pieces together the truth.

The Big Sleep is a euphemism for death, and there are six fatalities in *The Big Sleep*, none of them accidental. Chandler was a prolific short-story writer for the pulp fiction magazine *Black Mask* and he described his process of merging and expanding several of them to form his full-length novels as 'cannibalising'. *The Big Sleep* incorporates plots from *Killer in the Rain* and *The Curtain* as well as other details from *Finger Man* and *Mandarin's Jade*.

By comparing the sources with the finished novel it is possible to see Chandler's genius at work in expanded evocations of characters and settings. Where one short story for example has this detail – 'Ivory drapes of immense height lay tumbled casually on the white carpet' – General Sternwood's residence is described thus: 'the white carpet that went from wall to wall looked like a fresh fall of snow at Lake Arrowhead. ... The ivory furniture had chromium

on it, and the enormous ivory drapes lay tumbled on the white carpet a yard from the windows. The white made the ivory look dirty and the ivory made the white look bled out.' The suggestion of blood on the white carpet is left for the reader to imagine.

Philip Marlowe was an anti-hero for his times. Industrialised America had just emerged from decades of Prohibition and economic collapse, and was about to be drawn into another world war. Readers no longer cared about the monied classes depicted by Edith Wharton and F. Scott Fitzgerald. Marlowe's disrespect and earthy reality chimed perfectly with the public mood and inspired a host of similar gritty characters. It is no accident that two of film noir's greatest stars, Humphrey Bogart and Robert Mitchum, have been cast in film versions of *The Big Sleep*.

The success of *The Big Sleep* led to a further six novels featuring Marlowe. Although the earlier short stories are considered prototypes for Marlowe, none of them contained his name. Chandler's regular pulp detectives were called Mallory, Carmady and Dalmas; many of them became Marlowe stories for radio and TV series about the detective, but were never changed in print. *The Pencil*, the only short story to feature Marlowe, was written in the year of Chandler's death, 1959.

OPPOSITE: A First Edition cover of Chandler's most famous book.

LEFT: Chandler was educated at Dulwich College and worked as a reporter for the Daily Express before heading to the US.

The Grapes of Wrath

(1939)

John Steinbeck (1902–1968)

John Steinbeck's masterpiece is one of the most widely discussed books of the twentieth century. It is essential reading for its historical record of the Great Depression and the sympathetic portrayal of its Dust Bowl victims. It was the main reason for awarding Steinbeck the Nobel Prize for Literature in 1962.

*T*he *Grapes of Wrath* is an emotional journey. When their crops fail, Tom Joad and his family in Oklahoma pack up and head west to California where well-paid farm work is rumoured to be available. Merging with other desperate farmers on the route, the Joads lose members of the family to death and abandonment along the way. They arrive to discover that there is not enough work and that wages have been driven down below subsistence levels. Corporate farms and the police work together to suppress the migrants. Tom, who has already violated his parole by leaving Oklahoma, kills a man who murdered his friend Jim Casy, because Casy was trying to unionise the workers. Although still young, he has taken on the role of head of the family, but for the family's sake he must leave them to fend for themselves now that he is a wanted man.

There is hope at the end of the novel that the oppressed migrants will form a union, with Tom's help, and that the Joads, held together by Ma Joad's forceful character, will pull through this desperate time. An achingly touching final scene between Ma Joad, Tom's sister Rose of Sharon (whose child has just been delivered stillborn), and an old man on the verge of death by starvation finds the Joads at their lowest ebb yet still offering help and life to others.

The suffering endured by so many during the Great Depression was hard to exaggerate, although some accused Steinbeck of doing so. The book was banned in many states for its profanity, its left-wing views and its unflinchingly real depiction of humanity at its most desperate. Copies of the book were burned in public, and Steinbeck, who lived in California, was treated as an enemy by the landowners of the state. Nevertheless it was wildly popular and sold 430,000 copies in its first year of publication.

Steinbeck had worked among migrant workers on a sugar beet farm in California and wrote articles on their difficulties for the *San Francisco News* before he began work on *The Grapes of Wrath*. He also saw, unknown to her, field notes about migrants taken in 1938 by another author, Sanora Babb, for her intended novel *Whose Names Are Unknown*. The success of *The Grapes of Wrath* meant that Babb's novel was shelved. She accused Steinbeck of plagiarism, and when her novel finally got into print in 2004, there were some clear similarities of detail. Steinbeck, however, was a thorough researcher who drew on many sources, including his own experience of delivering aid to New Deal camps which housed many homeless migrants.

The title of the book quotes the 'Battle Hymn of the Republic', which includes the lines

> Mine eyes have seen the glory of the coming of the Lord;
> He is trampling out the vintage where the grapes of
> wrath are stored

The song in turn refers to a passage from the Book of Revelation. Steinbeck suggests, but does not show, in *The Grapes of Wrath*, that wrath of the down-trodden will eventually bear wine and deliverance.

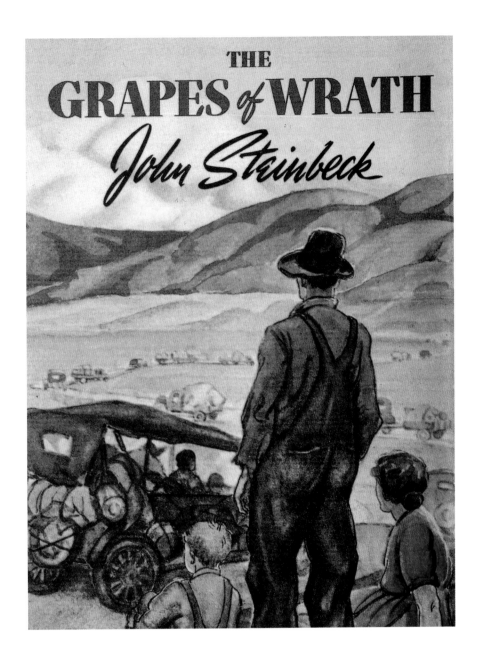

ABOVE: The cover of The Grapes of Wrath *showed migrant workers and their primitive vehicles heading west on roads such as Route 66. When they got to California their troubles were far from over.*

OPPOSITE: John Steinbeck in 1939. He picked up a Pulitzer Prize for his novel in 1940 and became a Nobel laureate in 1962 for work that included Of Mice and Men *and* East of Eden.

100 Novels That Changed the World_____117

Camus
L'étranger

folio

Texte intégral

ABOVE: *A 1970s cover. The book was originally published by Gallimard in France.*
OPPOSITE: *As a journalist, novelist and playwright, Albert Camus became the left-wing spokesman of his own generation and mentor to the next. His core theme was the isolation of man in an alien universe typified by* The Stranger.

The Stranger (USA) /
The Outsider (UK)

(1942)

Albert Camus (1913–1960)

L'Étranger, the original title for Camus' first published novel, has many meanings – Stranger, Estranged, Outsider, Foreigner. All of them imply a degree of alienation. Whether through detachment or rejection, Camus's anti-hero represents the absurdity of becoming involved in this world.

Albert Camus, a Frenchman born in Algeria when it was still a colony of France, was an outsider compared to the country's majority population of Berbers and Arabs. As a European he enjoyed privileges not allowed to the native Algerians, who were themselves considered foreigners by the ruling French. While in France, Algerian Europeans were looked down on. They were called Pieds-Noirs, Black Feet, as if merely by being born in Algeria they were contaminated by connection with the African population.

It was a racist slur, and Camus, who despite his European origins was raised in poverty, had considerable sympathy for the local people who were violently abused by their French masters. The pivotal moment in *The Stranger* finds the central character, Meursault, a Pied-Noir, shooting an Arab – at first in self-defence but then, even after that fatal shot, deliberately and calmly four more times.

The Arab – none of the Arab characters in the novel are given names, to emphasise the French attitude to them – is a foreigner to the Frenchman Meursault. Meursault is an outsider to the Arabs, but also to the mainland French. Furthermore he is estranged even from his own society, the Pieds-Noirs. Meursault has detached himself from care, and the novel opens with his curious lack of grief after the death of his mother. Later he tells his lover that he doesn't love her and doesn't care if they get married.

The only event which elicits any positive response from Meursault is the visit towards the end of the novel of the prison chaplain to his cell where he awaits execution for the Arab's murder. He snaps and angrily denounces the chaplain's patronising Christian world view. Confronted with the certainty of death which comes to everyone one way or another, Meursault knows, with more confidence than the chaplain ever can, that nothing matters. He consigns himself to 'the benign indifference of the universe'.

Camus divided his output into three phases, each thematically connected to a Greek myth and each consisting of a novel, a play and an essay. The first phase, to which *The Stranger* belongs, was guided by the story of Sisyphus, who tricked Death into releasing him and whom Hades therefore punished by making him endlessly roll a large boulder up a hill – an absurd, pointless and unsatisfying task, which would eventually make Sisyphus long for Death. The Sisyphus cycle also included Camus' play *Caligula* and his essay *Le Mythe de Sisyphe* (*The Myth of Sisyphus*).

Among the works of Camus published posthumously was a novel, *La Mort heureuse* (*A Happy Death*), which Camus wrote before *The Stranger* but then shelved. Its central character, Patrice, is a Pied-Noir. He murders the man who has advised him to pursue happiness, in order to use the dead man's wealth in that pursuit. Unable to find pleasure from conventional sources such as money, love or friends, he dies alone and therefore, at last, happy.

Brideshead Revisited

(1945)

Evelyn Waugh (1903–1966)

The country house has been a popular setting for novels since the English began building them. The convention is given a twentieth-century twist in what the author called his magnum opus. Waugh uses a nostalgic form to develop his theme of reconciliation, whether with the past, friends or oneself.

For Jane Austen, Daphne du Maurier and many others, the grand house represents family and fortune, social ascension and aristocratic decline. *Brideshead Revisited* projects all these meanings onto Brideshead, the fictional country estate to which Charles Ryder is posted during World War II. He knew the place twenty years earlier when he was drawn into its social circle by a fellow student, Sebastian Flyte. Brideshead is the Flyte family home, and the rest of the novel relives Ryder's memories of his relationships with the family.

It's complicated. Charles is in love with Sebastian's sister Julia, but chiefly because of her resemblance to Sebastian, with whom Charles is also in love. Sebastian has a difficult relationship with his mother, finding solace in Charles, in his childhood teddy-bear Aloysius, and in alcohol. The latter brings about his descent and retreat to a Tunisian monastery. Charles' and Julia's separate marriages fail but their own planned wedding collapses when Julia and Sebastian's unfaithful father returns to Brideshead from exile in Italy in order to die at the ancestral home. Charles, an atheist who was nevertheless moved by the father's reception of the Last Rites, closes the novel by praying in the chapel twenty years later.

Waugh himself became a Roman Catholic in 1930, and Catholic theology colours much of *Brideshead Revisited*. Sebastian's mother is from an ancient recusant Catholic family, one which refused to convert to Anglicanism after the English Reformation introduced by Henry VIII.

His father converted in order to marry his mother; and Charles, by speaking the catechism in the Brideshead chapel at the end of the novel, appears also to have converted. Cordelia, the most devout of the Flyte children, has a conversation with Charles in which she explains the principle of Catholic grace by quoting a story by G.K. Chesterton, who was also a convert to Catholicism – 'the unmerited and unilateral act of love,' as Waugh described it, 'by which God continually calls souls to Himself.'

Many of the characters undergo some sort of reconciliation. Sebastian's father returns to the Church on his deathbed after his infidelity. Julia withdraws from her intended marriage to Charles because it began in sin while she was still married to her husband. Even the alcoholic Sebastian ends up in the service of God by working as a porter in the monastery.

The novel courted controversy, like others of the period, in its veiled portrayal of homosexuality. The love between Charles and Sebastian was underplayed in the book, perhaps to satisfy laws against the promotion of same-sex relationships, and ignored by critics for the same reasons. Many still choose to interpret the relationship as chaste and platonic, in the tradition of Conan Doyle's Sherlock Holmes and Dr Watson. For most, however, there is no doubt, and when Julia asks Charles, as they embark on their affair, 'You loved him, didn't you?', Charles replies, 'Oh yes. He was the forerunner.'

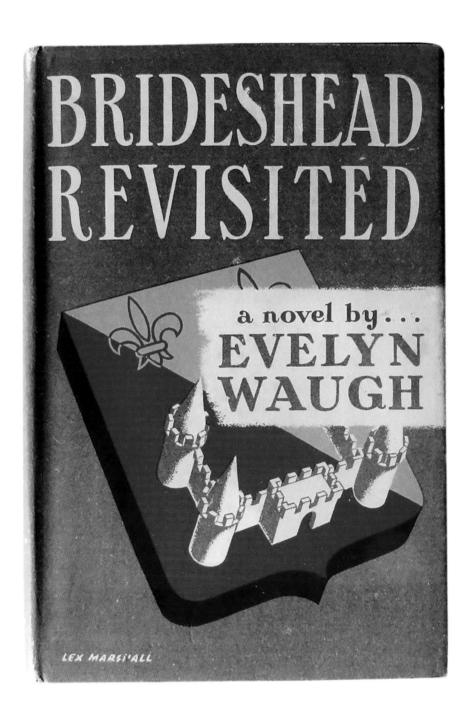

ABOVE: *An Australian First Edition, published in 1946 by Chapman and Hall. Madresfield Court, near Malvern, in Worcestershire, on which Brideshead was based, is far more country house than turreted bastion.*

OPPOSITE: *Evelyn Waugh photographed by Carl Van Vechten in 1940.*

1984

(1949)

George Orwell (1903–1950)

George Orwell's classic dystopian novel has proved prophetic in several ways. A world in which Big Brother is always watching, where a perpetual war is waged by the so-called Ministry of Peace, and over which the ruling party 'seeks power entirely for its own sake' – Orwell's future is many people's present.

*1*984 is the claustrophobic story of Winston Smith, hiding his rebellious thoughts and love affair from the autocratic rule of The Party, only to be uncovered by the Thought Police and, under torture, to betray his lover Julia. Orwell creates a nightmare world in which nothing is what it seems. Winston believes at first that Julia is a spy; that Mr Charrington, above whose shop they conduct their love affair, is a friend; and that O'Brien is a fellow rebel. None of these assumptions is true.

The Ministry of Love, for which both O'Brien and Mr Charrington work, is where dissidents are tortured and their unsanctioned passions converted into a love of Big Brother. The Ministry of Truth rewrites history. The Ministry of Plenty rations food and goods, which are scarce because of the constant war being fought between the three global superpowers of Oceania, Eurasia and Eastasia. The Party's sinisterly counter-intuitive slogans are 'War is Peace', 'Freedom is Slavery' and 'Ignorance is Strength'.

Orwell was a socialist, and had written, before *1984*, of the possibility of a socialist revolution in Britain. The novel imagines, as he once explained, 'what communism would be like if it were firmly rooted in the English speaking countries, and was no longer a mere extension of the Russian Foreign Office' – in other words, how life in Britain would be under a British Stalinist government. The cult of personality surrounding Big Brother in

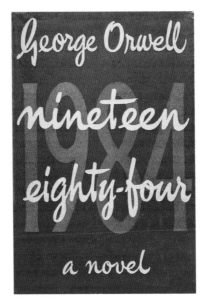

the book is based on Stalin's. Big Brother and his old enemy Goldstein have similar appearances to Stalin and Trotsky; and where Stalinist propaganda films showed Trotsky transformed into a goat, Orwell describes similar films in which Goldstein becomes a sheep.

It is interesting that Orwell wrote *1984* on the remote Scottish island of Jura, a place as far removed from the oppressive, crowded London of the novel as one could imagine. Jura, with an area of 142 square miles (367 square kilometres), has only one road, one village of any size, one whisky distillery and a population of less than two hundred. Perhaps Orwell needed the open, empty moorland and mountains as an antidote to the world he was creating.

The world of *1984* has made many contributions to the English language: Big Brother, in reference to intrusive abuses of power; Room 101, where the Ministry of Love exposes dissidents to their greatest fears; the Thought Police, applied to those who believe private thoughts can be as undesirable as public crimes. The very language of power which Orwell invented, Newspeak, has led to the adoption and creation of new words – doublethink (believing one idea while knowing another contradictory one to be the truth), unperson (someone erased from history), mediaspeak (jargon) and so on. It has even given rise to the adjective Orwellian, for a dystopian society such as the one he devised in *1984*.

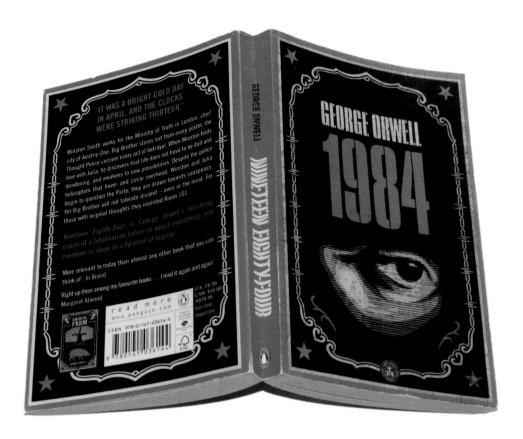

OPPOSITE AND ABOVE: *The original cover gave little hint of the oppression and terror within, while modern covers emphasise the unblinking gaze of a surveillance society.*
LEFT: *Eric Arthur Blair changed his name to George Orwell to save embarrassing his parents with his first book,* Down and Out in Paris and London, *which described his time as a tramp in London and a dishwasher in the French capital. Having spent time in Burma, during World War II he compiled programmes and broadcast on the Eastern Service of the BBC.*

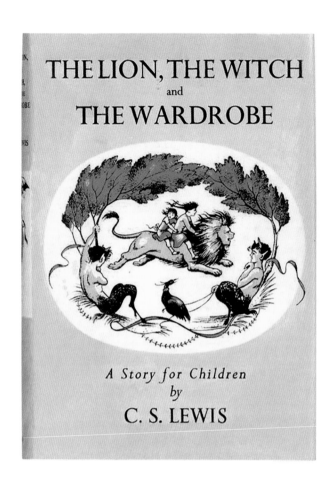

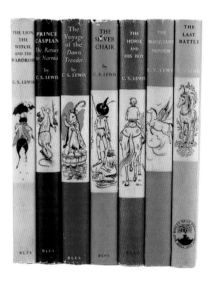

The Chronicles of Narnia

(1950–1956)

C.S. Lewis (1898–1963)

Starting with *The Magician's Nephew*, the Narnia series of seven novels charts the life from birth to death of a mythical land where good and evil fight for supremacy. A much-loved example of twentieth-century fantasy and a popular set of children's books, *The Chronicles of Narnia* are also an allegory of Christianity.

Clive Staples Lewis had already written four of the seven books before the first of them, *The Lion, the Witch and the Wardrobe*, was published in 1950. *The Magician's Nephew*, which describes the beginnings of Narnia, was actually last to be written and the sixth to appear; but it is now customary to read and number the volumes in the order of their Narnian chronology, not their publication date.

Narnia is a magical land populated by fantastical men and beasts, in which the eternal battle between good and evil is played out over 2,555 Narnian years – but only nine years in the lives of the young Pevensie children and their friends who discover Narnia through a mysterious portal at the back of a wardrobe. Aslan, a lion and a king, is the Christlike figure whose spirit runs through the series and who acts as a key to the allegory.

Lewis was a lapsed Christian as a teenager, but an interest in Celtic and Scandinavian folklore, which he shared with his fellow Oxford University academic J.R.R. Tolkien, helped renew his faith. He wrote several theological works including the delightfully witty *The Screwtape Letters* (1942), an imagined correspondence between a senior demon, Screwtape, and his nephew Wormwood, who is having trouble tempting his human target, 'the Patient'.

The Narnian landscape was inspired by the Mourne Mountains of Northern Ireland where Lewis grew up. The entry to it through a wardrobe was, Lewis acknowledged, a device which the children's author E. Nesbit had earlier used in a short story. Lewis found the name Narnia on a map of the ancient Roman and Greek world; it is a hilltown in Umbria, Italy, today called Narni. The Pevensie children began to take shape in Lewis's mind after three children, evacuated from London during the bombing of World War II, came to stay at his Oxfordshire home.

The 1950s was a Golden Decade for British fantasy fiction. Both *The Chronicles of Narnia* and Tolkien's *Lord of the Rings* were published during it, and both have become classics of the genre. Today the *Narnia* books still use the illustrations of the original editions, which were drawn by Pauline Baynes. Baynes was recommended to Lewis by Tolkien, for whom she had already illustrated the novella *Farmer Giles of Ham* (1949). For Lewis she returned to Narnia on several occasions, producing new images for the series until 1991.

The final book in the saga, *The Last Battle* (1956), won Lewis the prestigious Carnegie Medal for children's literature. *The Chronicles of Narnia* have, since their inception, been the focus of extensive academic research and comment for their allegorical allusions; but their primary audience, and their greatest admirers, are the children taking their first steps not only in Narnia but in the world of literature.

OPPOSITE: C.S. Lewis had been carrying some of the visions of Narnia, such as a faun carrying parcels in a snowy wood, since his teenage years. He wrote the books quickly, with one published every year between 1950 and 1956.

The Catcher in the Rye

(1951)

J.D. Salinger (1919–2010)

The classic American coming-of-age novel is beloved of teenagers but was written for an older readership. Frequently banned for its adult language, which includes profanity, sexually explicit descriptions and coarse 1940s colloquialisms, the controversy has only boosted its popularity.

The Catcher in the Rye revolves around the teenage angst of its central character, Holden Caulfield, who feels alienated by almost everything in his life except his younger sister Phoebe. The novel is narrated through his first-person thoughts about these disappointments, including his unsuccessful dates with girls and his perceived inferiority in the presence of other boys. He is, like all teenagers, self-obsessed; but the title refers to his one selfless ambition, the result of mishearing the lyrics of the Robert Burns poem 'Comin' Thro' the Rye'. He pictures his ideal occupation, rescuing children who are running through a field of rye before they fall over the cliff at the end of it.

The book is about innocence and the loss of it through the progress from childhood to adulthood, which in Holden's mind feels like falling off a cliff. When Holden finally makes a move towards growing up, it is not by accident, but by enjoying Phoebe's pleasure during a ride on a carousel for which he has paid. Although he wanted to be the Catcher in the Rye, in the end it is Phoebe who rescues him by showing him joy and talking him out of running away from home, which really would be like falling off a cliff.

Holden Caulfield had been in Salinger's mind long before *The Catcher in the Rye* was published. He first featured in a story called *Slight Rebellion off Madison*, which the *New Yorker* magazine accepted in 1941 but then cancelled in the wake of the attack on Pearl Harbor. Salinger wrote in 1946 to his friend Ernest Hemingway that

he was writing a stage play about Caulfield. Salinger's wartime experiences in Europe were harrowing: he spent some weeks in hospital with combat stress, and once admitted to his daughter that 'you never really get the smell of burning flesh out of your nose entirely'. He had landed on Utah Beach on D-Day and saw action in the Battle of the Bulge. Undoubtedly the horrors of war contributed to his interest in the loss of innocence behind *The Catcher in the Rye*.

The many bans placed on the book by adults offended by its language only served to promote the novel, which still sells about a million copies a year. It brought Salinger unwanted attention and he became increasingly reclusive. His last publication was a novella printed in the *New Yorker* magazine in 1965, forty-five years before his death. His wife left him the following year, claiming that his enforced isolation had made her a virtual prisoner.

Ironically, Salinger himself has banned several books, films and plays which were either unwelcome biographies about him or unauthorised adaptations and sequels of his work. One biographer was blocked from using any letters written by Salinger; and a fan fiction sequel to *The Catcher in the Rye*, titled *60 Years Later: Coming Through the Rye*, may only be published once the original novel has entered the public domain in North America.

LEFT: A long-lived recluse, Salinger was hounded in later years by fans following him with a camera.
OPPOSITE: The early cover of the book, adorned by a carousel horse.

the CATCHER in the RYE

a novel by J. D. SALINGER

The Lord of the Rings

(1954–1955)

J.R.R. Tolkien (1892–1973)

John Ronald Reuel Tolkien first drew sketches of his imaginary land, Middle-earth, in 1914. He developed it over decades with disciplined, painstaking imagination until it became a congruent, plausible world. It became the setting for the foundation stone of the high fantasy fiction genre.

Tolkien fought during World War I in the battle-scarred landscape of the Somme in northern France. The bloody experience may have directed his subsequent career as an academic historian: it is far safer to study the past than to live in the present. Between the world wars he became Professor of Anglo-Saxon at Oxford University, where he specialised in the sagas and origin myths of northern Europe. He was one of the first academics to take these epic tales of good and evil seriously as historic records, albeit much embellished with dragons and gods. He later wrote that 'Beowulf [the Old English narrative poem] is among my most valued sources'.

Such ancient literature is characterised by deeds of heroism at climactic battles, and its resonance with his wartime experiences inspired his own writing. Both *The Lord of the Rings* and its predecessor *The Hobbit* (1937), which unveiled Middle-earth for the first time, rely on scenes of pitched battle and the eternal struggle between darkness and light for their drama. Tolkien's descriptions of conflict in *The Lord of the Rings* are frighteningly real.

Tolkien was one of several authors who contributed to the revival of fantasy literature. He owed much to the ground-breaking books of George MacDonald in the nineteenth century. With C.S. Lewis publishing *The Chronicles of Narnia* in the same decade as *The Lord of the Rings*, the public was offered not one fantastical world but two. Tolkien and Lewis were both members of an informal group of Oxford writers known as the Inklings, which also included the historical children's author Roger Lancelyn Green. They happily shared ideas, and Tolkien's devout Christianity helped to revive Lewis's faith, which in turn gave rise to the Narnia books.

The Lord of the Rings was originally intended to be one of two novels set in that world. Its events take place in a Third Age of Middle-earth, and *The Silmarillion*, for which Tolkien made extensive notes, dealt with earlier history. Because of the costs involved in producing such a large book *The Lord of the Rings* was published in three volumes over the space of a year rather than one, as Tolkien had intended. After Tolkien's death his son, Christopher, took on the enormous task of editing his father's Silmarillion material, and *The Silmarillion* finally appeared in 1977.

A strong sense of morality runs through *The Lord of the Rings*. Its combination with large-scale adventures and the cohesive setting of Middle-earth are responsible for making fantasy, previously regarded as unsophisticated and childish, acceptable to an adult audience. *The Lord of the Rings* contains half a dozen appendices elaborating on aspects of Middle-earth life, including its history, some genealogy and notes on the languages of Middle-earth peoples and their 'translation' into English. They act not only as references for the complex story but expand on it with background information. Tolkien's overview of the world which he created was comprehensive, and set the standard for modern fantasy. Without it, Terry Pratchett's voluminous Discworld canon would not exist.

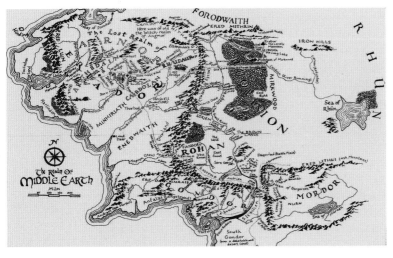

ABOVE: *The cornerstone of modern fantasy was painstakingly assembled.*
LEFT: *Tolkien's map of Middle-earth. In 2023 HarperCollins announced a new edition of* The Hobbit, *illustrated for the first time since original publication in 1937 with a greatly enhanced gallery of 50 Tolkien paintings, maps and drawings.*
OPPOSITE: *The small room at the back of the Eagle and Child pub where the Inklings would meet.*

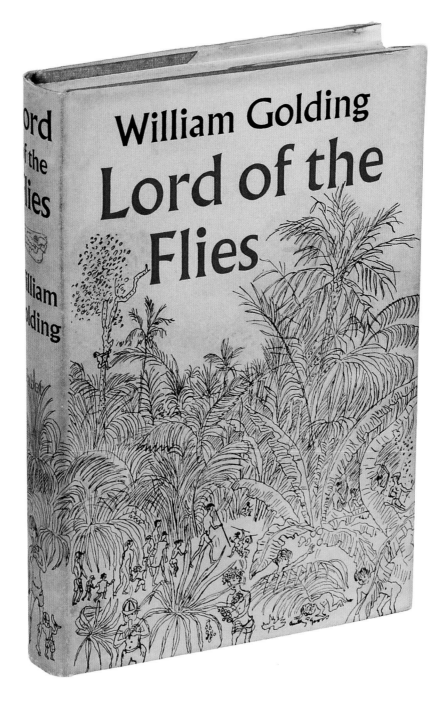

ABOVE: *The cartoon nature of this early cover of* Lord of the Flies *belied the savagery that would unfold.*

OPPOSITE: *With a modern readership more accustomed to visual shocks, publishers could market a more explicit cover.*

Lord of the Flies

(1954)

William Golding (1911–1993)

A bleak view of humanity underscores *Lord of the Flies*, William Golding's first and best novel, in which human nature is laid bare. Now a staple of many higher English literature classes, it has been suggested that it should also be read in courses on psychology, philosophy, biology and economics.

The plot describes the descent into feral anarchy of a group of supposedly well-educated schoolboys who are marooned on a deserted island. They begin well by organising themselves into hunting parties and maintaining a permanent smoke signal in the hope of rescue. But when collectively they convince themselves of the existence of a predatory beast on the island, self-preservation and tribalism lead them all down a very primitive path which ends in torture and murder among them.

The novel went through considerable changes from its first draft to its final publication. A reader at the publishers, Faber & Faber, advised rejection of the manuscript, which she described as 'an absurd and uninteresting fantasy'. Literary editor Charles Monteith, however, saw potential in it and worked with Golding to make major changes to the text. He recommended completely removing the opening section of the novel, which explained that the boys were being evacuated during a nuclear war. He erased a shadowy, God-like figure who advises Simon, one of the boys who retains some perspective on their situation, and reworked Simon's character so that he was less stand-offish from the rest of the group.

Simon is the closest thing to a hero in the book, resisting the groupthink which conjures up the beast. He gives the book its title when he describes an insect-festooned pig's head on a pole, which the others have erected as an offering to the beast, as Lord of the Flies. And when he tries to convince the boys that there is no beast, they decide that he is the beast and beat him

to death, the first but not the last murder committed by the group in defence of their superstitious beliefs.

Golding willingly made all the changes required, trusting Monteith's instincts and admitting that he was too close to the novel to see it clearly any more. After its publication, sales were slow at first; but perceptive reviewers understood it as an allegory of the human condition in which the desire for order and civilisation is constantly under tension with the urge to take and retain power. Throughout *Lord of the Flies* Golding illustrates the conflict between morality and immorality, between individuality and unquestioning collective acceptance. E.M. Forster declared it his Book of the Year.

The inspiration for *Lord of the Flies* was *The Coral Island*, a popular nineteenth-century boys' adventure by R.M. Ballantyne, in which boys cast away in a similar situation behaved with impeccable British stiff upper lips, demonstrating the values of leadership and Christianity. Golding found it preposterously unrealistic and determined to write something better. Some critics found Golding's more cynical view of humanity too one-sided, and a real-life incident eleven years after the novel's publication seemed to back up that assessment. When six boys were rescued in 1966 after fifteen months marooned on an uninhabited Pacific island, they had worked together to create a food garden, poultry run, water storage, a gymnasium and even a badminton court. The ship's captain who found them reported them all to be healthy and happy.

The Quiet American

(1955)

Graham Greene (1904–1991)

Drawing on his own experiences as a war correspondent in Indo-China, Graham Greene's prescient novel about the build-up to the Vietnam War was attacked in the US for being un-American. Since his predictions about the outcome came to pass, however, it has received renewed attention and praise.

The novel tells the story of a love triangle between a Vietnamese woman, Phuong, and her two admirers – an experienced English war reporter, Thomas Fowler, and a naïve CIA agent, Alden Pyle – the quiet American of the title. The two men vie for Phuong's attention as greater, imperial powers fight for domination of Vietnam itself. Both men's presence in the region disrupts the lives of its citizens, although Pyle proves to be considerably more of a threat when he orchestrates a terrorist attack in a crowded marketplace which kills many innocent Vietnamese. Fowler, shocked, assists an assassination which clears the way for him to be with Phuong and to remain in the country for which he has demonstrated a passion not shared by Pyle.

The novel is narrated by Fowler. It is set at a time when France, then the colonial power in the region, was losing its grip on Vietnam. America, which saw the country as a bulwark against encroaching communism, was beginning to play a part there. Greene, who reported on the conflict for British and French newspapers, uses the situation to criticise America's sense of exceptionalism. Pyle is convinced, based not on personal knowledge of Vietnam but on the foreign policy theories of fictional US author York Harding, that American intervention will succeed. Fowler, who like Greene, has reported from Saigon for two years, has an empathy and understanding of the region; Pyle blunders about clumsily. In one telling scene Fowler notes that Pyle, in his efforts to seduce Phuong, is a terrible dancer. On its

publication, Americans were offended not only by the criticism of American foreign policy but by the typical British sense of cultural superiority presented by Fowler.

If Hollywood is a useful measure of America's mood, the two film versions of *The Quiet American* are interesting indicators of change. The first, produced in 1958 at the height of the Cold War, reworked the plot so that instead of questioning US intervention in the region it became an anti-communist piece. In retrospect it's surprising that it was made at all. The second, from 2002, long after the end of the Vietnam War, when America was facing increasing opposition to its presence in the Middle East, was a faithful rendition of the novel's ideas.

Graham Greene, best known as a contemporary novelist, also wrote a series of books for children illustrated originally by the respected artist Dorothy Craigie and, in new editions in the 1970s, by the great Edward Ardizzone. He also wrote the screenplays for many of his novels which transferred to the cinema screen. Among those novels are *Brighton Rock* (1938), *The Third Man* (1950) and *Our Man in Havana* (1958). Many of his works centre, like *The Quiet American*, on characters caught up in situations overseas. *The Power and the Glory* (1940) is set in Mexico; *the Heart of the Matter* (1948) in Sierra Leone; *A Burnt-Out Case* (1960) in a Congo leper colony; *The Comedians* (1966) in Papa Doc's Haiti. They draw on Greene's own experiences, and on his unerring insights into human dilemmas.

ABOVE: Graham Greene, like John Le Carré, was recruited into MI6 and was posted to Sierra Leone during World War II. The infamous spy Kim Philby was his supervisor.

LEFT: The Quiet American was Greene's 16th novel and one that incensed his American readership.

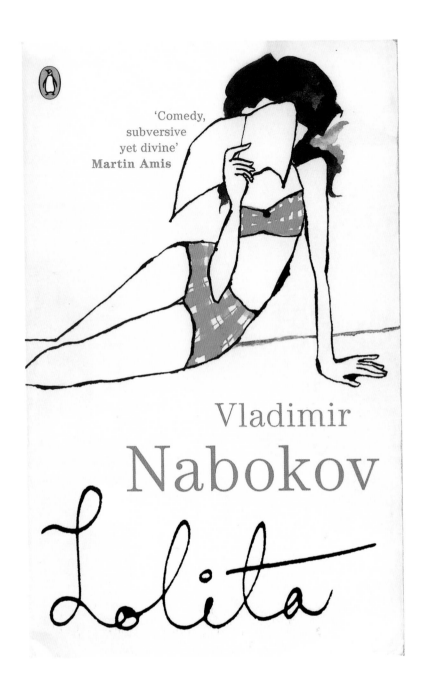

'Comedy,
subversive
yet divine'
Martin Amis

Vladimir

Nabokov

Lolita

*ABOVE: Though the 'cut-up' writing process was attributed to William S. Burroughs,
Vladimir Nabokov would write sections of text on index cards, add to them and then
rearrange them to form chapters. When he lectured at Cornell University he had little
interest in his students, who were known by their seat number.*

Lolita

(1955)

Vladimir Nabokov (1899–1977)

Lolita has courted controversy since the day it was published. Although social attitudes to child sexual abuse have changed since its publication, it still divides those who see it as erotic literature from those who consider it pornographic fantasy.

The name Lolita has entered the English language as shorthand for a seductive young girl. As Humbert Humbert, the unreliable narrator of *Lolita*, tells it, it was Lolita who seduced him, although she had been the object of his sexual fantasy for some time and he had intended to drug and rape her the night before. Humbert is twelve-year-old Lolita's stepfather, and they conduct their sexual relationship on the road from New England to Colorado until one night Lolita is kidnapped by a playwright who wants to put her in one of his pornographic films.

Five years later, seventeen-year-old Lolita is pregnant and married to a man who knows nothing of her past. Humbert tracks her down but has to accept that she has moved on. He murders the pornographer, is arrested, and writes his memoir, *Lolita*, from his prison cell.

Humbert is not Nabokov, and the literary merit of the book resides in Nabokov's ability to inhabit Humbert's self-justifying mind. This is Humbert's version of events, and the reader is left with almost no sense of Lolita's perspective. Humbert effectively silences her by telling only his side of the story; he doesn't even allow her her real name, which is Dolores. Even Humbert has to admit in the course of his memoirs that what he has done is statutory rape and that, however willing Dolores was (having lost her virginity not to Humbert but to a boy at summer camp a year earlier), consent is not applicable to minors. Humbert is every man who ever objectified a woman and denied her an existence as a human being, especially as a juvenile human being; and Nabokov has described him as 'a vain and cruel wretch'.

Although sex is a dominant theme of the novel, descriptions of sex only occur in its early pages. The bulk of the book is a study of personality, all the more ingenious because narrator Humbert deceives himself and only accidentally reveals his character. Are we to believe him when at the end he calls her Dolly for the first time, and decides that he has loved her all along? Even his belief that Dolly will outlive him proves to be a lie.

The book abounds in wordplay and in ironic observations of American life. The woman who aids the pornographer's kidnap of Dolores, for example, is Vivian Darkbloom – an anagram of Vladimir Nabokov. Nabokov, a native of Imperial Russia, fled with his parents after the October Revolution of 1917, first to Crimea, then to study at Cambridge University, and then to Berlin, where he wrote his first nine novels in Russian. Via Paris he emigrated to the United States in 1940, and *Lolita* with all its puns and double entendres was written in English. For Humbert's description of Dolores, Nabokov invented the word 'nymphet', which now has a life of its own, meaning a provocative young woman, and can be found in many English dictionaries.

LEFT: *The paperback First Edition cover from 1958 looked more like a movie poster than a classic novel.*

OPPOSITE: *The back cover of the Signet paperback was strong on sensation: 'buying cars, wrecking cars, stealing cars, dumping cars, picking up girls, making love, all-night drinking bouts, jazz joints, wild parties, hot spots ...'*

On the Road

(1957)

Jack Kerouac (1922–1969)

Jack Kerouac gave the Beat Generation its name, and his novel *On the Road* is its defining literary manifestation. It spoke for those who rejected the conventional values of family, stability and prosperity attached to America's post-war economic boom.

Middle-class America celebrated its victory in World War II and capitalised on the development of industry prompted by the war with a thriving peacetime economy. What felt like stability to most Americans seemed like stagnation to some. The Beat Generation rebelled against the rampant consumerism of the age, which they believed dulled the inquisitive mind until it was beat. Writers such as Allen Ginsberg, Neal Cassady and Jack Kerouac wanted more from life.

Kerouac took the label and turned it on its head. If one had been beaten down, he argued, all that remained was the core of one's being, a state of transcendental beauty from which the only way forward was up – up-beat. For him and the rest of the Beat Generation, this was not just the perpetual reaction of one generation against the previous one but a psychological, spiritual movement.

On the Road is Kerouac's memoir of several road trips which he undertook in the late 1940s with Neal Cassady. Looking back in 1961 he wrote, 'It was really a story about two Catholic buddies roaming the country in search of God. And we found him.' The book is a snapshot of American attitudes to class, race, conservatism and change. Each trip was slightly less carefree than the last and *On the Road* is a study of the ties and limits of friendship, of dreams and plans and their pragmatic outcomes, as the pair travelled through the post-war United States.

Kerouac made many attempts to write about the journeys but found

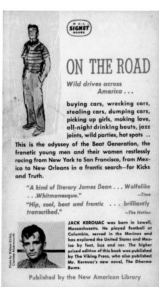

them all unsatisfactory until one day in 1950 he received a long, rambling, disjointed letter from Cassady. Its 10,000 words were like an improvised jazz solo: spontaneous, unpremeditated and direct from the heart. Kerouac was inspired by it to develop a theory of Spontaneous Prose, uninterrupted by new paragraphs or page breaks, and began once again to write about their travels together. In order not to break his stream of consciousness as he typed, he glued several pages together; and the finished manuscript of *On the Road* is a scroll 120 feet long.

He made a few changes before publication, adding some more literary passages. Some sexually explicit scenes were deleted, and he fictionalised the names of some of the participants – Neal Cassady turned into Dean Moriarty and Allen Ginsberg became Carlo Marx. William S. Burroughs was renamed Old Bull Lee, and Kerouac, the central character, changed his name to Sal Paradise.

The original scroll still exists. It was sold in 2001 for nearly $2.5 million, and is exhibited from time to time. To celebrate the fiftieth anniversary of its publication, *On the Road: The Original Scroll* was published, restoring deleted episodes and allowing its protagonists their real names. *On the Road* was a radical new form of literature, more like an impressionist painting than a novel. It inspired the hippie movement of the 1960s and still fuels that longing to be carefree. In an age where war once again threatens stability and where financial insecurity makes many question the value of materialism, *On the Road* has a renewed relevance.

Things Fall Apart

(1958)

Chinua Achebe (1930–2013)

Controversially written in English, *Things Fall Apart* paved the way for worldwide recognition of many African authors. It offered global audiences a new perspective on colonialism, and its success gave writers all over Africa the confidence to tell their own stories.

*T*hings *Fall Apart*, set in a Nigerian village in the 1890s, tells the story of Okonkwo, a champion wrestler and elder of his community, trapped by traditional machismo. In trying to excise the ghost of his weak father who died in debt and was afraid of blood, Okonkwo amasses his own wealth, but beats his wife and, tragically, follows tribal protocol by killing his adoptive son. When that act brings bad luck on the village he goes into exile; and in his absence, European missionaries come to the village. Their Christianity, white rule and English language undermine the cultural heritage of its people. When tensions arise, Okonkwo makes a typically bloody gesture of defiance, but not everyone is willing to reject the new ways.

One of the remarkable things about *Things Fall Apart* is the even-handedness of Chinua Achebe's narration. He presents a native tradition of government, religion, judiciary, economy and creativity which denies the dominant European discourse of a continent inhabited by godless savages, civilised by the white man. But he simply lets events unfold, without commentary, before the reader's eyes. Only the casual remark by a British district commissioner, as he symbolically oversees a native burial, that recent events will fill a chapter of the book he is writing, *The Pacification of the Primitive Tribes of the Lower Niger*, contains more than a hint of irony.

The setting and period of the novel reflect the experience of Achebe's own family. The culture of the fictional village is very close to that of the Onitsha and Igbo people among whom Achebe grew up. Achebe was born in 1930, when missionary influence on his village was already well established. Achebe's father Isaiah was among the first of his village to convert to Christianity; Achebe himself refused to adopt a European name, Albert, in place of his given Igbo name Chinua.

Achebe's decision to use the English language was part of the legacy of the missionaries, but not entirely in the way one might expect. He considered English to lend itself well to the novel as a literary form; and he argued that his native Igbo language had been corrupted by the influence of missionaries who, in seeking to create a standard Igbo from all the many local dialects and variations, had reduced it to a stilted, formal language, useful for communication, but not for poetry. 'There's nothing you can do with it to make it sing,' he once said. 'It's heavy. It's wooden. It doesn't go anywhere.'

The choice of English was therefore as much a commentary on the impact of the missionaries as the novel's plot is. *Things Fall Apart* depicts the moment when European and African cultures collided. Achebe shows the weaknesses of native tradition as well as their value. It is widely read in African schools and universities, and further afield it is admired by students of English literature and of African studies. At a time after World War II when colonial affiliations were being revisited in the light of the Cold War, it was the first novel to show Africa with an African voice, not an Imperial European one.

OPPOSITE: *Chinua Achebe photographed in the 1970s. He was often referred to as the 'Father of African Literature'.*

ABOVE: *Things Fall Apart was Achebe's debut novel. He supported Biafran independence when the region tried to break away from Nigeria.*

William
BURROUGHS

NAKED LUNCH

With an introduction by
J. G. Ballard

flamingo
MODERN CLASSIC

Naked Lunch

(1959)

William S. Burroughs (1914–1997)

A baffling, anarchic, utterly unique novel reflects its author's detachment from reality while under the influence of morphine, heroin and hashish among other mind-altering drugs. The book consists of a series of zany literary sketches, which Burroughs suggested could be read in any order.

Burroughs explained in his introduction that 'the title means exactly what the words say: naked lunch, a frozen moment when everyone sees what is on the end of every fork.' The naked clarity to which he refers is the sort of insight claimed by drug users like him during moments of heightened awareness. The results are impressionistic, unrealistic and often shocking; excesses of violence, sex and obscene language caused the book to be banned on the east and west coasts of America, and several of its European publishers to become the target of protests. Because of US obscenity laws the book was originally published in more liberal Paris – where it was partly written – and did not appear in an American edition until 1962.

The vignettes of which the book is composed are mostly surreal episodes in a disjointed set of locations, only very loosely connected by a few recurrent characters, including Burroughs' alter ego William Lee. There is no plot. The nearest thing to a storyline is the opening 'routine' (as Burroughs called the vignettes) in which Lee, in search of his next fix of drugs, is fleeing two police officers; a later routine finds the police catching up with Lee, who shoots them dead, then discovers that there is no record of them with the Narcotics Squad.

Some of the action takes place in Mexico, where Burroughs wrote part of the work; and Burroughs also invents places called Freeland, Annexia and Interzone. There are wild orgies, beheadings, child murder and paedophilia, and of course many references to drug-taking. Parts of the novel are written using the cut-up technique, in which bodies of original text are cut up and the parts reassembled at random. Singer David Bowie claimed to use a similar technique to write his lyrics in the late 1970s.

Naked Lunch (originally published in error as *The Naked Lunch*) is regarded as a pillar of Beat Generation literature, its chaotic structure a perfect example of the movement's need to distance itself from convention of any kind. It is the very model of the deconstructed novel.

Where Kerouac tempered the sexual content of his *On the Road*, Burroughs gave full details in his book. The Beat Generation paved the way for the sexual freedom of the hippie movement of the 1960s as well as the violent non-conformity of the era's motorcycle gangs. One may admire the spirit of liberation which the Beat authors promoted while at the same time being relieved that we have pulled back from some of the most liberal aspects of that culture.

OPPOSITE: *A modern cover from Flamingo.*

ABOVE: *William S. Burroughs said all forms of drug addiction were counterproductive, but it gave him insight into a junky's world.*

To Kill a Mockingbird

(1960)

Harper Lee (1926–2016)

If you only write one novel in your life, make it a good one. Harper Lee's study of smalltown America through the eyes of a child holds a mirror to its readers and asks questions about morality, hypocrisy and racism which still need to be raised today.

Harper Lee was not reclusive, but shunned the attention which *To Kill a Mockingbird* brought her. It was an immediate bestseller and is a regular on the reading lists of schools throughout the US. Its very success has led to a lack of critical study at an academic level, where 'popular' and 'good' are sometimes seen as mutually exclusive. The same success has deprived the literary world of more works by Lee, who said, 'I wouldn't go through the pressure and publicity I went through with *To Kill a Mockingbird* for any amount of money.'

Perhaps too, the experiences in the novel of tomboyish six-year-old Jean Louise Finch, nicknamed Scout, had revealed too much for comfort of Lee's own childhood. Lee wrote that an author 'should write about what he knows and write truthfully'. Scout lives in a fictional Alabama town, Maycomb, not unlike Lee's hometown Monroeville in that state. Scout's brother Jem is modelled on Harper's brother Edwin; and their friend Dill is based on Harper's childhood friend Truman Capote. Like Boo Radley's house in Maycomb, there was a house in Monroeville whose inhabitants were never seen or heard.

Harper Lee and Scout were both tomboys and both had morally upright fathers who, as lawyers, unsuccessfully defended Black men accused of horrific crimes. The Black man accused of the rape of a white woman and shot by a Maycomb lynch mob has many real-life precedents; and Lee's father defended two men accused of murder who were hanged and mutilated after their conviction on dubious evidence. Disgusted by the

justice system, he never took on another criminal case.

The shocking events surrounding the rape trial of falsely accused Tom Robinson are at the centre of *To Kill a Mockingbird*. The repercussions occupy the second half of the book. Scout's father, and even Scout and Jem, are attacked and branded by a community which sides with the Klan and prides itself on its Southern brand of Christianity but convicts a man it knows to be innocent, and murders him for embarrassing a white perjurer.

The charm of the novel is in its narration, by young Scout. Readers watch the story unfold through her innocent eyes and make their own judgement about its protagonists' behaviour. Scout merely observes, and does so with a finely balanced narrative which captures both her youthful, sometimes sarcastic, sometimes witty observations about the goings-on in Maycomb and her sense of moral surprise at what she sees. Some critics have found her language too mature for her age, but it is an author's prerogative to give their characters a voice.

The portrayal of moral standards in the novel offended some Americans at a time when the movement for racial equality was gathering pace. As Harper Lee reminded her editor, 'Surely it is plain to the simplest intelligence that *To Kill a Mockingbird* spells out in words of seldom more than two syllables a code of honor and conduct, Christian in its ethic, that is the heritage of all Southerners.' Asked why she had never written another book, she replied, 'I have said what I wanted to say, and I will not say it again.'

ABOVE: The US First Edition published by J.B. Lippincott Company.
OPPOSITE: Mary Badham, who played Scout in the 1962 film, posing on set with author Harper Lee.

ABOVE: *The US First Edition from Simon & Schuster.*
OPPOSITE: *In World War II, Joseph Heller flew missions on the Italian front as a bomb aimer in B-25 bombers.*

Catch-22

(1961)

Joseph Heller (1923–1999)

The archetypical satire of war was so popular at one point that it was said every student went to university carrying a copy. Written about one war but inspired by another, it chimed with objectors to a third. Its title has become a byword for a problem whose very nature precludes its solution.

Catch-22 is a fictitious clause in military regulations which justifies the denial of a soldier's request on the grounds that he has made the request. In the case of Heller's novel, Captain John Yossarian's tent-mate, Orr, has been driven crazy by repeated bombing missions. He should be grounded, and he would be mad to continue flying. By requesting to stop flying, he is however demonstrating a degree of sanity. By being sane he proves that he is safe to fly. As Heller explains in *Catch-22*, 'If he flew [the missions] he was crazy and didn't have to, but if he didn't want to he was sane and had to.'

Catch-22 oscillates between farce and tragedy, the one often leading to the other. It revolves around a US bomber squadron in World War II and the desire of airmen to escape the horrors of war. Although the narrative is centred on Captain Yossarian, events are told through several characters, sometimes repeatedly so that the reader gets a fuller picture of them. Yossarian's escape plans are constantly thwarted by his superiors, who raise the number of missions a pilot must fly before being sent home, whenever Yossarian reaches the existing total.

The novel grows darker as it proceeds. What starts almost as slapstick comedy ends with unflinching accounts of the madness and horror of war. The novel is set in 1944, with occasional flashbacks to show the origins of some situations. Heller himself flew some sixty missions in bombers during World War II, and *Catch-22* draws on his own experiences and comrades. He believed that his was a just war, and intended *Catch-22* to be

a veiled attack not on that but on what followed it: the Cold War, the Korean War and McCarthyism.

The Korean War ended soon after Heller began writing *Catch-22*, to be replaced by the unwinnable war in Vietnam. By the time the novel was published, that war had already been fought for six years, and opposition to it was growing. In Britain the novel was an immediate success, but in the US sales were slow at first. It was published in paperback in 1962, and as the prospect of conscription by draft loomed in 1963, sales took off. It has now sold more than ten million copies in the US alone.

One curious feature of *Catch-22* is the complete absence of an enemy. No hostile Germans or Italians appear in the text. The pain and death visited on Yossarian and his friends are inflicted by his own superiors and colleagues. The only German character is a pilot working for Milo Minderbinder, the American squadron's mess officer, whose entrepreneurial aptitude extends to bombing his own airbase because it is profitable. War is profitable for industry, and justifies the existence of military forces, creating a potentially dangerous industrial-military relationship, which Heller satirises through Minderbinder. As Yossarian reminds Minderbinder, President Coolidge once said, 'The business of government is business.' War is not about enmity but about profit and the resources that lead to profit.

If there is any doubt about the success of *Catch-22* in conveying its message, the United States Air Force Academy now uses the novel to 'help prospective officers recognize the dehumanizing aspects of bureaucracy.'

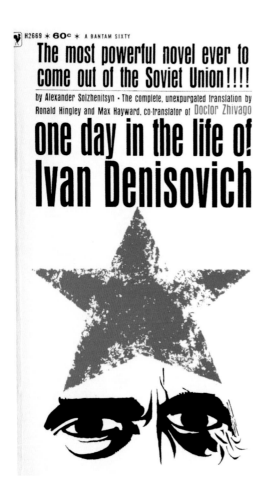

H2669 ★ **60¢** ★ A BANTAM SIXTY

The most powerful novel ever to come out of the Soviet Union!!!!

by Alexander Solzhenitsyn · The complete, unexpurgated translation by Ronald Hingley and Max Hayward, co-translator of *Doctor Zhivago*

one day in the life of Ivan Denisovich

ABOVE LEFT: *An early 1960s paperback edition, one of the few in this book with four consecutive exclamation marks.*

ABOVE: *Solzhenitsyn as a prisoner in a Kazakhstan labour camp, 1953.*

LEFT: *In 1994 Aleksandr Solzhenitsyn visited the Memorial to Victims of Repression who died in the gulags.*

One Day in the Life of Ivan Denisovich

(1962)

Aleksandr Solzhenitsyn (1918–2008)

Published during a brief easing of Soviet censorship, a unique portrait of life inside a prison camp opened the eyes of the world to the authoritarianism of the USSR. The fictitious narrative was a barely disguised autobiography of the author's own imprisonment and exile in the gulags.

Aleksandr Solzhenitsyn was imprisoned in 1945 for the crime of 'founding a hostile organisation' after he discussed the need for regime change in the USSR in letters to a friend. He was critical of Stalin's conduct of the Great Patriotic War, as World War II is known to Russians, in which he served as an artillery officer and witnessed war crimes perpetrated by Soviet troops. He was held in a series of labour camps, serving the last three years of an eight-year sentence in one reserved for political prisoners in Ekibastuz in Kazakhstan. It was his experiences there which he recorded in *One Day in the Life of Ivan Denisovich*.

Ivan Denisovich Shukhov is in prison for the crime of being a spy, of which he was convicted simply for having been captured by the Germans during the war. On the day in question he feels unwell and rises late, for which he is punished. Because of his punishment task he is too late to request a medical exemption from the day's hard labour on a construction site. This is a world where survival is a day-to-day affair, dependent on a currency of food and favours. Rations are short, but still Shukhov keeps some food back to trade when he needs to. The novel depicts his relationships with the other prisoners in his squad, and with its strict but kindly foreman Tyurin. At the end of this day, a day like every other, Shukhov celebrates the small victories which make life tolerable – he has not fallen sick; the day's labour has been productive; he has been able to steal a second ration at lunchtime; and he has smuggled a scrap of metal into the camp after work from which he can make a labour-saving tool.

Stalin died in 1953, to the cheers and tears of joy of prisoners like Solzhenitsyn. After the end of his prison sentence in 1953, Solzhenitsyn was nevertheless still required to live the rest of his life in exile in Kazakhstan. In 1956, Stalin's successor, Nikita Khrushchev, delivered a report to the Soviet Communist Party conference entitled 'On the Cult of Personality and Its Consequences', which was an attack on Stalin's legacy. In its wake Solzhenitsyn was released from exile in 1957 and, twelve years after his conviction, exonerated of any crime. He worked as a teacher and began to write *One Day in the Life of Ivan Denisovich* secretly. When it seemed safe to assume that the Stalinist years really were over, he submitted the manuscript to *Novy Mir* magazine.

Its subject matter was strictly taboo, and the magazine's editor wisely passed it to the Communist Party Central Committee for vetting. The Committee in turn passed it upwards, to the very top – and Khrushchev himself authorised its publication on the grounds that it was a good example of what was bad about Stalinism. *Novy Mir* published a slightly censored version in November 1962.

The novel sold well, particularly in the West, where it received three different translations in its first year. Emboldened, Solzhenitsyn wrote a further four outspoken books over the next three years, and became a more controversial figure. Khrushchev was replaced in 1964 by the hardliner Leonid Brezhnev, and the KGB began to persecute the author, confiscating his papers and even attempting to poison him. He was eventually deported to West Germany in 1974, a year after the publication in the West of his non-fiction masterpiece *The Gulag Archipelago*.

The Golden Notebook

(1962)

Doris Lessing (1919–2013)

A book like no other, deconstructing the very format of a novel, *The Golden Notebook* has been regarded as a feminist landmark. Its author disagreed: she thought that such a description was too narrow and overshadowed the work's greater theme.

The Golden Notebook tells the story of fictional author Anna Wulf, and her efforts to combine four notebooks in which she has recorded her life in one form or another, into a fifth, the golden notebook of the title. Extracts from the four are intertwined with a separate narrative called *Free Women* about Anna's friends, family and lovers, and the novel represents Anna's attempts to reconcile the formerly compartmentalised pieces of her life into one balanced whole.

Each of the four notebooks is revisited four times in the course of *The Golden Notebook*. One of them, a black notebook, records her time in southern Rhodesia, which formed the basis for Anna's successful novel. A blue one is Anna's personal journal of dreams, memories and emotional turmoil, and a yellow one contains Anna's fictionalised version of the unhappy end of a love affair. The red notebook is for Anna's political thoughts of her membership of the Communist Party.

The notebooks reflect aspects of Doris Lessing's own life. She grew up in southern Rhodesia, and was a member of the British Communist Party until she resigned following the Soviet Union's invasion of Hungary in 1956. *The Golden Notebook* naturally offers a female perspective on its characters and events; but although Lessing can be considered a feminist she did not want to fulfil the feminist movement's expectations of her. 'What they would really like me to say,' she said with regret in a *New York Times* interview in 1982, 'is, "Ha, sisters, I stand with you side by side

in your struggle toward the golden dawn where all those beastly men are no more." Do they really want people to make oversimplified statements about men and women? In fact, they do.'

In her own introduction to the novel she preferred to emphasise the fragmentation of Anna Wulf's psyche which the mosaic format of the book reflects. Anna's attempt to write her Golden Notebook is the result of a mental breakdown and reflects, in Lessing's view, the break-up of post-war European society. Anna's breakdown is a necessary prelude to her attempts to reunite the isolated areas of her life. By implication the social upheaval caused by World War II and its aftermath can serve to heal social divisions. This is the author's greater theme.

Lessing's skill is in her management of the many different narrative threads of *The Golden Notebook*, woven, like Anna Wulf, into one complex personal and political entity. Lessing was awarded the Nobel Prize for Literature in 2007 for 'subject[ing] a divided civilisation to scrutiny ... with scepticism, fire and visionary power'. She was at the time the oldest recipient, and only the eleventh female in its 106 years. She was eighty-seven and had by then written fifty novels. Her lecture given at the presentation of the award, was titled *On Not Winning the Nobel Prize*.

LEFT: Doris Lessing (front), playwright John Osborne, and Vanessa Redgrave at a Ban the Bomb protest in Trafalgar Square, 1961.
OPPOSITE: The US First Edition hardback.

A NOVEL

THE GOLDEN NOTEBOOK

BY DORIS LESSING

A Clockwork Orange

(1962)

Anthony Burgess (1917–1993)

Anthony Burgess's dystopian satire on juvenile delinquency was the author's least favourite of his works. Its depiction of ultra-violence divided critics and the public, who were, however, united in their admiration of its prose and its invented slang language, Nadsat.

Burgess was principally a comic writer. His first three novels form the comedic trilogy *The Long Day Wanes*, which was based on his time as a civil servant in Malaya. *A Clockwork Orange* was written soon after his return to England and may be regarded as a very, *very* black comedy of manners. Instead of jokes, the novella uses episodes of extreme violence to move its plot forward, but the rhythm and timing of the brutality are as precise as any comedian's. It is perhaps an anti-comedy.

The book concerns the progress of fifteen-year-old Alex and his gang as they perpetrate ultra-violence – Burgess coined the term to describe the unprovoked assaults which the gang carry out on innocent bystanders. Injured in an attack by a rival for the leadership of the gang, Alex is arrested and successfully treated with aversion therapy for his violent tendencies; but on his release from prison, he finds himself detached from his old life and attempts suicide. The treatment for his suicidal urges undoes the earlier aversion therapy and although Alex becomes a poster boy for the regime's medical treatment of individuals like him, he starts to dream of violence once more.

A Clockwork Orange has a final chapter in which Alex begins to question the senseless nightly rapes and assaults, and to contemplate a settled family life instead, wondering whether any children of his own would behave as he has. The chapter was omitted from American editions of the book on the grounds that the darker ending, without it, was more convincing and realistic. The final chapter does in truth feel like the obligatory moral ending of many films of the time, in which crime must never be seen to pay. Nevertheless, its omission completely alters the overall message of *A Clockwork Orange*. It was an American edition which persuaded Stanley Kubrick to make his notorious film adaptation. Looking back in 1985, Burgess wrote that 'The book I am best known for, or only known for, is a novel I am prepared to repudiate … (It) became known as the raw material for a film which seemed to glorify sex and violence. The film made it easy for readers of the book to misunderstand what it was about.'

One of the features of the novel is Burgess's invented slang language, called Nadsat. Burgess and his wife had recently returned from a trip to Leningrad (now St Petersburg) during which he learned Russian; and Nadsat is a mixture of Cockney rhyming slang and words derived from Slavic languages. For example, Alex calls a head a 'gulliver' – from the Russian word *golova*; and a criminal is a 'prestoopnick', from the Russian *prestupnik*. Burgess made other words up completely; Alex's companions in the gang, for example, are his 'droogs'.

There is much debate about the title of the novel. Burgess himself has offered differing explanations. Originally he claimed that it came from an old East London saying, that something is 'as queer as a clockwork orange'. But there is no record of such a phrase before 1962. At other times Burgess suggested that it was a pun on the Malay word for a man, *orang*; that the image was of something natural rendered unnatural by the mechanical age; or that Alex was 'a clockwork orange … just a toy to be wound up by either God or the Devil, or (what is increasingly replacing both) the State'.

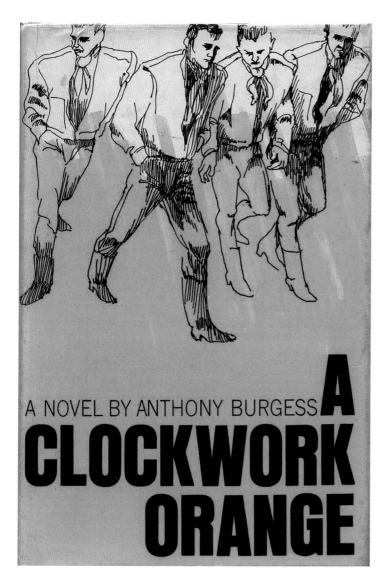

A NOVEL BY ANTHONY BURGESS **A**

CLOCKWORK ORANGE

ABOVE: Like many film adaptations of complex books, Burgess felt the Stanley Kubrick movie distorted his work with an overemphasis on the sex and violence.
LEFT: The cover from the US First Edition published by W.W. Norton.

The Spy Who Came in from the Cold

(1963)

John Le Carré (1931–2020)

Who better to write a spy story than a spy? John Le Carré's six years with the British secret services gave his novels a unique detail and authority, while his mastery of plot resulted in some of the most gripping, complex tales of espionage and subterfuge ever published. In Le Carré's hands, no one is whom they seem to be.

John Le Carré was recruited by MI5, Britain's internal security agency, in 1958. His work included phone-tapping and interrogation. His boss Lord Clanmorris wrote crime fiction under the name John Bingham and encouraged Le Carré to try his hand as an author. *The Spy Who Came in from the Cold* and two earlier novels – *Call for the Dead* and *A Murder of Quality* – were all written while he was serving with MI6, the British version of the CIA, to which Le Carré was transferred in 1960. They feature Le Carré's best-known character George Smiley, head of intelligence, who was modelled partly on Clanmorris and partly on Le Carré's old history teacher, Vivian Green.

In *The Spy Who Came in from the Cold*, Smiley is retired and the story centres on Alec Leamas, a British spy who is demoted, sacked and imprisoned in order to give East German Intelligence the impression that he would be willing to betray his country. Leamas's real mission is to give East Germany false information and to discredit Hans-Dieter Mundt, now the head of East German espionage but first encountered by readers as an assassin in *Call for the Dead*. The Cold of the title is the No Man's Land between the two security services which Leamas must inhabit during the operation.

He successfully convinces Liz, a British Communist Party official, of his treachery, and travels to the German Democratic Republic. There he becomes caught up in a turf war between Mundt and his deputy, Jens Fiedler. Mundt is portrayed as an amoral gun for hire, while Fiedler seems to have a genuine ideological faith in his country. Mundt and Fiedler accuse each other of treason in a tribunal, in the course of which Leamas's cover is blown. With the help of testimony from Liz, it is however Fiedler who is discredited and arrested, and Mundt who quietly helps Liz and Leamas escape. Mundt is not what he appears to be; nor has Smiley retired; and even Leamas, kept in the dark about the true purpose of his mission, decides, in the end, not to come in from the Cold.

The Cold War was at its height in 1963 and *The Spy Who Came in from the Cold* was revolutionary in portraying both British and foreign agents in the same unflattering light of amoral expediency, willing to do anything for their respective employers. Leamas, Fiedler and Mundt are all pawns in the game, the Great Game as the to-and-fro of the international power struggle used to be called in the nineteenth century. They are all unwittingly manipulated by MI6's Control to achieve Smiley's aim – the fall of Fiedler and the preservation of Mundt, despite Mundt's previous assassination of a British spy in *Call for the Dead*. The reading public had become accustomed to the easy but inaccurate fiction of west-good, east-bad, or the playboy-adventurer model of Ian Fleming's James Bond. Le Carré's undercover world was a much grubbier, more ambiguous and far more believable place.

John Le Carré's Secret Service career ended a year after the publication of *The Spy Who Came in from the Cold* when the double agent Kim Philby betrayed British agents to the KGB. The mole in his later novel *Tinker Tailor Soldier Spy* (George Smiley's finest hour) was based on Philby.

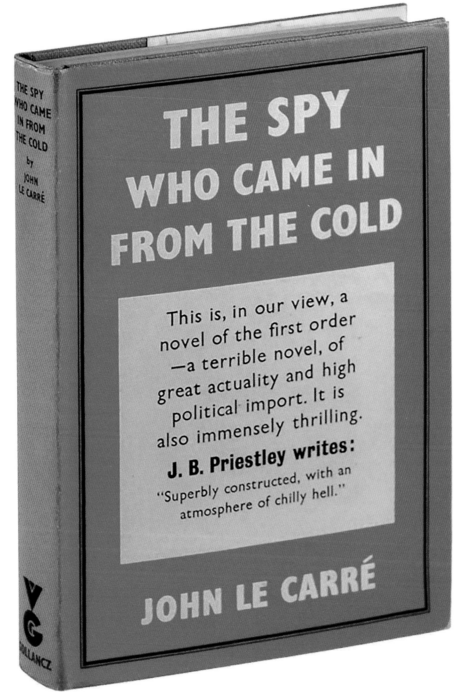

THE SPY WHO CAME IN FROM THE COLD

by
JOHN LE CARRÉ

This is, in our view, a novel of the first order —a terrible novel, of great actuality and high political import. It is also immensely thrilling.

J. B. Priestley writes:
"Superbly constructed, with an atmosphere of chilly hell."

JOHN LE CARRÉ

ABOVE: The original cover with a pre-publication quote that Victor Gollancz regarded as a ringing endorsement.

OPPOSITE: No one had written as convincingly about the secret services until John Le Carré produced his third novel.

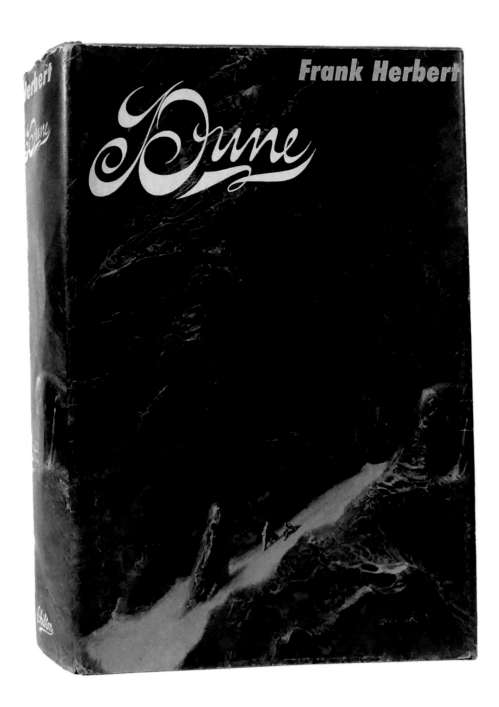

ABOVE: The original cover eschewed the terrifying giant sandworms of Arrakis.

OPPOSITE: Frank Herbert was instrumental in creating the epic science fiction series. Dune *was followed by* Dune Messiah, Children of Dune, God Emperor of Dune, Heretics of Dune, *and* Chapterhouse: Dune.

Dune

(1965)

Frank Herbert (1920–1986)

The best-selling science fiction novel of all time is a blend of ancient myth-telling and futuristic imagination. Originally inspired by Frank Herbert's interest in the environment, at its heart it is a powerful allegory of modern man's dependence on oil, which threatens the planet we live on.

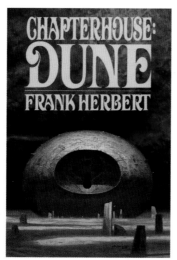

The science fiction in *Dune* is almost incidental. The plot, of dynasties fighting for control of a vital resource, was fed by Herbert's interest in Caucasian history's recurring wars between the Turks and Russians, and owes more than a little to the Arthurian legends of old. Herbert is convincing in his imagining of future technologies and worlds; but it is secondary to his power as a storyteller of an age-old narrative.

The planet Arrakis is the only source of a spice called melange, which extends life and enables interstellar navigation (and is not a million miles from the modern need for rare earth minerals). Arrakis is a valuable possession but an inhospitable one, turned to desert by the exploitation of its resource. The House Atreides, which rules the planet, must defend itself against a conspiracy by the Emperor Shaddam IV and the House Harkonnen to destroy Atreides' power. When a rebellion by Arrakis's native population, the Fremen, threatens the supply of melange, and Shaddam's imperial fleet prepares to intervene decisively, the climax of the novel is an old-fashioned knife fight between Shaddam's chosen warrior and Duke Atreides' son Paul for control of the Empire.

The world of *Dune* was shaped by several strands. On a visit to the northwest in 1957, Herbert was struck by the shifting sands of the Oregon Dunes which, as he marvelled in a letter to his agent, could 'swallow whole cities, lakes, rivers, highways'. One of Herbert's closest friends, Howard Hansen, was a Native American, who complained that the deforestation of his reservation risked turning it into a desert. As Herbert became more fascinated by the idea of a sand-covered world, it struck him that many of history's messianic religions and figures, notably in the Middle East, emerged from desert environments. David Lean's film *Lawrence of Arabia* was released in 1962, telling the story of one such leader, T.E. Lawrence, and his role in the Arab Revolt during World War I. Lawrence was undoubtedly one inspiration for the character of Paul in *Dune*.

The environmental damage caused by the extraction of melange on Arrakis is a clear reference to man's destructive pursuit of fossil fuels on Earth. The uses to which melange are put, however, offer closer parallels with the psychedelic drugs of the Swinging Sixties. In *Dune* it prolongs youth and increases vitality, and as a navigational aid it makes interstellar travel possible by bending space. The eyes of the Fremen are the same blue as magic mushrooms, which Herbert is known to have experimented with and which stimulated the mystical aspects of the book.

Mysticism, myth, religion and ecology are brought together in *Dune*, widely considered one of the pinnacles of science fiction. Herbert was already working on sequels before he had finished the first book. He published five more Dune books in his lifetime, and his son, Brian Herbert, has worked with sci-fi author Kevin J. Anderson to produce many prequels and sequels, some based on Frank Herbert's notes and unfinished work. The Dune universe is still expanding.

Wide Sargasso Sea

(1966)

Jean Rhys (1890–1979)

A new perspective on an old character applies twentieth-century social standards to a figure originally written and judged according to those of the nineteenth. How different things can seem a hundred and twenty years after they were created. Times change, and we change with them.

Literature inspires by offering new perspectives, challenging its readers, and sometimes its writers, to see things differently. But all literature views things from its own point in time. When Charlotte Brontë invented Bertha, Mr Rochester's first wife, for the novel *Jane Eyre*, she did so with the tropes and assumptions of the 1840s. It was believed that those born of mixed race were at risk of mental illness; and so Bertha, a child of the West Indian sugar plantations, became, in Brontë's hands, a madwoman, locked in the attic of Mr Rochester's Thornfield Hall to avoid embarrassment. She was a character firmly in line with the prevailing sexist and racist attitudes.

In the 1960s, new platforms for Black and women's voices started a move towards equality for marginalised sectors of society. It was in these more enlightened times that Jean Rhys set out to challenge the nineteenth-century perception of Bertha and women like her on which Brontë played. Was she really mad? And if so, why?

Wide Sargasso Sea is Bertha's back story, a partial prequel to *Jane Eyre*. It traces her life from childhood in the wake of Britain's abolition of slavery in 1834, an event which had a complex impact on the Caribbean economy. Bertha, whose impoverished Creole family own a once-wealthy plantation, was christened Antoinette. When angry emancipated slaves burn down their family home, Antoinette is struck on the head, her brother dies and grief drives her mother to mental illness. An Englishman in need of money is persuaded to marry Antoinette in return for a generous dowry, but he is uncomfortable among her Black friends.

Her marriage is undermined by suggestions made to her husband that she comes from a family of deadbeats with poor mental health. Mistrust, infidelity and mental abuse follow, and Bertha – as her husband has taken to calling her – is sidelined. In a desperate attempt to save the marriage she takes a traditional love potion, but its only effect is to disturb the balance of her mind, a condition only worsened by her husband's decision to take her to England, far away from her familiar surroundings.

The novel concludes with a glimpse of her disturbed life in the attic of Thornfield Hall. Haunted by traumatic memories, she frequently dreams of liberating herself by burning down the house with lighted candles. Determined to break free, she at last escapes from her room and sets off, lighted candle in hand. Readers of *Jane Eyre* will know what happens in the final scene.

In addition to its commentary on gender and race, *Wide Sargasso Sea* criticises Britain's imposition of its own culture on its colonies. It is her husband's rejection of her heritage (and imposition of his own) which tips Bertha into madness, and his mistreatment of his wife has won *Wide Sargasso Sea* recognition as an important feminist and anti-imperialist novel.

OPPOSITE: The First Edition cover from 1966. Author Jean Rhys was 76 when it was published.

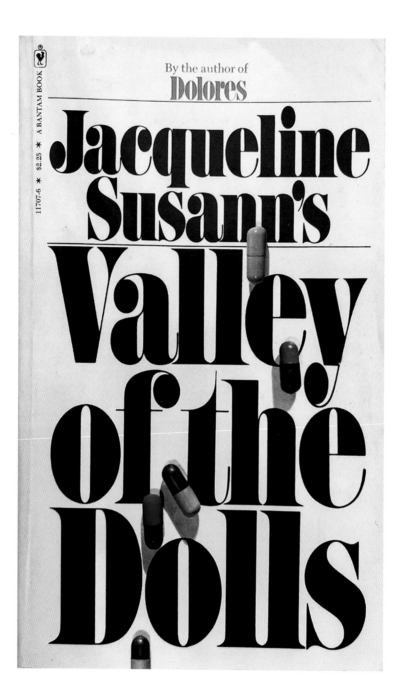

By the author of
Dolores

Jacqueline Susann's Valley of the Dolls

11707-6 ★ $2.25 ★ A BANTAM BOOK

ABOVE: The success of Valley of the Dolls *was a lesson to publishers in how to market popular fiction.*
OPPOSITE: Jacqueline Susann revelled in her success, while the literary establishment sniped from the sidelines. Gore Vidal said, 'She doesn't write, she types.'

Valley of the Dolls

(1966)

Jacqueline Susann (1918–1974)

At the time of the author's death, *Valley of the Dolls* was the best-selling work of fiction in history. Its tale of three actresses, their romances and their drug habits, was the first chick-lit blockbuster. Despite having little literary merit it made an indelible mark on the history of the novel.

Valley of the Dolls was not well reviewed on publication. Even *Publishers Weekly* described it in advance as 'poorly written'; *Time* magazine's headline declared it its 'Dirty Book of the Month' and called it 'a highly effective sedative'. Nevertheless it caught the public imagination and within nine weeks it was at #1 in the *New York Times* bestseller list, where it remained for a further twenty-eight weeks. To date it has sold well over 30 million copies.

The book relates the ups and downs of three actress friends over the course of twenty years in work and in love. They are in one sense the Dolls of the title; but 'dolls' was also slang for the uppers and downers, on which to a greater or lesser extent the women rely on to get them through tough times. *Valley of the Dolls* is a *roman à clef*, a veiled account of real lives, and the central characters are all based on entertainers whom Jacqueline Susann knew well.

Susann decided at an early age that she wanted to be an actress and had some moderate success on Broadway. Between jobs she wrote plays with another actress, Beatrice Cole. She also found some success on TV, even hosting her own show *Jacqueline Susann's Open Door*, which helped members of the public find work. By the late 1950s she was the public face of a lace and embroidery company, where she learned how to market products but felt that her acting career had run out of steam. Her only son was acutely autistic and had to be institutionalised: Susann turned to pills to deal with the distress. She also turned to writing, and *Valley of the Dolls* was her first novel.

Its central character, Anne Welles, was based on her friend Bea Cole. Anne's friend Neely O'Hara, whose career takes her to Hollywood, is a close fit for Judy Garland. Jennifer North, another friend of Anne's who finds success in European nude arthouse films, is a combination of Joyce Mathews (wife of comedian Milton Berle), Carole Landis (a Hollywood star with whom Susann once appeared on Broadway) and Susann herself.

Jennifer's sometime boyfriend Tony Polar, a dim-witted, sex-mad popular singer, was drawn from Rat Pack regular Dean Martin; and ageing, unhappy Helen Lawson, who reluctantly gives Neely her first break, was derived from the Broadway legend Ethel 'There's No Business Like Show Business' Merman. Susann and Merman had once been friends and Merman did not appreciate being the source for Helen. As Susann later observed, 'we didn't speak before the book came out. Let's just say that now we're not speaking louder.'

Susann promoted *Valley of the Dolls* energetically at signings and as a guest on chat shows. Her husband, press agent Irving Mansfield, who had wooed her by getting mentions for her in the society pages of New York's newspapers and magazines, organised her press campaigns. Together the couple are credited with inventing the modern book tour. Susann had a performer's instinct for marketing, acquired when she was promoting lace on TV, and she is recognised as the first author to achieve mainstream success as a brand in her own right, regardless of the mediocre reviews. 'A new book is like a new brand of detergent,' she observed. 'You have to let the public know about it. What's wrong with that?'

One Hundred Years of Solitude

(1967)

Gabriel García Márquez (1927–2014)

In the mind of Gabriel García Márquez time can speed up, or slow down, or go back to the beginning and repeat. Memory and forgetfulness are two sides of the same curse; and in his imaginary history of smalltown Colombia, the test for humanity is its ability to learn from the past.

A new player made its entrance onto the world's literary stage in the 1960s. Latin American literature brought a new genre of magic realism to bookshelves. In naturalistic settings, realistic characters unfolded fantastical histories in which the magical was as likely as the conventionally possible. South America was itself undergoing a magical transformation at the time, caught between the powerful myths and rituals of its people and the modernisation brought by global industries. The period was a more peaceful echo of the impact, centuries earlier, of Spanish missionaries who imposed western religion and language on the continent.

In Márquez's *One Hundred Years of Solitude* he creates an imaginary town, Macondo, and follows the lives of seven generations of descendants from the town's founder José Arcadio Buendía. Haunted by the eternally bleeding ghost of a man he killed in a duel, Buendía leaves home and dreams of a city of mirrors, founding Macondo on the spot where he had the dream. He is strong, quiet and intelligent but goes mad and is tied to a tree for the rest of his life. His strong-willed wife, Úrsula, oversees the next six generations of the family. Each generation has a little less of José Arcadio's fine qualities: his influence is gradually reduced, and Úrsula herself physically shrinks as she witnesses the degeneration of the family until at her death she is no bigger than a baby. In this cyclical world, Macondo itself eventually disappears and the Buendía descendants descend into animalistic behaviour.

Márquez described his magic realism as 'outsize reality'. *One Hundred Years of Solitude* is set in a convincing world of poverty and squalor, an all-too-realistic description of parts of South America at the time. Within that believable world, however, extraordinary things happen: a child is born with a pig's tail; a priest levitates; spells of rain or insomnia last for years. Time is flexible, and its passage does not mean progress. As Macondo becomes, like so many civilisations in South American and global history, a dictatorship, it is clear that modernity is worthless without a code of ethics.

The Buendías pass on Christian names from generation to generation, reinforcing the idea that they are inward-looking, resistant to change, and closed to the influence of the wider world. Theirs is the solitude of the title; and the words 'solitude' and 'solitary' occur on almost every page of the novel.

One Hundred Years of Solitude was welcomed on publication as the finest work in Spanish since Cervantes' *Don Quixote*. The pride of the Hispanic world in the work was only heightened by Márquez's award of the Nobel Prize for Literature in 1982. Macondo has become a byword in many Latin American states for two things – one's hometown with its quirks and foibles, or any small settlement where extraordinary events unfold. When Chilean refugees fled to Austria to escape the dictator Augusto Pinochet, they named their new settlement Vienna Macondo. They and their descendants still live there.

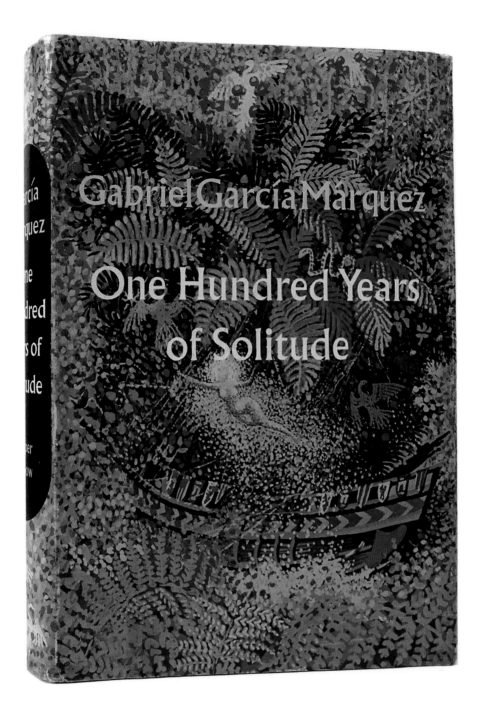

ABOVE: *Márquez got the idea for the book while driving his family to Acapulco in Mexico. He turned the car round mid-journey so he could start writing immediately and took the next eighteen months completing it.*
OPPOSITE: *The book helped 'Gabo' become a Nobel laureate in 1982.*

Slaughterhouse-Five

(1969)

Kurt Vonnegut (1922–2007)

'All this happened, more or less,' the narrator begins in Kurt Vonnegut's semi-autobiographical anti-war novel. With his trademark black humour, economy of words and science fantasy, it took the author twenty-five years to be able to write about his experiences as a prisoner of war in Dresden. And his kidnap by aliens.

Kurt Vonnegut served with the US Army during World War II and was taken prisoner during the Battle of the Bulge in December 1944. He was incarcerated in a slaughterhouse south of Dresden and survived the three-day firebombing of the city by Allied aircraft (which completely destroyed it and killed up to 25,000 civilians) by sheltering in a meat locker three floors underground. Afterwards he was put to work recovering bodies from the ruins.

This traumatic episode forms the central narrative of *Slaughterhouse-Five* whose anti-hero Billy Pilgrim shares Vonnegut's experience of the war and Dresden. Although the wartime elements of the novel are told in more or less chronological sequence, other elements of his life are not. Billy is 'unstuck in time', and travels back and forward in time to review significant moments. Several of those moments, including Billy's death and his abduction to Tralfamadore, are revealed in the first chapter, which serves as a preface where Vonnegut describes the difficulty of writing the novel. Thus forewarned, the reader is granted Billy's ability to see the past and the future.

The Tralfamadorians also have the power to see every point in time at once. This gives them a fatalistic approach to life and death, since all the moments when a person was alive are just as visible as the one in which he or she dies. Their response to fatality, which Billy adopts on his return to Earth, is a shoulder-shrugging 'So it goes.' The phrase occurs 106 times in the course of *Slaughterhouse-Five*.

There are, inevitably, many deaths in the novel besides Billy's. His hawkish comrade in arms, Roland Weary, dies of gangrene after they are captured, and blames Billy for it, something which will eventually lead to Billy's own death. Billy's friend Edgar Derby is shot in Dresden for stealing a teapot – something which really did happen to a friend of Vonnegut's – while another prisoner dies simply from excessive retching.

Death clouds the pages of *Slaughterhouse-Five* as it clouded Vonnegut: his mother committed suicide on the eve of Mother's Day 1944, three months before his unit was posted to Europe; and his sister and her husband died within two days of each other in 1958 while he was writing his second novel, *The Sirens of Titan*, in which the planet Tralfamadore makes its first appearance. *Slaughterhouse-Five* also includes several characters who recur in other novels, notably the failed science fiction author Kilgore Trout. Bertram Copeland Rumfoord, a historian whom Billy meets while in hospital for post-traumatic stress disorder (PTSD) after the war, is a relative of Winston Niles Rumfoord who appears in *The Sirens of Titan*.

Slaughterhouse-Five is notable for its early and accurate depiction of PTSD, a condition which Vonnegut also endured and which – when he was writing *Slaughterhouse-Five* – had not yet been recognised.

LEFT: *Kurt Vonnegut photographed in 1988.*
OPPOSITE: *The original UK cover of the novel used the number 5 and omitted the US strapline 'or the Children's Crusade'.*

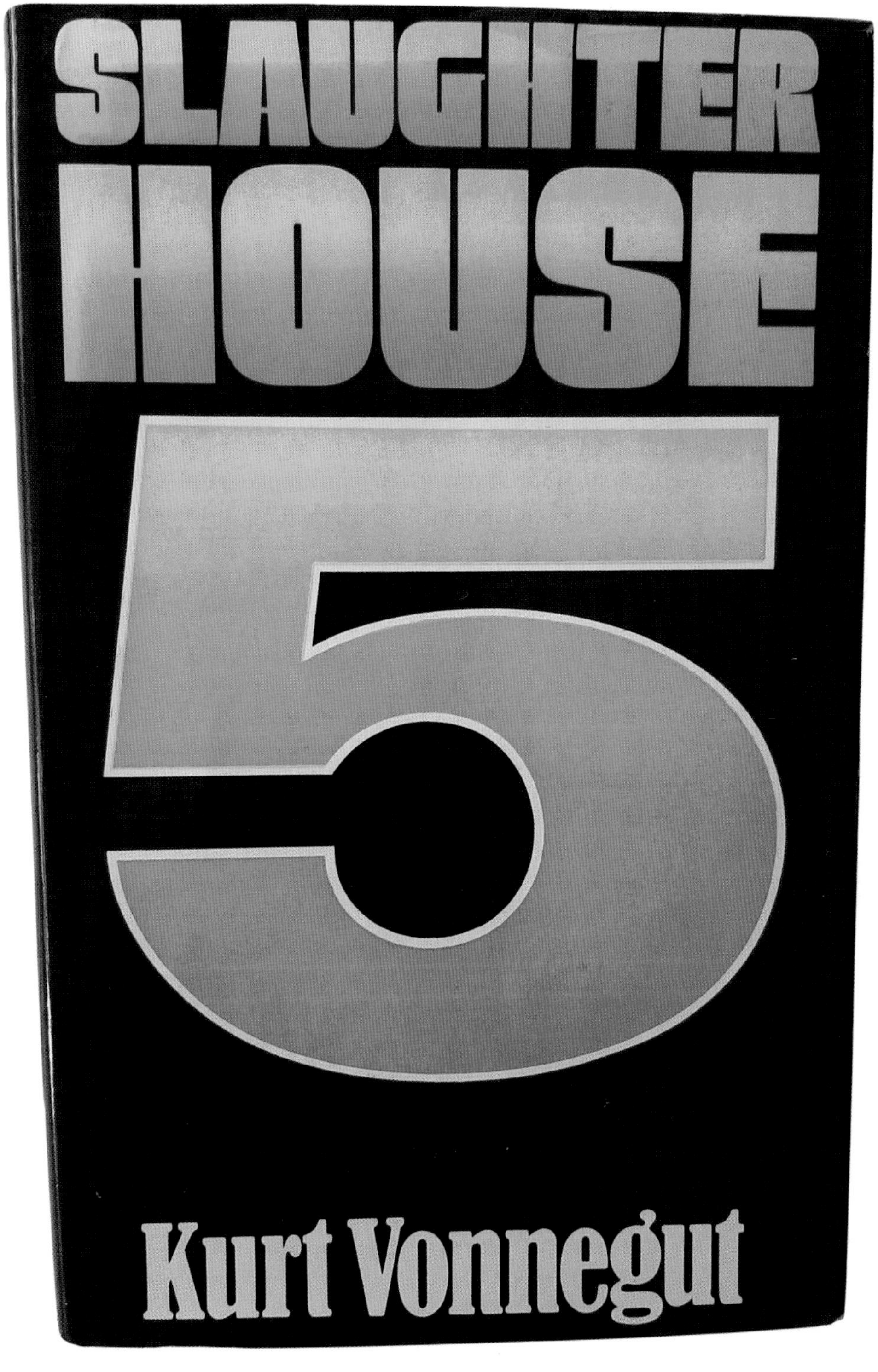

SLAUGHTER
HOUSE
5

Kurt Vonnegut

Portnoy's Complaint
Philip Roth

ABOVE: *In France the novel was translated as* Portnoy et son complexe *and, bizarrely, appeared as a backdrop to a 1970 Jane Birkin fashion show.*
OPPOSITE: *Philip Roth photographed in the late 1960s revisiting old haunts in Newark, New Jersey.*

Portnoy's Complaint

(1969)

Philip Roth (1933–2018)

A product of its time, when psychoanalysis was becoming a mainstream form of treatment for personal anxieties, *Portnoy's Complaint* takes the form of a sexually explicit comic monologue, delivered to his psychoanalyst by Alexander Portnoy, a self-confessed 'lust-ridden, mother-addicted young Jewish bachelor'.

The first page of Philip Roth's novel offers a medical definition: 'Portnoy's Complaint: A disorder in which strongly felt ethical and altruistic impulses are perpetually warring with extreme sexual longings, often of a perverse nature.' Roth chose the psychoanalytical setting of the novel because the presumed patient-doctor confidentiality of that situation would allow his character to describe his shameful acts and thoughts freely. In another context, Roth argued, the themes of the novel would be considered simply pornographic. In fact, the detailed nature of Portnoy's descriptions, especially of various acts of masturbation, ensured the novel a high degree of controversy – and publicity – even in the sexually liberated times which enabled its writing.

Portnoy's complaint, in the sense of his dissatisfaction, is that his highly moral Jewish upbringing prevents him from enjoying his sexual exploits, and that the resulting frustration drives him to ever more extreme, more shaming acts of sexual gratification, which he describes to psychoanalyst Dr Spielvogel with considerable frankness. Between Portnoy's recounting of the key moments of eroticism in his life, there are also comparisons of Jewish life in America and in Israel, and of the advantages and disadvantages of growing up in a Jewish family. The novel thus managed to offend not only those of prudish sensibilities but the Jewish community in America, who found it irreverent.

Philip Roth was, until the publication of *Portnoy's Complaint*, not known for this sort of material. His previous novels had been compared to the work of Henry James. *Portnoy's Complaint* began life as a satirical monologue which Roth intended for inclusion in the sexually risqué stage revue *Oh! Calcutta!*, which would accompany a slideshow of celebrity genitals. The monologue was not used, but Roth reworked parts of it in a piece called 'Whacking Off', which was printed in the left-wing literary magazine *Partisan Review*. Although he tried to work it up into a novel, his progress was hampered by the knowledge that he would have to pay half of any royalties to his ex-wife under the conditions of their divorce. Only her death in 1968 removed his writer's block and allowed him to complete the book.

Portnoy's Complaint has the distinction of being the last publication whose censorship came before the courts of Australia. Victoria and Queensland banned it; two New South Wales prosecutions foundered on hung juries; Western Australia allowed it on artistic grounds; and South Australia permitted sales as long as the book was hidden from view below the counter. As a federal country, decisions of censorship were matters for individual Australian states, but the absurdity of contiguous states imposing different degrees of prohibition led in 1971 to the lifting of the ban on importing the novel.

Fear and Loathing in Las Vegas

(1971)

Hunter S. Thompson (1937–2005)

Two wild trips to Las Vegas are the factual basis for Hunter S. Thompson's fictional account, a manifesto for gonzo journalism and one of the first books to assess the legacy of the 1960s. What was left after a decade when free love, drug use and the energy of youth made real change seem possible?

Freelance journalist Hunter S. Thompson set off in March 1971 to cover Mint 400, an annual off-road race which took place in the desert around Las Vegas, sponsored by The Mint hotel-casino. Travelling with him was Oscar Zeta Acosta, with whom Thompson was also writing an article about police abuse of Mexican Americans. His report, commissioned by *Sports Illustrated* magazine, was rejected; but the pair returned the following month to cover a district attorneys' conference on illegal drug use. On both trips Thompson and Acosta indulged extensively in those illegal drugs, and found themselves examining the state of the American Dream. Their conclusion, recorded through a filter of drugs and anarchic abandon in *Fear and Loathing*, was that it had failed to fulfil its promise.

Thompson developed an entirely new form of journalism. He felt that pure objectivity in reporting was impossible – that any material was inevitably coloured by the perspective of the person writing it. From that point of view, it was more truthful for a journalist to insert himself into the story, reporting on his own reactions to the events he was covering. Thompson's breakthrough was *Hell's Angels* (1967), the first-hand record of a year which he spent with Hell's Angels bikers, experiencing their lifestyle for himself.

He went further in 1970, when he covered the annual horse-racing festival in Louisville with an iconoclastic magazine feature entitled 'The Kentucky Derby is Decadent and Depraved'. Racing aficionados were incensed by the way in which they were portrayed by both Thompson and the illustrator of the article, the British cartoonist Ralph Steadman. Steadman's grotesque style suited Thompson's; the pair became lifelong friends and Steadman also drew the illustrations for *Fear and Loathing*.

The final piece of the gonzo jigsaw puzzle was Thompson's admiration for novelist William Faulkner's diktat, that fiction was often more truthful than fact. He further developed his theory of journalism by not only reporting on himself but staging events through which to comment on the subject of his reports. So, in Las Vegas, his drug-fuelled escapades – which included hallucinatory experiences and the destruction of motor vehicles and hotel rooms – became additional ways of looking at the Mint 400 and the American Dream. As he writes in *Fear and Loathing*, 'What was the story? Nobody had bothered to say. So we would have to drum it up on our own. Free Enterprise. The American Dream. Horatio Alger [a popular nineteenth-century young-adult novelist] gone mad on drugs in Las Vegas. Do it now: pure Gonzo journalism.'

ABOVE: *Illustrator Ralph Steadman set the perfect tone for Hunter S. Thompson's*
radical approach.
OPPOSITE: *Hunter S. Thompson in the Baccarat Lounge of Caesars Palace,*
Las Vegas, 1971.

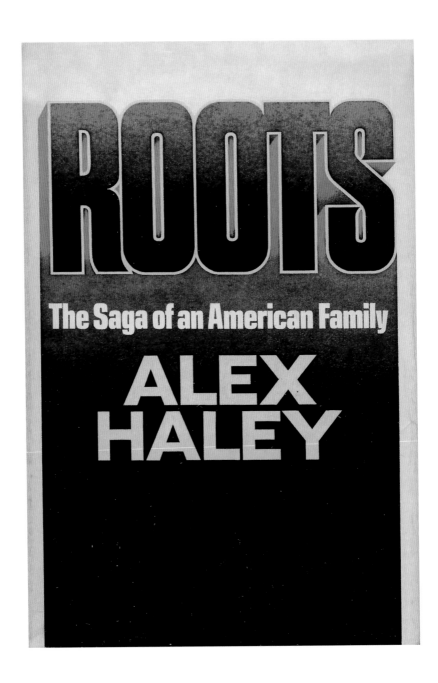

ABOVE: Roots *achieved a rare double in 1977, winning a Pulitzer Prize and a* National Book Award, *in both cases a 'special citation'. Its success emboldened American publishers and opened doors for Black novelists.*
OPPOSITE: *Alex Haley's profile was raised considerably by his collaboration with Malcolm X.*

Roots: The Saga of an American Family

(1976)

Alex Haley (1921–1992)

Although many were familiar with the struggle for Civil Rights and the protests of Black Power, it took the fictional biography of a slave and his descendants to open American eyes to the full history of a slave's journey from their continent of birth.

Alex Haley served with the US Coastguard for twenty years before retiring and taking up journalism. He conducted the first ever interview for *Playboy*, in which his subject, Miles Davis, spoke about his experience of racism in the music industry. *Playboy* published many more such interviews by Haley with, among others, boxer Muhammad Ali, NFL star Jim Brown, music producer Quincy Jones and – in the longest interview which the great man ever granted – Martin Luther King Jr.

Another important Civil Rights leader was the subject and co-author of his first book, an autobiography of Malcolm X, whom Haley interviewed many times between 1963 and Malcolm X's assassination in February 1965. The book remains required reading for anyone interested in Black pride and history.

Roots was the result of Haley's research into his own history. He traced his ancestry back seven generations to Kunta Kinte, who was abducted from his family home in the Gambia in 1767 and sold as a slave in Annapolis. The book follows Kunta's life before and after his kidnap, and describes the experiences of his descendants as slaves bought and sold at their owners' convenience and, after the American Civil War, as free men and women, moving up into the professions; Alex Haley's father was a Professor of Agriculture.

In the final chapter of *Roots* Haley describes the research process which led him to the facts of his ancestors.

It included archive research of shipping records and slave sales, and the oral histories retained and retold by griots, traditional historians in the Gambia. The saga was so compellingly told that *Roots* could be found in bookshops in both the fiction and non-fiction sections. Haley himself described it as 'faction'.

It later emerged that Haley's research was severely flawed. Documentary evidence could not be found of the nineteenth-century part of the story, and the griot who was his only source in the Gambia may have been telling him what he wanted to hear. In the US, records before the Civil War were scarcely more accurate, and further distorted by misinformation which Haley had received as truth in Africa and searched for in the archives.

Nevertheless *Roots* made its point, that African Americans had a long history about which few knew. Apart from enhancing Black pride and raising awareness among white Americans, the novel stimulated a new interest in genealogy around the world, which continues to this day.

The television series based on the book was aired within a few months of its publication. It was shown over eight consecutive nights rather than eight weeks because ABC network executives were afraid that the subject of Black history would turn off viewers and advertisers. In fact the series was watched by 130 million Americans and the final episode attracted the third largest television audience of all time.

The Color Purple

(1982)

Alice Walker (born 1944)

The emotional journey of Celie, an uneducated black teenager living in the Southern States at the start of the twentieth century, is told in a series of ninety letters, mostly from Celie to God and between Celie and her lost sister Nettie. The novel exposes racism, and challenges traditional gender stereotypes.

The Color Purple covers a period of thirty years in which Celie suffers terrible abuse at the hands of her father and her husband, loses her sister Nettie and her children, and eventually finds love, peace, acceptance and contentment by taking control of her own fate. Reunited with those she thought dead, she also comes to a new understanding of the God to whom she has written so often.

The epistolary form of The Color Purple serves several useful functions. Celie's letters to God act as a diary for her thoughts and, in the course of the novel, show her transformation from submissive, unknowing young woman to mature, wise adult who, ironically, ends the novel, feeling 'the youngest us ever felt'.

Celie is kept ignorant of Nettie's life because her husband withholds Nettie's letters to her, just as slaves were kept in ignorance by being denied the opportunities for education. Nettie escapes the uneducated prison of the family home and travels the world, also learning about God and about people who are kind to each other; and she writes to Celie about what she has seen. Through this enlightenment she also finds Celie's children, long assumed dead.

Although Celie's letters to God are her private thoughts and confessions, most letters need a reader, an audience for the writer's news and reflections. Without one, the writer is invisible, pointless. While her husband withholds Nettie's letters, Celie thinks that her sister, as well as her children, must be dead; and when Nettie receives no replies to hers, she feels alone and isolated.

The patriarchy of society comes in for substantial criticism in The Color Purple, not least in the fact that for almost the entire novel Celie's husband is known only as Mister, without even a surname to humanise him. Mister treats Celie cruelly, and encourages his son Harpo to behave in the same way to his own young wife. Misogyny teaches misogyny, and racism, too, is passed from generation to generation, as Harpo's wife Sofia finds when the children of the woman she works for treat her as badly as her mistress does. God also comes under the microscope: it is only when Celie is encouraged to think of God as a creative force and not as an old man with a beard that she can really appreciate the miracle of creation. She has suffered too much at the hands of older men.

Purple is the colour of blood and bruises. It is however one of the many things that Celie comes to thank God for at the end of the novel. Strong bright colours are a theme of hope running through The Color Purple. When Celie tries to buy a new dress she is disappointed by the drab colours. By contrast, when Celie and Sofia make a quilt from yellow fabric, it is a happy occasion. And when Mister has a chance to start afresh (and Celie is able at last to call him by his Christian name), he paints every room in the house 'fresh and white', a blank page on which to write the future.

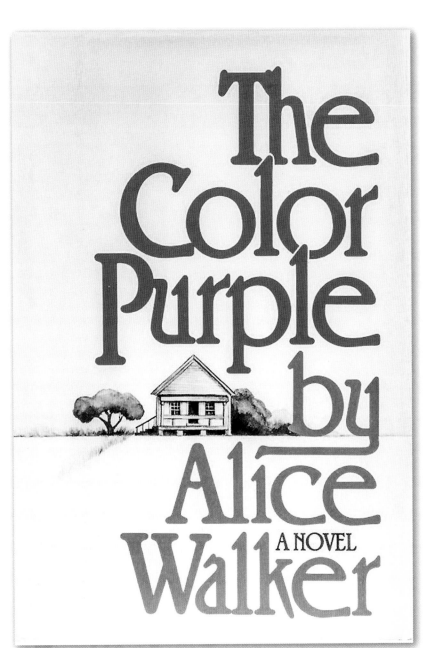

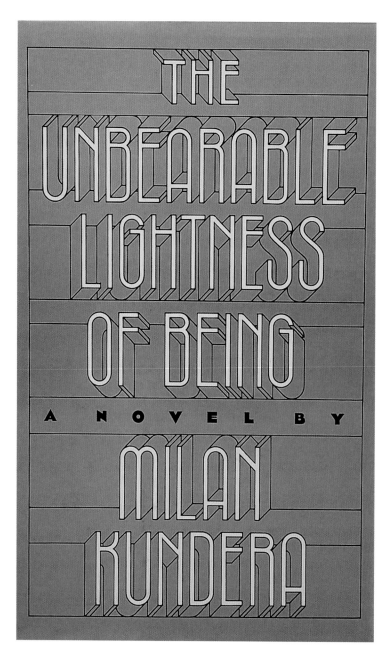

ABOVE: *Milan Kundera became an exile by moving to France in 1975.*
LEFT: *The novel was first published in Britain by Faber and Faber. It was adapted for film in 1988 and in a subsequent Czech edition of the book, Kundera noted that the film version had little to do with the 'spirit of the novel' or the characters in it, and he would no longer allow any adaptations of his work.*

The Unbearable Lightness of Being

(1984)

Milan Kundera (born 1929)

Existentialism lies at the heart of a novel set in Czechoslovakia during and after the heady days of the Prague Spring. Should one bear personal problems and the burdens of the world? Or should one shrug them off and float away, free but unconnected?

The Unbearable Lightness of Being follows the lives of five characters in the late 1960s and early 1970s. The Prague Spring was a period beginning in January 1968 when demonstrations against communism increased and won a degree of liberalisation from the Czech leader Alexander Dubček, until in August of that year the Soviet Union and its allies in the Warsaw Pact (Poland, Hungary and Bulgaria) invaded the country to restore communist order. Officials who had instigated liberal reforms were purged, and some dissidents fled, like husband and wife Tomáš and Tereza in *The Unbearable Lightness*, to neighbouring countries. Others, including Milan Kundera, remained and urged liberals to keep faith in Dubček's reforms. Within a year, however, Czechoslovakia had been 'normalised' back to strict communist rule.

Tomáš lives lightly. He is a gifted surgeon and enjoys his work. He finds his marriage to Tereza burdensome sometimes, but draws an uncomplicated distinction between his undoubted love for her and the sex which he enjoys with many other women, including Sabina. Although he is the sort of intellectual that communists despise, he considers himself apolitical and does not stay to oppose the new regime. Tereza, by contrast, is weighed down by her political idealism. She is a controversial photo-journalist opposed to Soviet influence and lives with a heavy heart because of the invasion and Tomáš's infidelity. As she discovers that her political and romantic beliefs can never match reality, she must learn to live a less burdened life.

Sabina, Tomáš's mistress, is the lightest of all the characters. Faced with aspects of life and art which displease her – kitsch, patriarchy, totalitarianism – she simply walks away from them; and she keeps on walking away, abandoning one influence after another until she ends the novel living in America and (like Kundera who eventually left Czechoslovakia for France) never returning. She and Tomáš play together, erotically but without any pretence of attachment or romance. Yet she is impressed by the philosophically heavier Tereza; and she has another lover, Franz, who is her polar opposite, a painfully burdened man. Franz is passionately engaged in politics and compassionately attentive to his fellow men and women. He makes decisions with difficulty, weighing up all the moral and practical arguments according to his own strict laws. His task in *The Unbearable Lightness* is to lighten up and realise that not everything is quite as serious and inflexible as he thinks.

The fifth character is Karenin, Tomáš and Tereza's dog, who dislikes the changes in circumstances which their life dictates, from liberalisation to communism, from Prague to Zurich, back to Prague and eventually to a house in the country. Karenin settles down after this last move, as Tereza does, accepting life, befriending a pig called Mefisto and facing her imminent death from cancer with great lightness.

There is a balance to be struck, Kundera tells us, between being so weighed down like Franz with the burdens of life, that we are pressed hard up against reality and flattened by it, and so unburdened that we drift off into fantasy and isolation from truth. If Tereza and Franz must learn to live more lightly, Kundera writes, Sabina's is the *unbearable* lightness of being.

The Handmaid's Tale

(1985)

Margaret Atwood (born 1939)

Written long before the storming of the Capitol and the overturning of Roe vs Wade, Margaret Atwood foresaw a world in which extreme right-wing religious fundamentalists would overthrow the US government. Nearly forty years later, her dystopian vision seems closer than ever.

The Handmaid's Tale is a harrowing piece of speculative fiction set in a near future in which the United States of America has been violently replaced by the Republic of Gilead, a radical regime characterised by an extreme fundamentalist misinterpretation of the Old Testament. Gilead is a totalitarian, militaristic state in which social order is strictly maintained; and women, whatever their ordained status – from senior wife to lowly domestic servant – have the lowest standing in society. Their precise rank is indicated by the colour of their clothing.

Rampant pollution has caused a rise in infertility among women, which threatens the very future of the state. Handmaids are a class of fertile women assigned to men whose wives are infertile (in Gilead husbands are never considered infertile). A handmaid is required to take part in so-called Ceremonies with the husband, at which the wife is also present, the sole purpose of which is conception. Handmaids are stripped of all personality, including names. The red-cloaked handmaid who narrates Atwood's novel is known simply as Offred, indicating that she is the handmaid of Fred, a Gilead commander and one of the founders of the Sons of Jacob.

Offred is of a generation which remembers life before Gilead. She recognises the Commander's wife Serena Joy as a former televangelist whom Offred watched on TV while waiting for her cartoons. Offred's growing emotional relationship with the Commander, and her interest in an underground organisation, Mayday, which helps Gilead dissidents escape to Canada, form the dramatic narrative of *The Handmaid's Tale*.

Atwood was inspired by the Islamic Revolution of 1979 in Iran, which robbed Iranian women of their human rights and imposed strict dress codes on them. The appearance of the handmaids, completely covered in modest red dresses and cloaks, with winged white bonnets which limit their vision and conceal their faces, harks back to the Puritans who founded modern America. Far from escaping Europe to find religious freedom, they were actually, Atwood believes, a sect determined to establish a strict society in which religious dissent was forbidden. *The Handmaid's Tale*, she argues, is a response to those who claim, despite evidence to the contrary, that such things 'couldn't happen here'. The speculation of her fiction is only in how such a turn of events might evolve. 'I didn't put in anything that we haven't already done, we're not already doing, we're seriously trying to do, coupled with trends that are already in progress,' she has said, 'and therefore the amount of pure invention is close to nil.'

Despite its satire of religious fundamentalism, Atwood insists that the behaviour of the Sons of Jacob is not the fault of religion, but of human nature. She cites the former Soviet Union as an example of an atheist state which similarly oppressed its peoples. 'It is a question of human beings,' she explains, getting power and then wanting more of it.' And it is always the men who want the power.

MARGARET ATWOOD
THE HANDMAID'S TALE

ABOVE: The success of the television adaptation of The Handmaid's Tale *has taken the story arc well beyond the original novel .*
OPPOSITE: Margaret Atwood reads from her book The Year of the Flood *at St James's Church, Piccadilly, in 2009.*

Oranges Are Not the Only Fruit

(1985)

Jeanette Winterson (born 1959)

Repression and defiance of convention drive a debut novel about growing up and coming out. The central character's intensely religious childhood and adolescent discovery of her homosexuality are a thinly veiled autobiography of an author who was trained to deliver evangelical Christian sermons at the age of six.

Both Jeanette Winterson and her fictional double (also called Jeanette) were raised in the bosom of the Elim Pentecostal Church, having been adopted by evangelical parents. In the novel the adoption is because her mother wanted a child without having to go through a sexual experience. Jeanette is raised to be a servant of God and educated at home, mainly through readings of the Bible. When she does attend school she is regarded as a freak because of her devout religious beliefs.

She seems destined for evangelical greatness, but her apparent holy rapture proves to be merely a hearing defect. When that is repaired, Jeanette is exposed to a wider world. Her friendship with a market stallholder, Melanie, deepens and Jeanette introduces her to the church; but their private Bible study sessions become a love affair. Jeanette, in all innocence, announces her love for Melanie to her mother, who believes that her daughter must be possessed by demons and enlists the church to conduct an exorcism in the form of a fourteen-hour-long laying on of hands and prayer.

The church concludes that, by being given too much responsibility as an evangelist at too young an age, Jeanette has somehow become a man; and so she is prevented from giving any more lessons and sermons. Jeanette leaves home, and the church, as Winterson did when she came out as a lesbian at the age of sixteen.

Oranges Are Not the Only Fruit is steeped in biblical references, and its eight sections are named for the first eight Old Testament books of the Bible. Many episodes in the book have parallels in stories from the Old Testament, or from Arthurian legend. Despite the fictional Jeanette's narrow education, there are many references to classic English literature, evidence that she is trying to broaden her mind. One symbolic scene, after her hearing has been restored, finds her decorating Easter eggs with characters from Wagner's *Ring of the Nibelung* operatic cycle, who are all from pagan Northern European legends.

This, Winterson's first novel after coming out, leaving home and moving to London, won the Whitbread Prize for a debut work of fiction and launched a successful career which has regularly returned to themes of gender, sexuality and physicality. *Oranges Are Not the Only Fruit* is taught in twentieth-century literature studies in English and Welsh schools. It is often regarded as a lesbian novel, but Winterson resents this tag. 'I've never understood why straight fiction is supposed to be for everyone,' she has argued, 'but anything with a gay character or that includes gay experience is only for queers.' The novel is about making personal choices and not merely accepting the role, or the fruit, which one has always been given.

Jeanette Winterson's 2011 memoir, *Why Be Happy When You Could Be Normal?*, gives a non-fiction account of many of the elements of *Oranges Are Not the Only Fruit*.

LEFT: *Jeanette Winterson in 2006.*
OPPOSITE: *The novel was published by Grove Atlantic in the US in 1997.*

WINNER OF THE WHITBREAD PRIZE
FOR BEST FIRST FICTION

"Winterson's great gift is evident. . . . She has mastered both comedy and tragedy in this rich little novel."—*The Washington Post Book World*

JEANETTE WINTERSON
Oranges Are Not the Only Fruit

BELOVED

TONI MORRISON

With an introduction by BERNARDINE EVARISTO

ABOVE: *A recent cover of Toni Morrison's acclaimed book.*
OPPOSITE: *Morrison won the Pulitzer Prize for Beloved in 1988, and gained worldwide recognition when she was awarded the Nobel Prize for Literature in 1993.*

Beloved

(1987)

Toni Morrison (1931–2019)

One of the crowning achievements of African American literature paints an unflinching picture of the legacy of slavery in the years after the American Civil War. The first in a trilogy of novels, with Jazz *and* Paradise, *written over eleven years,* Beloved *deals in loss, pain, memory and the need for family.*

Among Toni Morrison's many landmark achievements, she was the first Black senior editor in Random House's fiction department. Before becoming an author herself, she played a key role in bringing Black literature into the mainstream. *Beloved* was inspired by an article from the *American Baptist* newspaper of 1856 which she came across while compiling *The Black Book* (Random House, 1974), an anthology of Black history resources. The article was headlined 'A Visit to the Slave Mother Who Killed Her Child'.

It reported on a fugitive slave, Margaret Garner, who was recaptured as she prepared to murder her own children rather than see them taken back into slavery – she had already killed her youngest daughter when she was interrupted by the marshals. This became the starting point for Morrison's novel, which catches up with a mother, Sethe, who still lives in the house in which she murdered her daughter. The house is said to be haunted, as Sethe is haunted by the memory of the cruelty she experienced as a slave.

The unexplained appearance of a young woman on Sethe's doorstep, the same age that Sethe's dead daughter would have been, triggers Sethe's mothering instincts. She is all too willing to believe that this young woman, called Beloved, is the reincarnation of her daughter; and destitute Beloved is ready to accept Sethe as the mother she lacks. Sethe is entranced by her and begins to lose herself as, in her mind, she becomes a mother again. It takes the arrival of a man who used to work on the same plantation as Sethe to break the spell which Beloved has

cast over the home. Paul D, a friend of Sethe's absent husband, has suffered mental, physical and sexual abuse on the chain gang, the memories of which are prompted by having sex with Beloved.

We are all at risk of being enslaved – Paul by reminders of his brutal treatment, Sethe by Beloved and her dead daughter. If Paul cannot understand Sethe's unfettered devotion, he does manage to throw off the shackles of his own memories. In the end, Beloved is driven away like a bad memory after an exorcism by the local community, and over time she is completely forgotten.

The novel remains ambiguous as to whether Beloved is real or an apparition. She is central to all the novel's themes. Her arrival (or return) stops the haunting of the house; but while Sethe welcomes her openheartedly as her long lost daughter, Beloved also invokes all the suppressed memories of the murdered girl and of Sethe's tortured life. She brings both pain and joy, neither of them sustainable, because they are built on the false relationship which she and Sethe willingly foster.

Morrison dedicated the novel to the '60 million and more' Africans who died in transit to America, for whom, she said, there was no memorial, not even a bench by the road. Since that remark, the Toni Morrison Society has begun to erect memorial benches across America. The first was on Sullivan's Island, South Carolina, where around 40% of those who survived the Atlantic crossing entered the United States.

V for Vendetta

(1988)

David Lloyd (born 1950), Alan Moore (born 1953)

The sinister mask worn by anonymous anti-government protesters around the world from London to Hong Kong has its roots in a graphic novel begun in 1982, which in turn took its inspiration from a notoriously unsuccessful anti-government protest in 1605.

When a group of thirteen Jesuit conspirators failed in their attempt to assassinate the Protestant King James I of England by blowing up the Houses of Parliament in 1605, they were sentenced to be hanged, drawn and quartered for their treason. One of them, Guy Fawkes, escaped the fate of his brothers in arms only because he jumped off the scaffolding and broke his neck before they could hang him.

Writer Alan Moore and artist David Lloyd began to create their graphic novel *V for Vendetta* in 1982. The central character, V, is a revolutionary dedicated to bringing down the fascist government in the near-future Britain of a post-nuclear holocaust. V is an anti-hero: not for him the usual trappings of a comic book superhero. Instead he wears a mask with the face of Guy Fawkes, a fellow anti-establishment figure.

Moore's story is a battle between anarchy represented by V, and fascism in the form of a totalitarian government called Norsefire, whose various avenues of enforcement are nicknamed after body parts. The secret police are The Finger; the propaganda ministry is The Mouth; The Eye is the department for surveillance. V's sidekick and aide is Evey, whom he rescues from attempted rape and murder by The Finger at the beginning of the novel.

In the first two books of the trilogy, V exacts revenge on those who tortured him in a prison camp for enemies of the state. The third builds to a climactic battle between V and Finch, the policeman

who is trying to bring him to justice. V declares that he cannot be killed because he is not only a man but an idea, 'and ideas are bulletproof'. Evey assumes V's identity and completes the overthrow of Norsefire; but the ensuing chaos begs a final question about the new so-called Land-of-Do-As-You-Please. Is anarchy enough?

Moore has cited an impressive list of influences on V, the central character of the series: they include other anti-establishment characters such as Robin Hood and Dick Turpin; heroes from other comics including The Shadow, Night Raven and Batman; science fiction authors like Thomas Disch and Harlan Ellison; dystopian novelists George Orwell and Aldous Huxley; the horror films of Vincent Price; the chameleon-like persona of David Bowie; and a painting by Max Ernst, *Europe after the Rain*. (Book One of *V for Vendetta* is called *Europe after the Reign*.)

V for Vendetta was originally published in parts and in black and white, in the British anthology *Warrior*. When *Warrior* folded with two instalments of *V for Vendetta* still to go, the series was picked up and colourised by DC Comics, with whom it was extended to the full three-volume saga, and sold (in America alone) over half a million copies. Anti-capitalists who wear the *V for Vendetta* mask may be disappointed to learn that Warner Bros, who made the film, hold the rights to the image and get royalties from each sale. It is the best-selling mask on Amazon.

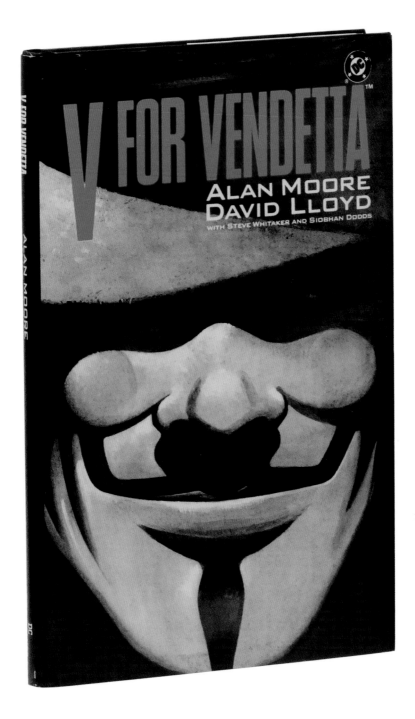

ABOVE: *Moore and LLoyd's character has become the face of international protest.*
OPPOSITE: *The mischievous Alan Moore at a signing for his book* Fashion Beast *at*
Waterstones, Piccadilly, in 2013.

The Satanic Verses

(1988)

Salman Rushdie (born 1947)

If only *The Satanic Verses* was as well-known as the controversy which surrounds it. In a work of magic realism, Salman Rushdie's central theme is the immigrant experience of Indians in Britain and the competing demands of assimilation, and preservation of native culture.

The Satanic Verses is Rushdie's fourth novel. It tells the story of two Indian Muslim actors, Gibreel Farishta and Saladin Chamcha, who at the start of the novel miraculously survive a terrorist attack on their flight to England. Farishta is a Bollywood film star and is frequently cast as Hindu gods. Chamcha has no connection with his Indian roots and does voiceover work in England. As they fall from the exploding aircraft, Farishta becomes the Archangel Gabriel and Chamcha turns into a devil. Separated, they gradually try to rebuild their lives; but Chamcha resents Farishta for abandoning him after their fall from the sky and takes revenge by inciting Farishta's fierce jealousy to destroy his relationship with Allie, an English mountain climber. When they return to India, Farishta kills Allie and himself, but Chamcha rediscovers his roots and settles once again in the country of his birth.

Framed by this narrative are a series of dream sequences experienced by Farishta, concerning the prophet Muhammad. One is a thinly veiled attack on the Ayatollah Khomeini, Iran's religious and spiritual leader at the time. Another describes a vision of the Archangel Gabriel which persuades a peasant girl to lead her village on a pilgrimage by foot to Mecca, during which she assures the villagers that they will be able to walk across the Arabian Sea. As they wade into the water and disappear, no one is sure whether they have drowned or not.

The dream sequence which caused the greatest controversy retells an episode in Muhammad's life in which he was hoodwinked by the Devil into accepting some verses dedicated to three pagan goddesses of Mecca, a city which Muhammad was hoping to convert to Islam. Realising his mistake, Muhammad revoked his declaration that the goddesses should be honoured. These are the Satanic Verses, about whose existence Islamic scholars still argue today. In Farishta's dream-vision, however, it is revealed that the verses were not written by the Devil but by Gabriel himself. Furthermore, one of Muhammad's companions in the dream casts doubt on the prophet's authenticity and quietly rewrites sections of the Quran as Muhammad dictates them.

Rushdie's revision of a well-known episode in the history of Muhammad caused widespread offence, particularly among Muslims who regard the Prophet as infallible and believe he would never have adopted the satanic verses in the first place, or mistaken Gabriel for the Devil. Opposition to the book increased when Pakistan banned it; and after a mob rioted in Islamabad in February 1989, the Ayatollah Khomeini proclaimed a fatwā, a legal decision under Islamic law, calling for the righteous murder of Rushdie and his publishers.

The fatwā has been seen in Christian countries as an attack on freedom of speech and the arts. At least four translators of *The Satanic Verses* have been assaulted – a Japanese one fatally. Numerous attempts have been made on the life of Rushdie himself, including one at a literary event in 2022 in which he lost an eye and the use of one hand. Rushdie has commented that the novel would probably not be published if it were submitted today, because of the atmosphere of fear and nervousness which the fatwā has created.

OPPOSITE: Author Salman Rushdie and his translators have paid a high price for creating works of fiction.

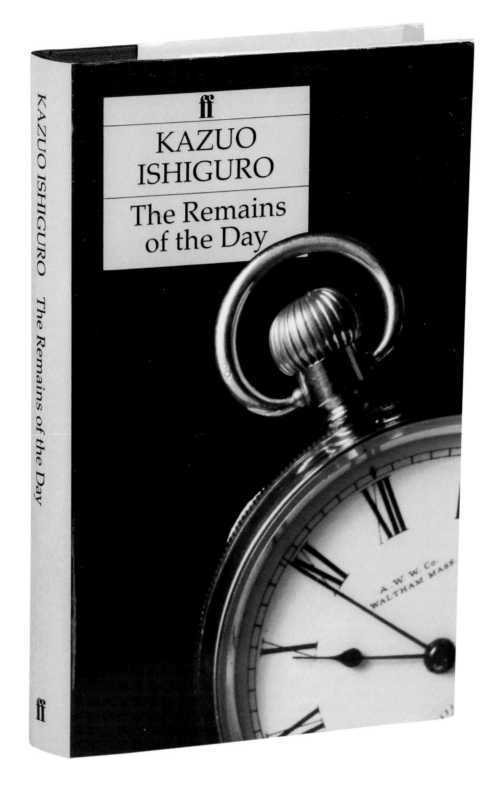

The Remains of the Day

(1989)

Kazuo Ishiguro (born 1954)

Kazuo Ishiguro came to Britain from Japan in 1960, at the age of five. His finest novel, a painfully sad portrait of what it is to be British, could only have been written by an outsider. His portrait of dignity, reserve and the stiff upper lip, before and after World War II, is drawn with remarkable fondness and restraint.

That quintessential Englishman, the butler to an English lord, is the embodied spirit of *The Remains of the Day*. Such is his pride in his work that we never learn the first name of Mr Stevens, the butler in question and first-person narrator of the novel. The narrative consists of his reflections on life before and after the war, after he receives a letter from a former fellow servant, the housekeeper Miss Kenton.

As he travels to meet her, and as they reminisce about old times, Ishiguro slowly unfolds his picture of Mr Stevens, a butler of impeccable modesty in awe of his father who was a butler before him. Such is his devotion to duty and his unquestioning loyalty to his employer, Lord Darlington, that as his father lay dying of a stroke, Mr Stevens' priority was to make sure that the doctor attended to the sore feet of one of Lord Darlington's guests.

Lord Darlington, we learn, argued for appeasing Germany before the war. Now, after the war, Darlington is dead and an American who lacks the British notion of formality has bought Darlington Hall; he even tries to banter with Mr Stevens. Mr Stevens' old world has gone; and so has Britain's. With the gentlest of nudges, Ishiguro uses Darlington Hall and Mr Stevens to reflect on Britain's loss of status in the wake of World War II – its empire was shrinking rapidly, and the new players on the world stage were America and Russia.

Britain, ever backward-looking, was clinging on to former glories and outdated customs which – it was becoming clear by the time Ishiguro was writing – were leaving it on the sidelines of world affairs. Mr Stevens'

unquestioning dignity, respect and service may, he begins to suspect, have led him, like Britain, to miss out on life's opportunities. Should he have been with his father at his death? Should he have been so unswervingly loyal to Lord Darlington, a Nazi sympathiser like many of the upper class in pre-war Britain?

These suspicions are at their most personal when he considers his relationship with Miss Kenton. Although neither would acknowledge it at the time, there were the beginnings of a romantic connection between them. Miss Kenton did on one occasion attempt a rapprochement, but any feelings between them remained unspoken. Now Miss Kenton is the happily married Mrs Benn, only fleetingly wondering whether she should have married Mr Stevens (if Mr Stevens had ever asked). The opportunity, like so many, has passed. Circumstances have changed.

When he confides his doubts to a friendly stranger on his way back to Darlington Hall, the man suggests that it is better to make the most of the present than to dwell on the past. The evening, he remarks, is, after all, the best part of the day. Mr Stevens resolves to do so, to focus on his service to the new owner and on the evening of his own life, which is what remains of his day.

LEFT: *Sir Kazuo Ishiguro was born in Nagasaki, Japan, in 1954, but moved to England with his family in 1960.*
OPPOSITE: *An early cover of the Booker Prize winner.*

The Joy Luck Club

(1989)

Amy Tan (born 1952)

Amy Tan's first novel is a rare study of the Chinese American experience. Four women born in China and their four daughters born in the USA must come to terms with both generational and cultural clashes to know themselves and their place in a post-war world.

The Joy Luck Club is an informal get-together for four Chinese immigrants to west-coast America, at which they play mahjong, chat and reminisce about their former lives. Its founder, Suyuan Woo, has recently died, and her place at the mahjong table is taken by her daughter. The novel is divided into four sections corresponding to the four winds of mahjong, two containing stories of the daughters and two those of the mothers. Each section is also introduced by an invented parable in the style of a Chinese folk tale. The resulting twenty short stories build up a detailed picture of life in America for first- and second-generation immigrants in 1949, when the novel is set. The search for a Chinese identity frustrates the daughters' attempts to find their own in America; but although mothers and daughters often hurt each other, love and forgiveness bring reconciliation.

Although not autobiographical, *The Joy Luck Club* draws heavily on Amy Tan's own life. Tan had an extremely difficult relationship with her own mother, and one of the reasons she chose not to have children of her own was the fear that a depressive gene might be passed on to them: Tan's grandmother committed suicide; her mother made several attempts to take her own life; and Tan herself suffers from chronic depression.

This genealogy is portrayed in the novel's An-Mei Hsu, whose mother committed suicide. An-Mei herself does not, but it is a subject never far from the surface. An-Mei's daughter Rose was responsible, through inattention, for the death of her brother Bing, who drowned. She is careful and passive in everything, and only later in the novel does she find a voice with which to resist her bullying husband.

Tan herself has had traumatic encounters with death. Her father and older brother died within months of each other when Tan was only fifteen; and as a student it fell to her to identify a fellow student who had been murdered, a shocking experience which, for the next ten years, left her mute on the anniversary.

The novel has been criticised for its reinforcement of crude stereotypes of Chinese social culture, which Tan often portrays as cruel, misogynistic and primitive. Tan's female characters are warm, rich, fully formed people; but the men and boys in *The Joy Luck Club* are all negative figures, pastiches of villains in one way or another. Some have said that these obvious stereotypes are part of the novel's commercial success, offering readers the racist characteristics they expect instead of challenging them. Nevertheless, *The Joy Luck Club* has given an important voice to Chinese Americans, who have often been overlooked among American immigrants in favour of Americans of African, Hispanic and Japanese descent.

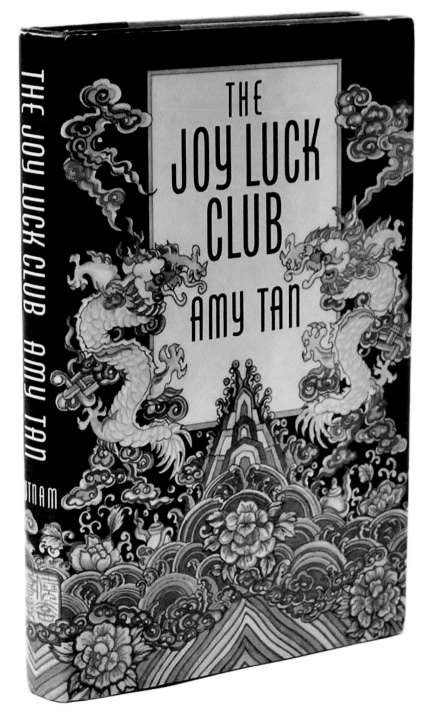

ABOVE: *An original dust jacket of the Putnam First Edition.*
OPPOSITE: *Amy Tan's back story is one of immense upheaval and a succession of traumatic events, not least the discovery that she had three Chinese half-sisters.*

A Suitable Boy

(1993)

Vikram Seth (born 1952)

Set in the early years of India's newly won independence from Britain, Vikram Seth's ostensibly domestic tale of finding a suitable husband considers all the challenges and choices facing an emerging country as it learns to make decisions for itself.

Beginning in 1950 with the wedding of Lata Mehra's older sister, *A Suitable Boy* follows Lata's determination to make her own choice of a husband alongside her mother's attempts to find a suitable boy for her daughter. There's Kabir, with whom Lata first falls in love – but he's a Muslim and she a Hindu. There's Amit Chatterji, her sister-in-law's English-educated brother – but Lata's mother disapproves of the Chatterjis. And there's Haresh, a businessman. He is in love with another woman, whose family disapprove of him; and Lata doesn't think of him as husband material, although her mother does. Yet something about Lata attracts Haresh to her, and there's something about his company that she enjoys.

As the supporters and detractors of each candidate try to influence Lata's choice, Seth makes time to look at the institutions of Indian society – the caste system, the old order of provincial rulers, land reform and the impending first democratic elections in India, which took place in 1952. Although much of the novel takes place in Brahmpur, a fictional town, events also use Calcutta, Delhi and Lucknow as settings, giving Seth the opportunity to observe and comment on choices of greater import to India than that of an appropriate spouse.

Vikram Seth takes his time to tell his story, weaving his intimate plot through a weft of Indian socio-politics and culture. That combination of the personal with the historical has drawn comparisons with Tolstoy's *War and Peace*. There is another similarity: at 1,488 pages in paperback, *A Suitable Boy* is one of the longest novels ever published in English in one volume. This is not a novel for hand-luggage. Seth has acknowledged the influence during the gestation

of the novel of one of the great works of Chinese literature, *Dream of the Red Chamber*, an eighteenth-century epic by Cao Xueqin which charts the fortunes of one family against a backdrop of China's culture, society and place in the world of the time. *Dream of the Red Chamber* is known for the psychology and philosophy with which Cao imbued his characters, and the same can be said of Seth's novel.

Seth began his writing career as a poet, and each of the nineteen chapters of the book is introduced on the contents page at the start of the book by a rhyming couplet. The author has been working on a sequel, *A Suitable Girl*, for at least six years. Originally scheduled for publication in 2017, it remains unfinished because, according to Seth, he has been unable to decide on a suitable ending.

OPPOSITE: Apart from the eventual publication of A Suitable Girl, *Seth plans to return to the 'universe' of* A Suitable Boy *in the future.*
BELOW: Vikram Seth photographed in 1995.

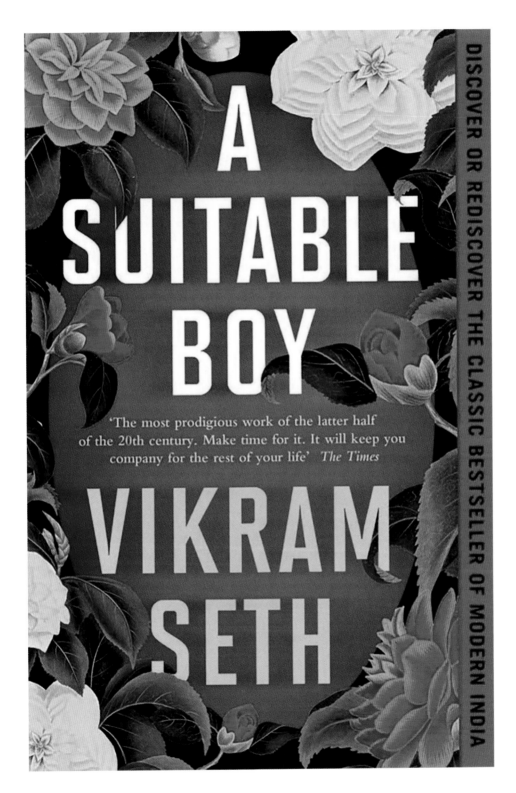

A SUITABLE BOY

'The most prodigious work of the latter half of the 20th century. Make time for it. It will keep you company for the rest of your life' *The Times*

VIKRAM SETH

DISCOVER OR REDISCOVER THE CLASSIC BESTSELLER OF MODERN INDIA

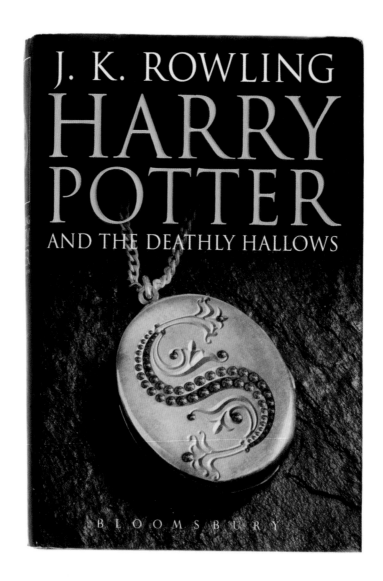

ABOVE: Philosopher's Stone started the series, but the final novel in the Harry Potter story became the fastest-selling novel of all time.
LEFT: J.K. Rowling has named Jessica Mitford as her greatest influence, having received a copy of her autobiography as a teenager.

Harry Potter and the Philosopher's Stone

(1997)

J.K. Rowling (born 1965)

The seven volumes in the series of novels about schoolboy wizard Harry Potter are a publishing phenomenon. It is the best-selling book series in history, with well over half a billion copies sold in over eighty different languages. The final instalment sold 8.3 million copies in the first twenty-four hours of its release.

The first book in the series, *Harry Potter and the Philosopher's Stone* (*Sorcerer's Stone* in the US), remains the third-best-selling individual novel of all time, behind Cervantes' *Don Quixote* and Charles Dickens' *A Tale of Two Cities*. It introduces the major characters of the saga: Harry Potter, and his friends Hermione Granger and Ron Weasley; the teaching staff at Hogwarts, a school for young wizards; and Lord Voldemort, Harry's archenemy, a villain determined to rid the wizarding world of Muggles (those, like Harry, who were not born into a family of pure wizard blood).

Philosopher's Stone describes the circumstances of Harry's admission to Hogwarts, and his attempts to thwart the theft by Voldemort of a magical stone which turns metal to gold and gives its user immortality. The book also introduces Quidditch, an aerial sport played at the school on flying broomsticks with three different kinds of ball. Such is the popularity of the Harry Potter series that a real-life ground-based version of the game has now been devised by fans which even has its own regulating body, the International Quidditch Association. Quidditch has now joined Muggle in the *Oxford English Dictionary*.

Such is the richness of the world which Rowling creates in *Philosopher's Stone* that it contains the seeds of many plotlines in the subsequent volumes in the series. Incidental characters from this first book, such as Sirius Black, take on major roles in later stories. Rowling has been compared to Jane Austen in her plots, her wry observation of social behaviour and the frequent need of Harry and others to re-evaluate their preconceptions in the light of each novel's dramatic events. Like Charles Dickens, Rowling takes great delight in choosing names for her characters which reflect their attributes, often using classical or literary allusions. One of Harry's schoolboy enemies, for example, is Draco Malfoy (from the French for 'bad faith'), whose henchmen are ungainly Vincent Crabbe and ugly Gregory Goyle. Rowling's writing is playful, reflecting her own pleasure in literature.

Despite the magical premise of *Harry Potter and the Philosopher's Stone*, J.K. Rowling has said that the main theme of the series is death. The first novel begins with an explanation of the death of Harry's parents at the hands of Lord Voldemort (whose name is French for 'flight of death'). Voldemort's quest for immortality is aided in later episodes by frightening spirits called the Death Eaters.

The book connects with a number of classic literary genres. There are elements of mystery and detection, fantasy and the supernatural, horror in the very real threat of Voldemort, a central battle between Good and Evil, all framed in a very traditional British schoolboy story. Although the young age of the protagonists in *Philosopher's Stone* encouraged the publishers to aim the book at children (among whom it has been popular from the beginning), J.K. Rowling objects to any distinction between young and adult fiction; and editions of the books have been published with more nuanced covers for adults who did not want to be seen reading a so-called 'children's book'.

The God of Small Things

(1997)

Arundhati Roy (born 1961)

Love, leading only to sorrow, separation and death, haunts the pages of Arundhati Roy's first novel, set in the province of Kerala, India. Social convention and discrimination make it impossible to form untainted relationships; and without love, each character's life is destroyed by deception and betrayal.

It is the small things of the title which make the difference in life. The great central tragedy of *The God of Small Things* is caused by a glimpse, by a child, Rahel, of a family servant, Velutha, at a political rally. Everything spirals from there.

Rahel's aunt, Baby Kochamma, humiliated at the rally, victimises Velutha, whom Rahel and her twin brother Estha therefore befriend. Pleased at the friendship, Rahel and Estha's mother Ammu begins an affair with Velutha. When the affair is discovered, Ammu blames Estha and Rahel, who decide to run away from home with their cousin Sophie. As they cross a river by boat, Sophie drowns. Velutha, wrongly held responsible for Sophie's death because of false testimony, is beaten by police and dies in prison.

Ammu and the twins are expelled from the family home for their supposed negligence around Sophie's death. Ammu dies alone; and the twins are split up, only to be reunited years later in a forbidden act of love in which they share 'not happiness, but hideous grief'. The novel closes with memories of the only genuinely happy love affair in the book, but one made impossible because Ammu is a Christian of the business class and Velutha an untouchable Hindu.

The God of Small Things is not told chronologically but pieced together episodically, in flashes backwards and forwards in time. As Roy writes in the novel, 'the Great Stories are the ones you have heard and want to hear again. The ones you can enter anywhere and inhabit comfortably.'

The third-person narrative is broadly from Rahel's perspective, but some events are returned to and seen through different eyes. This apparently disjointed form of storytelling is designed to convey the complexity of the lives of the characters, and of society in India.

Indian society has many divisions – of language, of religion, of caste, of race. All these socially accepted barriers seem designed to thwart rather than ease social interaction in post-colonial India. Sophie, whose mother was English, is racially disadvantaged compared to the twins because they are 'all wog', while she is only 'half-wog'. In this India of the 1960s, even language is a barrier: some Indians still hold England and English in the highest regard while others look to a political future. Love is forbidden, Roy suggests, which does not fit in with these social constructs: the love between the twins, between Ammu and Velutha. Even within the same religion there are barriers: Baby Kochamma earns the disapproval of her Syrian Christian family by joining a Catholic Christian monastery in order to be near her forbidden love, a Catholic priest.

Roy's non-chronological narrative reflects the many obstacles and interruptions which all the characters experience, and those which lie in India's path. Love, the Great Story to which she refers, is too powerful to be constrained by convention; but convention seeks to destroy love, that most anarchic of emotions, because of its threat to social stability. Love is a tragedy.

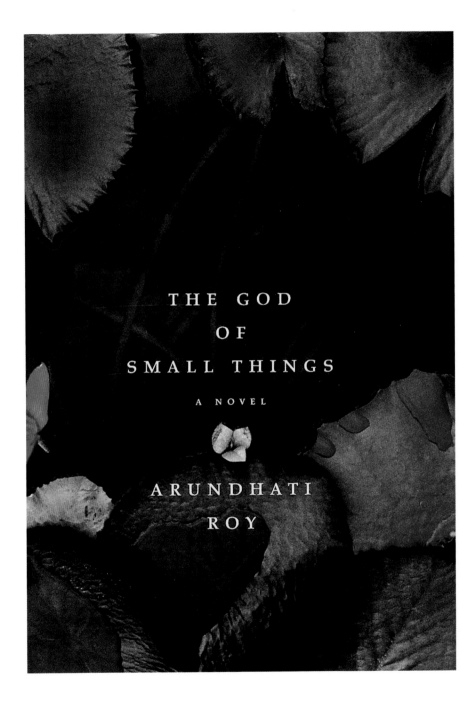

ABOVE: *After writing two screenplays,* The God of Small Things *was Roy's debut novel.*

OPPOSITE: *Arundhati Roy in 1997. A ceaseless activist, she has used her platform to campaign on many social and environmental issues.*

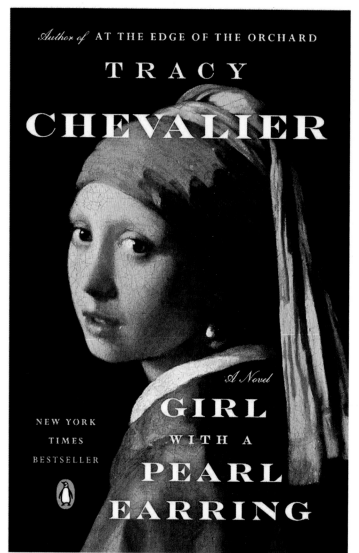

ABOVE: Before writing Girl with a Pearl Earring, *Tracy Chevalier worked as an editorial assistant on Macmillan's* Dictionary of Art.

LEFT: The novel and subsequent film helped Amsterdam's Rijksmuseum sell out 450,000 tickets for their 2023 Vermeer exhibition in record time.

Girl with a Pearl Earring

(1999)

Tracy Chevalier (born 1962)

By an extraordinary coincidence, not one but four fine novels about Dutch artists arrived in bookshops in 1999. Only one of them managed to recreate with words the subtlety and restraint which Johannes Vermeer, the painter of *Girl with a Pearl Earring*, achieved with light and colour.

Tracy Chevalier has had a poster of Vermeer's painting on her wall since she was nineteen. That girl, that glance, that earring – they have watched over her wherever she has lived, from Washington, D.C. to London, England. At the age of thirty-five, having been in its company for sixteen years, Chevalier's curiosity about what lay behind that intriguing stare – knowing yet innocent, a word or a gasp hanging on her lips – drove her to write *Girl with a Pearl Earring*.

The model for the painting has not been identified, and very little is known of the artist's life. He lived all his life in Delft, and with his wife he had fifteen children. Was the girl one of his daughters, or a mistress, or a member of the household staff? Chevalier took clues from the few paintings definitely painted by Vermeer – fewer than three dozen, several of which are incorporated into the novel's plot.

In Chevalier's imagination the girl is Griet, a housemaid from a poor family sent to work in the Vermeer household. Housemaids are regarded with suspicion because they have a reputation for stealing, or for seducing their masters; and one of Vermeer's daughters, Cornelia, distrusts her. Another daughter, Maertge, befriends her. Griet becomes interested in the work of her master and shows an understanding of the craft, and Vermeer entrusts her with errands to buy art materials.

They develop a friendly relationship, although on the advice of Vermeer's friend Antonie van Leeuwenhoek (in reality the executor of the artist's will) she is careful not to overstep the mark. One of Vermeer's patrons, Pieter van Ruijven (who was the sitter in Vermeer's painting *The Concert*), is attracted to Griet and takes advantage of her lowly status. He asks Vermeer to paint a double portrait of the pair, but Vermeer suggests discreetly that it would be better to paint such a portrait of van Ruijven and his wife, and to paint a separate picture of Griet which van Ruijven can buy. Vermeer asks Griet to have her ears pierced so that, for the portrait, she can wear earrings belonging to Vermeer's wife. When Cornelia reveals this to her mother, Griet is sacked. Only years later, after Vermeer's death, does she discover the depth of Vermeer's feelings for her.

Girl with a Pearl Earring is painstakingly written, with a great deal of visual description, as befits its artistic world. The narrative proceeds at a gentle pace, emphasising the restraint exercised by both Griet and Vermeer and evoking the subtle use of colour of which Vermeer was a master. Chevalier's detail of seventeenth-century Dutch life and of Vermeer's painting process are completely convincing and the result is that, by the end, the reader feels that they have read a Vermeer.

As evidence of the impact of *Girl with a Pearl Earring*, an exhibition of works by Vermeer and the Delft School at the Metropolitan Museum of Art in New York in 2001 attracted twice as many visitors as another Vermeer show at the National Gallery of Art in Washington in 1996, before the novel was published. The other novels drawing on Dutch art in 1999 were Susan Vreeland's *Girl in Hyacinth Blue*, Katharine Weber's *The Music Lesson* and Deborah Moggach's *Tulip Fever*.

Atonement

(2001)

Ian McEwan (born 1948)

A story whose happy ending the novel's fictional author admits to having made up, *Atonement* is a metafictional enquiry into whether it is possible to atone for past mistakes; and if so, how. In a tale of wilful misidentification and misdirection, can one trust an author of fiction to tell the truth?

Briony, a thirteen-year-old girl, misunderstands the nature of sex. When she discovers her older sister and boyfriend making love, she perceives it as a violent attack by the young man, Robbie. When she later witnesses the genuine sexual assault of her fifteen-year-old cousin, she assumes that Robbie is again to blame and reports him to the police. Four years later, as World War II erupts, Robbie is released from prison on the condition that he join the British Army, and as a member of the British Expeditionary Force he is caught up in the underprepared army's disastrous retreat to Dunkirk. On the eve of evacuation from the French coast, injured Robbie falls asleep ...

What happens next is not entirely true. It transpires that an adult Briony is the author of this story. Having realised her mistake and the effect of it for Cecilia and Robbie, she wants to atone. But some things cannot be undone. Should she try to clear Robbie's name? Should she apologise to Cecilia? Should she rewrite history by admitting her juvenile ignorance and error? Or by denying its consequences? *Atonement* concludes with a diary entry written by Briony in 1999 in which she tries to justify her approach to atonement, however fictitious it may be, as an act of kindness to the lovers whose happiness she destroyed.

Briony's mistake is compounded by class as well as by her youth. Her family own land and property; Robbie is the son of their housekeeper. Briony's father paid for Robbie to go to university; but Robbie is nevertheless from servant stock in Briony's eyes. His use of lewd language in a love letter to Cecilia, which Briony reads, plants the idea that he is a crude and violent man.

Ian McEwan's novel is as much a reflection on writing as it is a work of fiction. Fiction is by its very nature an invention, an idealisation of events manipulated by

the author to suit his plots and themes. As readers we know that novels are made up, and in that sense not true. However we willingly suspend our disbelief for the pleasure of reading them; and in so doing we rely on the author to be truthful about the world which he or she has created for us.

To what extent then does a fiction writer tell the truth? McEwan's use of historical events in World War II heightens the plausibility of Briony's storyline and we believe Ian McEwan's initial version of his story; but Briony doesn't tell the truth and Briony is herself a fiction created by McEwan for his own purposes. *Atonement* is Briony's fictional reality cloaked in McEwan's fictional reality.

Truth and fiction mingle in both McEwan's novel and Briony's. The agonising difference between Briony's fiction and McEwan's truth about the fates of Cecilia and Robbie are the book's emotional knockout blow. The possibility of atonement for the past remains an open question.

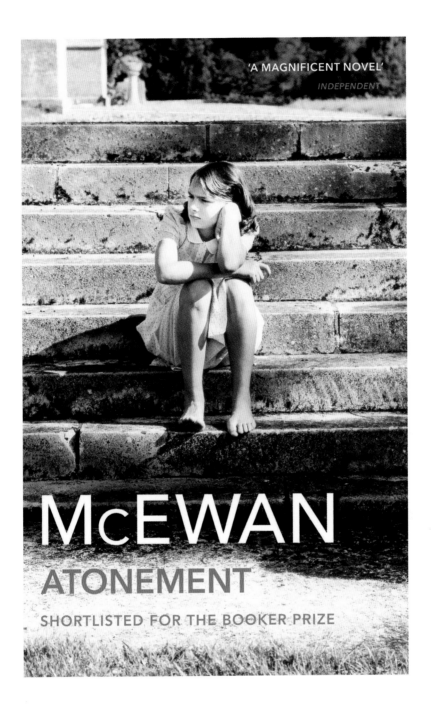

'A MAGNIFICENT NOVEL'
INDEPENDENT

McEWAN
ATONEMENT

SHORTLISTED FOR THE BOOKER PRIZE

ABOVE: *McEwan was nominated for, but didn't win, the 2001 Booker Prize for Atonement, one of six Booker nominations to date.*
OPPOSITE: *Ian McEwan at the 2007 Edinburgh Book Festival.*

Life of Pi

(2001)

Yann Martel (born 1963)

A novel rooted in philosophy and religion invites questions about reality, credibility and belief. Why, Yann Martel asks, is one unbelievable fiction more acceptable than another? And why do we need stories, or religions, at all?

Pi is the son of a zoo manager in the Indian city of Pondicherry. The central story of *The Life of Pi* is Pi's narrative description of his 227 days lost at sea in a lifeboat shared with a Bengal tiger called Richard Parker, which emerges from beneath a tarpaulin and devours a hyena (that has killed a zebra and orangutan), but with whom Pi develops a relationship of mutual respect and support.

This charming but unlikely tale is introduced, in the manner of *Don Quixote*, by a note from Yann Martel describing how he came across the story while searching for inspiration in India after the failure of his first two novels. He tells of his meetings with Pi, in the course of which Pi showed him newspaper cuttings and his diaries to confirm the events he was describing to Martel.

The novel closes in similar fashion, with a supposed transcript of conversations with Pi in hospital where he was recovering from his ordeal. It is noted that some of his two Japanese interviewers' remarks to each other have been translated from the original recording, and the layout of the text reflects that. The idea of a tape recording, like Martel's version of the genesis of his book, is designed to convey the impression that all of this really happened, however improbable it sounds.

The reader is not taken in by these devices, but nevertheless willingly suspends their disbelief for the pleasure of the story. It's what fiction readers do. Pi's interviewers, on the other hand, do not believe his version of events, and Pi therefore offers them another. Following the shipwreck which cast him adrift, he finds himself in a lifeboat with his mother, the ship's cook

and a young Chinese sailor, whose broken leg the cook amputates to use as fishing bait. When the sailor dies the cook eats him, to the horror of Pi and his mother. The cook then kills her and hurls her severed head at Pi, who kills the cook in fury and eats parts of his flesh and organs. Afterwards, Pi tells his interviewers, 'Solitude began. I turned to God. I survived.' Which story is more acceptable? And which more credible? Pi's interlocutors choose, on balance, the one with the tiger.

Pi has indeed turned to God. At the age of fourteen, long before the shipwreck, although he was raised a Hindu, he has embraced Christianity and Islam, because he just wants 'to love God'. Each religion has advantages and philosophical insights; and from their three stories Pi gains a greater understanding of God. Episodes in the first part of the novel suggest that it is perfectly possible to have more than one story, or one God: Pi recalls an occasion when two visitors to his father's zoo – one an atheist and one a devout Muslim – both had exactly the same name.

In real life an extraordinary coincidence was one of Martel's inspirations for the book. Prompted by a character called Richard Parker in Edgar Allan Poe's *The Narrative of Arthur Gordon Pym of Nantucket* (1838), a mutineer who is cannibalised, Martel came across another Richard Parker who was lost at sea. This third Richard Parker came to light in a story by Jack London based on the 1846 sinking of the *Francis Spaight*. Richard Parker was drowned, but the cabin boy, who escaped on a lifeboat, was cannibalised. Truth can be brutally stranger than fiction.

OVER
FOURTEEN
MILLION
COPIES
SOLD

WINNER
OF THE
MAN
BOOKER
PRIZE

a novel

Life of Pi

Yann Martel

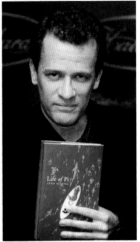

ABOVE: Canadian author Yann Martel's first language is French, but he writes in English.
LEFT: The novel became an international bestseller, spending sixty-one weeks on The New York Times bestseller list. It has been adapted for the theatre in a variety of forms; the most recent version transferred to London's West End winning five Olivier awards in 2022.

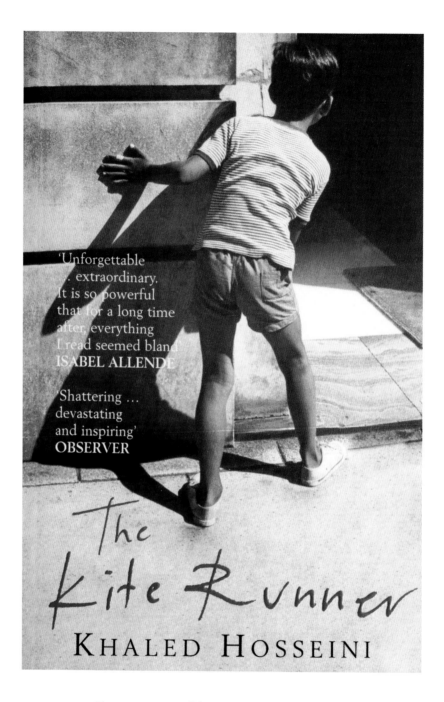

'Unforgettable
... extraordinary.
It is so powerful
that for a long time
after, everything
I read seemed bland'
ISABEL ALLENDE

'Shattering ...
devastating
and inspiring'
OBSERVER

The
Kite Runner
KHALED HOSSEINI

ABOVE: The Kite Runner *started life as a 25-page short story, which was rejected by* The New Yorker *magazine and temporarily put aside by Hosseini.*
OPPOSITE: Hosseini has subsequently become a Goodwill Envoy for the United Nations High Commissioner for Refugees.

The Kite Runner

(2003)

Khaled Hosseini (born 1965)

Afghanistan, divided by ethnic distinctions, invaded by Russia and oppressed by the rise of the Taliban, is the setting for a tale of guilt and redemption, of fathers and sons, and of poetic justice. The unhappy country's rifts amplify fractures in families and friendships.

The Soviet Union invaded Afghanistan in 1979, fighting a long and futile war there before withdrawing. The Taliban, Afghanistan's Islamic fundamentalist movement, ruled the country from 1996 until its overthrow by the United States in 2001 in the wake of the 9/11 terrorist attacks. Khaled Hosseini and his parents were able to flee the country in 1980 and found asylum in the US. Many of his childhood friends were not so lucky. The survivor guilt which he experienced at having avoided both the Soviet-Afghan War and the Taliban's regime found expression at last in *The Kite Runner*. It was published in the same year that he returned to his native country for the first time since he left as a fifteen-year-old.

The Taliban announced in 1999 that it was banning kite-flying. The news shocked Hosseini, who grew up in Kabul enjoying the sport of kite-fighting. His response, initially a short story, became his first novel. It is the story of two inseparable childhood friends, Amir (a Pashtun) and Hassan (a Hazara). Amir's father has always treated the boys as if they were brothers, even favouring Hassan on occasion and paying for the treatment of Hassan's harelip. Amir sometimes resents this.

Another boy, Assef (half-Pashtun, half-German) criticises Amir for his friendship with a Hazara, threatening to beat him up. Hassan comes to Amir's defence, promising to shoot Assef's eye out with his slingshot if he tries to bully Amir again. Assef swears to avenge this humiliation and one day beats and rapes Hassan in an alley. Amir witnesses the assault but is too cowardly to step in. The friendship is irreparably damaged.

This is the guilt which Amir must assuage. He did not come to Hassan's rescue in the alley because he was trying to salvage a kite to please his father. Divided loyalty – the choice between a father and a friend, a friend who has been like a brother – is the universally understood central theme of *The Kite Runner*. Amir has betrayed the paternal care shown by his father to Hassan, and redemption is required.

There is an air of Greek tragedy in the way that Hosseini manipulates his characters. Many years later, Hassan is dead at the hands of the Taliban, and beyond any act of redemption which Amir could make. The bully Assef, on the other hand, has thrived under Taliban rule. It is only when Hassan's son Sohrab fulfils a promise made by his father that Amir can carry his own father's kindness forward to the next generation, adopting Sohrab as his own son. Thus, redemption is achieved.

The tensions between fathers and sons, and the bonds between generations, drive the story of *The Kite Runner*. Afghanistan may be the setting but these themes cross all borders. *The Kite Runner* is part of a healthy globalisation of fiction which has introduced authors to an international readership, and readers to cultures far beyond their own with which, they may find, they have far more in common than they realised.

Cloud Atlas

(2004)

David Mitchell (born 1969)

A mind-bending fusion of six different stories in a multitude of literary styles, the novel spans several ages and contains contemporary, speculative, historical and science fiction, metafiction, comedy, mystery, and even – for one of the tales – an imaginary language.

David Mitchell is no novice in the matter of multiple threads. His first novel, *Ghostwritten* (1999), is told by nine different narrators through nine different stories. *Cloud Atlas*, his third book, may have fewer threads; but its ambition to tell them in so many different ways sets the novel apart.

The stories of *Cloud Atlas* are presented in their chronological order, with settings in the mid-nineteenth century, 1931, 1975, 2004, and near and distant futures. The narrator of each is aware of all the previous ones, and the first five are left on a cliffhanger. Each story is further framed as a story within a story by its narrator. The sixth is told from beginning to end, and then the others are concluded in reverse order.

This mirroring device allows Mitchell to lead the reader forwards and then backwards in time. It reinforces the idea of humanity's unchanging instincts, which is central to the novel. All the principal characters with the exception of Adam Ewing, the first, are reincarnations of earlier ones, identified symbolically in the novel by all having the same birthmark. By failing to learn the lessons of history they are doomed to repeat them. Mankind's best and worst acts are the product of unchallenged beliefs as a result of which, Ewing concludes, 'a purely predatory world shall consume itself'. One must break the cycle of violence by changing one's beliefs, as Ewing does by deciding to support the abolition of slavery.

Mitchell has acknowledged the influence of other authors on the structure of *Cloud Atlas*. Italo Calvino's *If on a Winter's Night a Traveler* (1979)

similarly frames a number of incomplete narratives with the device of a reader trying to read a book called *If on a Winter's Night a Traveler*. Calvino further challenges the form of the novel by directly addressing the reader in the second person about the coming chapter; Mitchell adds to Calvino's device by providing endings to the unfinished stories of *Cloud Atlas*.

Mitchell has also paid tribute to Russell Hoban's *Riddley Walker*. Both that novel and the sixth tale in *Cloud Atlas* are set in a post-apocalyptic world whose inhabitants speak a curious dialect, an imagined evolution of English which their respective authors transliterate on the page. The texts are an entertaining challenge both for the English-speaking reader and the literary translator.

The title of the novel is a reference to the ever-changing sky under which humans live, a contrast to the fixity of human nature. It is borrowed from a piece of music by Japanese composer Toshi Ichiyanagi, which

Mitchell bought purely for the poetry of the title. Ichiyanagi was Yoko Ono's first husband; Mitchell's second novel *number9dream* (2001) was named after a song by Ono's third husband John Lennon, a pattern which amused Mitchell but which (he has joked) he couldn't sustain indefinitely.

LEFT: Following university, Mitchell moved to Hiroshima, Japan, and absorbed Japanese cultural influences while teaching English to technical students.

OPPOSITE: The First Edition US paperback published by Random House.

CLOUD ATLAS

"Not just dazzling, amusing, or clever but heartbreaking and passionate, too.
I've never read anything quite like it." —MICHAEL CHABON

CLOUD ATLAS

A Novel

David Mitchell

AUTHOR OF *GHOSTWRITTEN* AND *NUMBER9DREAM*

Vintage Canada

The Girl with the Dragon Tattoo

(2005)

Stieg Larsson (1954–2004)

The novel originally called *Men Who Hate Women* is better known to the world by the title under which it was translated into English. Powered by the author's anger at injustice, both moral and legal, in Swedish society, the novel was the first in a series which has sold more than 100 million books to date.

Stieg Larsson was, like his central character Mikael Blomkvist, an investigative journalist. He was incensed by persistent violence against women, immorality in big business and the Nazism of a significant minority in Sweden. He believed that it was a reporter's duty to uncover evil rigorously wherever it occurred, and not to be cowardly about doing so. Larsson had revealed enough corruption and cruelty to irritate many powerful people, and he was cautious about protecting his private life. For example, he did not marry his long-term partner, because under Swedish law he would then have had to publish his home address, which he did not want his enemies to discover.

There must have been many stories which he did not have enough evidence to report; and Larsson poured all his anger that perpetrators were escaping justice into *The Girl with the Dragon Tattoo* and its two sequels. One shocking starting point for his move into fiction was that as a teenager he witnessed, or (accounts differ) heard of someone who witnessed a brutal sexual assault of a woman by several men and did nothing to intervene. Two violent honour-killings by men of women in Sweden took place when he was starting to write *Dragon Tattoo*, which further fuelled his anger. During the writing of the novel Larsson corresponded regularly with his niece Therese, a teenage goth who longed to get a tattoo of a dragon, to ask how she would react in certain situations. His partner, Eva Gabrielsson, also contributed to the discussion of plot and character, as many partners of authors have.

The plot of *Dragon Tattoo* concerns the discovery of the abuse and murder of

women by men at the highest levels of Swedish industry. The truth about the disappearance of a woman forty years earlier is painstakingly pieced together by Blomkvist and his unusual sidekick Lisbeth Salander, an asocial computer hacker. It's written with dark, ironic humour and – despite its disturbing subject – a playfulness of language and plot which confirm Larsson's genius for the genre.

Its hero Blomkvist writes for *Millennium* magazine, and Larsson intended to write ten books in his projected Millennium series. Only three were complete at the time of his sudden death of a heart attack in 2004. All three were published posthumously, and the Millennium Decalogy became a Trilogy. Larsson had made extensive notes for the plots of several future books in the series, including one almost complete novel, on Gabrielsson's laptop, which she felt competent to complete.

Without a marriage or a legal will, however, all rights and royalties from his novels reverted to his surviving father and brother, and Gabrielsson was not legally

allowed to complete the unfinished work. Instead, in 2013, Larsson's Swedish publishers commissioned another author and crime journalist, David Lagercrantz, to write another three Millennium novels; and eight years later, when the rights changed hands again, a new publisher commissioned a further three volumes, from the Swedish author Karin Smirnoff. None of these additions to the series can draw on Larsson's surviving outlines for the series.

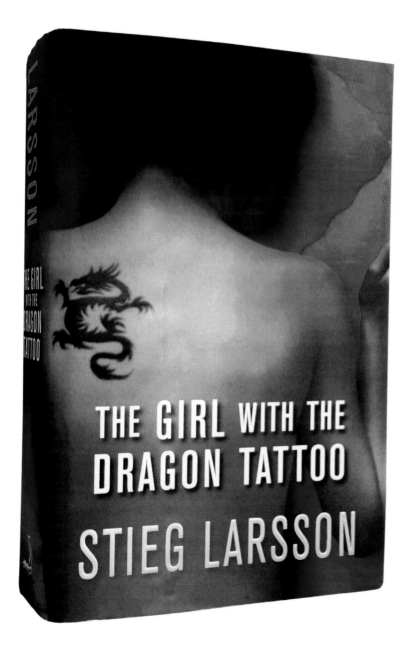

LEFT: What had started out as a decalogy with Män som hatar kvinnor (Men Who Hate Women) *became a trilogy after Larsson suffered a heart attack.*
OPPOSITE: Stieg Larsson photographed at his desk of the Swedish news agency TT in 1994.

CORMAC McCARTHY

THE ROAD

"His tale of survival and the miracle of goodness only adds to McCarthy's stature as a living master. It's gripping, frightening and, ultimately, beautiful. It might very well be the best book of the year, period."
—*San Francisco Chronicle*

The Road

(2006)

Cormac McCarthy (born 1933)

'When everything's gone, the only thing left to eat is each other.' Thus the author of a novel of post-apocalyptic America has described the premise for a father-and-son road trip with a difference. After a massive extinction event, starvation and cannibals stalk the ash-blanketed land in a literary horror landmark.

The Road is dedicated to Cormac McCarthy's son, and the initial inspiration for the novel was a visit to El Paso by the pair, during which the author wondered what the place would look like a hundred years hence, and what his son's future might hold. Conversations between them also steered the book, and McCarthy has on occasion credited his son as a co-author. Separately, McCarthy and his brother used to toss around ideas about what form a possible apocalypse might take, and one of their imagined outcomes involved cannibalism.

Thus The Road sets the vast, ruined North American landscape against the intimate conversations shared and dangers faced by a father and a son together. That close relationship, under the most harrowing of circumstances, is the warm heart of the novel, while the threats which they meet along the way – kidnap, hunger, and the desperation of others in this grey, post-industrial world – are its chilling atmosphere.

It is part coming-of-age story, part killer-chiller. The Road rises above mere horror schlock by virtue of McCarthy's striking prose style. He is terse, and his short direct sentences drive the narrative along. More than that, he eschews a lot of punctuation. He regards inverted commas for speech as 'weird little marks' that unnecessarily 'blot the page up'; and although he is prepared on occasion to use a colon, he considers semi-colons idiotic.

The comma is his worst enemy and he prefers to use the word 'and' in its place, often stringing many main clauses together in a single sentence this way. Without the comma, which is generally an indication to the reader to pause and take a breath before the next clause or phrase, we are left breathless in McCarthy's writing. The Road is a new way to tell a story.

McCarthy is notorious for the violence in his novels, which also include Blood Meridian (1985) and No Country for Old Men (2005). In an interview with Richard Woodward of the New York Times he said, 'There is no such thing as life without bloodshed' and was labelled 'the great pessimist of American literature'. Although his vision in The Road is certainly bloodshot, the closeness of the unnamed father and son which he creates suggests a reluctant softer side to the author. Early in the novel

the father tells his son that, in a dog-eat-dog world, they are the good guys; and at the novel's conclusion the son meets up with another wandering family, who reassure him that they too are the good guys. There are, even for McCarthy, some grounds for hope in the future of mankind.

LEFT: Cormac McCarthy has won many plaudits in a long writing career, but The Road *won him his first Pulitzer.*
OPPOSITE: The Road *was based on many conversations with his son John.*

Half of a Yellow Sun

(2006)

Chimamanda Ngozi Adichie (born 1977)

Set against the backdrop of bitter Nigerian civil war in the 1960s, a novel of loyalty and betrayal moves back and forth in time to look at the causes and consequences of the conflict through the eyes of five people caught up in it. Post-colonial politics and the strength of women are central themes.

After Nigeria won its independence from Britain in 1960, long suppressed ethnic tensions rose to the surface in the country. The Igbo people, dissatisfied with the ruling Hausa and Fulani ethnic groups, seceded from Nigeria and established the independent state of Biafra. In the ensuing war and blockade, hundreds of thousands of Igbo men, women and children died of deliberate starvation and slaughter by the Nigerian army. International interest centred on access to the lucrative oil fields of the Niger delta. Biafra, whose flag carried half a yellow sun on a background of red, black and green, fell in 1970. More than fifty years later, tensions still simmer close to the surface in Nigeria.

Chimamanda Ngozi Adichie was born in 1977 to an academic Igbo family. The family lost everything it owned in the war, and both Adichie's grandfathers were killed. In the novel, the much-loved aunt and uncle of one of the central characters die in a massacre.

Naturally all the protagonists in *Half of a Yellow Sun* are changed by the war. The novel opens and closes with young Ugwu, a houseboy who is conscripted into the Biafran army and forced to commit atrocities. Ugwu works for Odenigbo and Olanna, whose relationship is put under severe test by the war and by Odenigbo's infidelity – their baby is not Olanna's but the result of Odenigbo's affair.

The war forces Odenigbo to flee the university at Nsukka (at which Adichie's parents worked) where he was the centre of an intellectual circle. Ugwu, Olanna and Odenigbo escape to a refugee camp run by Olanna's twin sister Kainene and Kainene's boyfriend Richard, a white journalist.

Through Richard, Adichie explores the attitudes of the white world to Black Africa and to the war. Richard enthusiastically and romantically embraces the creation of Biafra and feels himself to be Biafran. He wants to write a novel about the new country, but is unable to complete it – and as Adichie has commented, perhaps it's time for African stories to be told by Africans. Richard is more effective in reporting the Biafran war to the world, and is shocked at the obsession of the press corps with the disappearance of one white man in the conflict which was claiming the lives of so many thousands of Biafrans. He notes this, 'the rule of Western journalism: One hundred dead black people equal one dead white person.'

It's been a long time coming, but the rest of the world is finally waking up to the riches of literature from the African continent. The spark lit by Chinua Achebe's *Things Fall Apart* in 1958 is now a living flame. Adichie grew up in a house on the campus of Nsukka University once occupied by Achebe. *Things Fall Apart* (also centred on an Igbo character) is a standard text taught in African schools, and Achebe has praised Adichie's storytelling ability and her bravery in writing about the war, which erupted long after *Things Fall Apart* was published. *Half of a Yellow Sun* in turn inspired Achebe's last book, published in 2012 just before his death in 2013: the non-fiction memoir *There Was a Country: A Personal History of Biafra*.

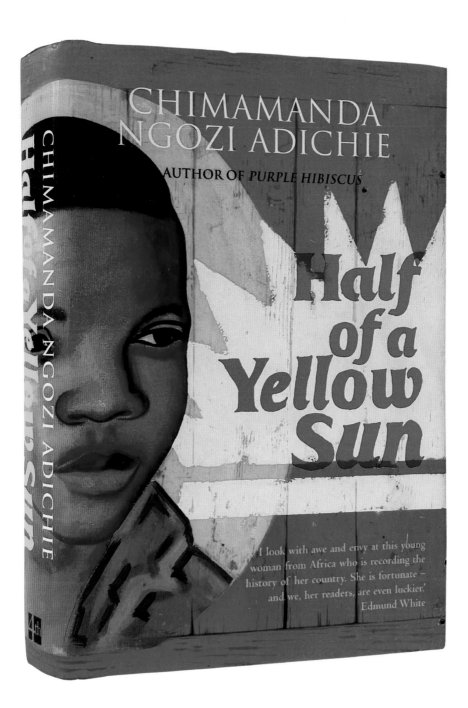

ABOVE: *Published by 4th Estate in the UK,* Half of a Yellow Sun *was Adichie's second novel following the critically acclaimed* Purple Hibiscus *(2003).*
OPPOSITE: *Chimamanda Ngozi Adichie photographed in 2009.*

100 Novels That Changed the World_____209

Wolf Hall

(2009)

Hilary Mantel (1952–2022)

A historical novel in its setting, a contemporary study of human behaviour in its plot and characters, Hilary Mantel's Tudor saga is so authentic on both counts that it changed the British public's perception of its own history. Her narrative places the reader at events which shaped a nation.

Hilary Mantel's trilogy about the life of Thomas Cromwell was the spectacular finale to a successful career as a novelist which encompassed both contemporary and historical fiction. Her subjects for the latter have included central figures in the French Revolution, and the pioneering Scottish anatomist John Hunter's efforts to procure the skeleton of a living Irish giant.

Thomas Cromwell (1485–1540) was the son of an innkeeper who rose by his own ability and opportunism to occupy the highest offices in the court of Henry VIII. The facts of that period of history are well documented. Cromwell's personal reputation was cemented in the public consciousness by Robert Bolt's 1960 play *A Man for All Seasons*, which portrayed him as a calculating, scheming figure. Bolt's characterisation was a dramatic device to contrast with the moral rectitude of the play's hero Thomas More, a Catholic philosopher and statesman.

Mantel, who was raised as a Catholic, offered in *Wolf Hall* a far more sympathetic portrait of Cromwell. In her hands he becomes a talented, tolerant man making pragmatic decisions for the good of the country as he saw it, at a time of great religious upheaval – the Reformation of the Church in England.

Cromwell's long career makes him a useful figure through whom to witness many significant moments of English history. Most of Henry VIII's six marriages were made for political advantage, although the family home of his one love match, Jane Seymour, gave *Wolf Hall* its title. The Tudors modernised the British monarchy and greatly expanded the nation's bureaucracy. Henry VIII broke away from the Catholic influence of the Vatican and established the Protestant Church of England. Mantel's research was meticulous, and extended to keeping retrospective diaries for all her historic characters, to ensure that their interactions were historically possible in time and place.

Mantel's authoritative account of history combines in *Wolf Hall* with her undisputed ability to tell a good story, and her warm understanding of human nature. Those in high Tudor office made difficult decisions from which the rest of us should be grateful for being spared, because they chose paths without our twenty-first-century advantage of knowing how things turned out. It was Mantel's intention to draw the reader so completely into the events which she described that they were too close to judge – to be present during hunting parties and royal audiences, lacking information which might have changed the course of history, proceeding as wisely as possible towards a future not yet known, and not knowing what good or bad luck may later affect the outcome.

The same combination of wisdom and ignorance guides all our actions, and Mantel's Cromwell trilogy – *Wolf Hall*, *Bring Up the Bodies* and *The Mirror and the Light* – is about as contemporary a work of historical fiction as it is possible to be.

ABOVE: *A copy of the US First Edition hardback.*

OPPOSITE: *Hilary Mantel set an almost unmatchable standard for historical fiction with her trilogy about the life of Thomas Cromwell.*

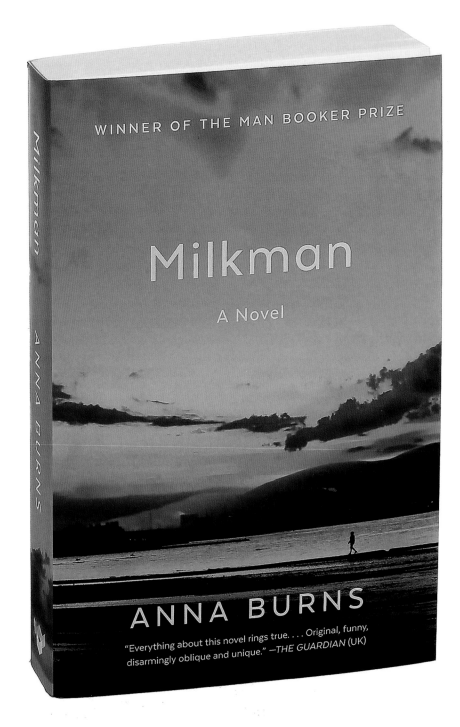

WINNER OF THE MAN BOOKER PRIZE

Milkman

A Novel

ANNA BURNS

"Everything about this novel rings true. . . . Original, funny, disarmingly oblique and unique." —THE GUARDIAN (UK)

ABOVE: *The unnamed narrator of Milkman is known simply as 'middle sister'.*
OPPOSITE: *In 2018 Anna Burns became the first woman from Northern Ireland to win the Booker Prize.*

Milkman

(2018)

Anna Burns (born 1962)

When the violence of 'The Troubles' in Northern Ireland was at its height in the 1970s, every act, or failure to act, became a political statement of whose side one was on. Dark humour, in the inimitable accent of the Northern Irish people, was a vital weapon in the battle for sanity.

Euphemistically referred to as 'The Troubles', the civil war in Northern Ireland pitted Catholic against Protestant, those who wanted reunification with the Republic of Ireland against those who wished to remain in the Union of Great Britain and Northern Ireland – itself the result of the earlier civil war which won independence for most of Ireland from Britain. In the Troubles, paramilitary forces fought each other, the Northern Ireland police and the British Army.

Carrying far greater authority than any of the legal forces of law and order, paramilitary leaders ruled their communities through fear and violence, and the eighteen-year-old protagonist of *Milkman* is being stalked by one such man – older, married, powerful, a dangerous man to be seen with and a hard man to say no to.

There are no proper names in *Milkman*. The girl, the narrator, has no name; her stalker is simply 'the milkman'; her male friend is 'maybe-boyfriend'; her best friend is 'longest friend from primary school'; even the city in which *Milkman* is set is unnamed. Milkman's persistent stalking causes her friends to speculate that the girl really is having an affair with him. She is shunned by her community, and maybe-boyfriend becomes distant. In an attempt to hide from awkward conversations the girl takes to reading-while-walking, burying her head in books to escape from politics; but even this distances her further from her peers, as longest-friend points out.

Mere reading can be seen as a political act; even not engaging with politics is political; and when maybe-boyfriend buys a new supercharger for his car, the fact that it is labelled 'Made in Great Britain' puts him at political risk.

A woman gives the girl pills which make her ill. When the woman, 'tablets girl' is found dead the following day, Milkman is suspected of murdering her in revenge for making the girl sick. Maybe-boyfriend becomes not-boyfriend and reveals that he is actually in love with his (male) best friend. The girl resigns herself to going on a date with Milkman, but he is shot dead by the British Army before their tryst. When another suitor, Somebody McSomebody, is chased away by the women of the community, the girl is at last free to return to some sort of normal life amidst the Troubles.

Northern Ireland remains a divided country, and the setting for Anna Burns' novel can still stir deep and violent emotions. Burns is eminently qualified to tackle it. She grew up in a Catholic area of Belfast at the time in which *Milkman* takes place. Her narrator speaks with an authentic Belfast accent, a rare thing to find on paper. Furthermore, Anna Burns is a woman; and it has always been left to the women of Northern Ireland, while the men were out fighting and maiming and stalking, to heal wounds with bandages or humour. Like so many novels of grim and violent times, *Milkman* has won hearts for its compassionate understanding of the everyday in the midst of the extraordinary.

Girl, Woman, Other

(2019)

Bernardine Evaristo (born 1959)

Girl, Woman, Other follows the lives of twelve Black British women in the early years of the twenty-first century. It looks at the ways in which women are excluded by racial, social, sexual, and gender discrimination, and how these same women sometimes discriminate against others.

The novel revolves around the fictional opening night of the first play to be produced at London's National Theatre expressly for a Black audience. Some of the women know each other, usually through work, school or family, and the book presents their interconnected stories. In the final chapter they are all present in the audience for the play, their individual stories both commenting on, and being reflected in, the drama. An epilogue, however, springs a surprise which further emphasises the shared experience of all the protagonists.

All have experienced discrimination. For example, the playwright Amma has been marginalised for most of her career, while her best friend Dominique was made so unwelcome in England that she now lives in Los Angeles. Bummi works for Penelope, a white teacher, as her 'African cleaner'. Penelope has advised Bummi's daughter Carole to assimilate white culture. Morgan, who is non-binary, has suffered from other people's narrow attitudes to gender. Morgan's mother and her siblings resist identifying themselves as Black because of the racism to which they were exposed, growing up on a farm in a small, very traditional English village.

Despite their experience of exclusion, many of the women in *Girl, Woman, Other* also discriminate against others in one way or another. Penelope has been a lifelong feminist, winning important advances for her gender at the school; but she cannot recognise the similar struggle being fought by Britain's Black population. Her young Black colleague Shirley is full of idealistic zeal for improving the lot of her Black students; but she cannot see the real progress which Penelope achieved through her activism. Amma has always rejected the white, wealthy world of mainstream theatre, of which she is now a part. Amma's politically engaged daughter Yazz scoffs at her mother for being out of touch, but she doesn't understand Amma's struggles to be heard as a Black voice.

Some issues in the novel derive from problems inherent in the English class system. Others are from unhappy marriages or the eternal misunderstandings between generations. Racism magnifies all of them. Bernardine Evaristo avoids stereotypes with this many-faceted approach to her protagonists. Yazz's Egyptian friend Nenet, for example, comes from a privileged background and pays a retired academic to write her essays for her. Yazz realises that she has more in common with a lower middle-class white schoolmate, Courtney.

Girl, Woman, Other has been received as a milestone in fiction about being Black in Britain. 'If you want to understand modern-day Britain,' British-Nigerian novelist Sarah Ladipo Manyika has written, 'this is the writer to read.'

LEFT: Bernardine Evaristo speaking at the Hay Festival Winter Weekend in 2019 about Girl, Woman, Other.

OPPOSITE: Girl, Woman, Other *was joint winner of the 2019 Booker Prize with Margaret Atwood's* The Testaments.

'Bernardine Evaristo can take any story from any time and turn it into something vibrating with life' Ali Smith

Girl, Woman, Other

BERNARDINE EVARISTO

ABOVE: *Thomas Hardy's novel,* Tess of the d'Urbervilles: A Pure Woman Faithfully Presented *(1891) is seen as the author railing against the treatment of women and so strikes a chord with Stieg Larsson's* Girl With a Dragon Tattoo *(2005).*

Index

LEFT: Agatha Christie's books are popular in Spain and she has a flight of steps dedicated to her novels in Puerto de la Cruz, Tenerife.

ABOVE: The Hound of the Baskervilles *was
the third of Conan Doyle's four Sherlock
Holmes novels.*
BELOW: *The illustration from the frontispiece
of the 1831* Frankenstein, *shows a far less
monstrous monster .*

LEFT: Margaret Atwood's The Testaments *(2019) is a sequel to* The Handmaid's Tale, *set fifteen years after the original. Like its predecessor it will be adapted for television.*

RIGHT: The Paseo de Ernest Hemingway is a panoramic walkway in Ronda, Andalusia, a town with its own historic bullring.

ABOVE: You can share a drink with James Joyce in The Temple Bar in Dublin. Ironically, little of his major work was written in Ireland.
RIGHT: A statue of another of literature's free thinkers, Franz Kafka stands above the Národní třída metro station in Prague.

LEFT: *The estate at Yasnaya Polyana in Russia where Tolstoy wrote* War and Peace *and* Anna Karenina.

Acknowledgements

The publisher wishes to thank all the publishing houses (particularly Penguin) of the books used in this review of the world's greatest novels. In addiction pictures were supplied by:

Alamy: 9, 11 (top), 14 (bottom), 15, 16,17, 19, 22, 25 (top), 27, 30 (top left), 37 (bottom), 40, 41 (bottom), 45, 47 (top), 48, 51, 53, 58, 59, 61, 63 (top), 65, 73, 75, 78, 79, 81, 84, 87 (top), 87 (bottom right), 92, 93 (top), 95, 98, 107, 105, 106, 108, 111, 112, 115, 117, 119, 123, 128, 131, 133 (right),138, 140, 141, 142, 143, 145, 148, 151 (right), 159, 160, 169, 172 (right), 174, 176, 179, 180, 185, 186, 190,192, 194 (right), 196, 199 (right), 200, 201, 202, 204, 207, 208, 210, 213, 214.

Getty Images: 162, 165, 171, 183, 188

Library of Congress: 25 (bottom), 49, 50, 55, 68, 77, 90

Shutterstock: 11 (bottom), 12, 13, 14 (top), 63 (bottom), 113 (bottom), 216, 217, 218 (top), 219, 220, 221, 222, 223

Also in this series:

100 Children's Books That Inspire Our World ISBN: 978-1-911641-08-7
Colin Salter (2020)

100 Posters That Changed the World ISBN: 978-1-911641-45-2
Colin Salter (2020)

100 Science Discoveries That Changed the World ISBN: 978-1-911663-54-6
Colin Salter (2021)

100 Symbols That Changed the World ISBN: 978-1-911216-38-4
Colin Salter (2022)

Publishing Director: Stephanie Milner
Commissioning Editor: Frank Hopkinson
Design Director: Laura Russell
Designer: Cara Rogers
Cover design: Lily Wilson
Production: Louis Harvey

About the Author

Colin Salter is a history writer with degrees from Manchester Metropolitan University, England and Queen Margaret University in Edinburgh, Scotland. He is currently working on a memoir based in part on letters written to and by his ancestors over a period of two hundred years.

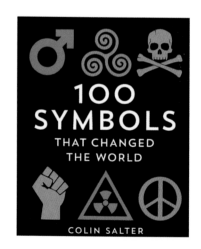